Fodor's

First New Edition

Denmark

by Karina Porcelli

D0170093

The complete guide, thoroughly up-to-date

Packed with details that will make your trip

The must-see sights, off and on the beaten path

What to see, what to skip

Mix-and-match vacation itineraries

City strolls, countryside adventures

Smart lodging and dining options

Essential local do's and taboos

Transportation tips, distances and directions

Key contacts, savvy travel tips

When to go, what to pack

Clear, accurate, easy-to-use maps

Books to read, videos to watch

Reprinted from *Fodor's Scandinavia*

Fodor's Travel Publications, Inc.
New York • Toronto • London • Sydney • Auckland
www.fodors.com/

Fodor's Denmark

EDITOR: Caragh Rockwood
Area Editor: Karina Porcelli

Editorial Contributors: Robert Andrews, David Brown, Christina Knight, Jennifer Paull, Heidi Sarna, Helayne Schiff, M. T. Schwartzman (Gold Guide editor), Dinah A. Spritzer

Editorial Production: Tom Holton

Maps: David Lindroth, *cartographer*; Steven K. Amsterdam, *map editor*

Design: Fabrizio La Rocca, *creative director*; Guido Caroti, *associate art director*; Jolie Novak, *photo editor*

Production/Manufacturing: Mike Costa

Cover Photograph: Bob Krist

Copyright

First Edition

ISBN 0–679–03615–6

Special Sales

Fodor's Travel Publications are available at special discounts for bulk purchases for sales promotions or premiums. Special editions, including personalized covers, excerpts of existing guides, and corporate imprints, can be created in large quantities for special needs. For more information, contact your local bookseller or write to Special Markets, Fodor's Travel Publications, 201 East 50th Street, New York, NY 10022. Inquiries from Canada should be directed to your local Canadian bookseller or sent to Random House of Canada, Ltd., Marketing Department, 2775 Matheson Blvd. E., Mississauga, Ontario L4W 4P7. Inquiries from the United Kingdom should be sent to Fodor's Travel Publications, 20 Vauxhall Bridge Road, London, England SW1V 2SA.

PRINTED IN THE UNITED STATES OF AMERICA

10 9 8 7 6 5 4 3 2 1

CONTENTS

On the Road with Fodor's   v

About Our Writers *v*
New This Year *v*
How to Use This Book *v*
Don't Forget to Write *vi*

The Gold Guide   xii

Smart Travel Tips A to Z

1   **Destination: Denmark**   1

Fairy Tales and Fjords 2
New and Noteworthy 3
What's Where 4
Pleasures and Pastimes 4
Fodor's Choice 6
Festivals and Seasonal Events 7

2   **Copenhagen**   8

3   **Sjælland and Its Islands**   44

4   **Fyn and the Central Islands**   58

5   **Jylland**   70

6   **Bornholm**   84

7   **Greenland**   95

8   **The Faroe Islands**   105

9   **Portraits of Denmark**   114

Denmark at a Glance: A Chronology 115
The Utterly Danish Pastries of Denmark 118
Tivoli 121
Books and Videos 124

Danish Vocabulary   125

Index   127

Maps

Denmark *vii*

Scandinavia *viii–ix*

World Time Zones *x–xi*

Copenhagen *12–13*

Copenhagen Dining and
Lodging *24–25*

Sjælland and Its Islands *47*

Fyn and the Central Islands *60*

Jylland *72*

Bornholm *87*

Greenland *99*

The Faroe Islands *108*

ON THE ROAD WITH FODOR'S

WE'RE ALWAYS THRILLED to get letters from readers, especially one like this:

It took us an hour to decide what book to buy and we now know we picked the best one. Your book was wonderful, easy to follow, very accurate, and good on pointing out eating places, informal as well as formal. When we saw other people using your book, we would look at each other and smile.

Our editors and writers are deeply committed to making every Fodor's guide "the best one"—not only accurate but always charming, brimming with sound recommendations and solid ideas, right on the mark in describing restaurants and hotels, and full of fascinating facts that make you view what you've traveled to see in a rich new light.

About Our Writers

Our success in achieving our goals—and in helping to make your trip the best of all possible vacations—is a credit to the hard work of our extraordinary writers and editors.

Freelance writer **Karina Porcelli** divides her time between Copenhagen and Washington, D.C.

New This Year

We're proud to announce that the American Society of Travel Agents has endorsed Fodor's as its guidebook of choice. ASTA is the world's largest and most influential travel trade association, operating in more than 170 countries, with 27,000 members pledged to adhere to a strict code of ethics reflecting the Society's motto, "Integrity in Travel." ASTA shares Fodor's devotion to providing smart, honest travel information and advice to travelers, and we've long recommended that our readers consult ASTA member agents for the experience and professionalism they bring to the table.

On the Web, check out Fodor's site (www.fodors.com/) for information on major destinations around the world and travel-savvy interactive features. The Web site also lists the 85-plus radio stations nationwide that carry *Fodor's Travel Show,* a live call-in program that airs every weekend. Tune in to hear guests discuss their wonderful adventures—or call in to get answers for your most pressing travel questions.

How to Use This Book

Organization

Up front is the **Gold Guide,** an easy-to-use section divided alphabetically by topic. Under each listing you'll find tips and information that will help you accomplish what you need to in Denmark. You'll also find addresses and telephone numbers of organizations and companies that offer destination-related services and detailed information and publications.

The first chapter in the guide, Destination: Denmark, helps get you in the mood for your trip. What's Where gets you oriented, Fodor's Choice showcases our top picks, and Festivals and Seasonal Events alerts you to special events you'll want to seek out.

Chapters in *Fodor's Denmark,* each dealing with a major region or city, contain recommended walking or driving tours. Within each city, sights are covered alphabetically. Within each region, towns are covered in logical geographical order, and attractive stretches of road and minor points of interest between them are indicated by the designation *En Route.* Off the Beaten Path sights appear after the places from which they are most easily accessible. Within town sections, all restaurants and lodgings are grouped together. The A-to-Z section at the end of each region or city covers getting there, getting around, and helpful contacts and resources.

At the end of the book you'll find Portraits, with a chronology of the history of Denmark, two essays highlighting Denmark's charms, followed by suggestions for any pretrip research you want to do, from recommended reading to movies on tape with Denmark as a backdrop.

Icons and Symbols

★ Our special recommendations
✕ Restaurant
🏠 Lodging establishment
✕🏠 Lodging establishment whose restaurant warrants a special trip
⚠ Campgrounds
☾ Good for kids (rubber duckie)
☞ Sends you to another section of the guide for more information
✉ Address
☎ Telephone number
☾ Opening and closing times
🎟 Admission prices (those we give apply to adults; substantially reduced fees are almost always available for children, students, and senior citizens)

Numbers in white and black circles that appear on the maps, in the margins, and within the tours correspond to one another.

Dining and Lodging

The restaurants and lodgings we list are the cream of the crop in each price range. Price charts appear in the Pleasures and Pastimes section of Chapter 1.

Hotel Facilities

We always list the facilities that are available—but we don't specify whether they cost extra: When pricing accommodations, always ask what's included. Assume that all rooms have private baths unless otherwise noted. Breakfast is almost always included in the price of Scandinavian hotels.

Restaurant Reservations and Dress Codes

Reservations are always a good idea; we note only when they're essential or when they are not accepted. Book as far ahead as you can, and reconfirm when you get to town. Unless otherwise noted, the restaurants listed are open daily for lunch and dinner. We mention dress only when men are required to wear a jacket or a jacket and tie.

Credit Cards

The following abbreviations are used: **AE,** American Express; **D,** Discover; **DC,** Diners Club; **MC,** MasterCard; and **V,** Visa.

Don't Forget to Write

You can use this book in the confidence that all prices and opening times are based on information supplied to us at press time; Fodor's cannot accept responsibility for any errors. Time inevitably brings changes, so always confirm information when it matters—especially if you're making a detour to visit a specific place. In addition, when making reservations be sure to mention if you have a disability or are traveling with children, if you prefer a private bath or a certain type of bed, or if you have specific dietary needs or other concerns.

Were the restaurants we recommended as described? Did our hotel picks exceed your expectations? Did you find a museum we recommended a waste of time? If you have complaints, we'll look into them and revise our entries when the facts warrant it. If you've discovered a special place that we haven't included, we'll pass the information along to our correspondents and have them check it out. So send us your feedback, positive *and* negative: email us at editors@fodors.com (specifying the name of the book on the subject line) or write the Scandinavia editor at Fodor's, 201 East 50th Street, New York, New York 10022. Have a wonderful trip!

Karen Cure

Karen Cure
Editorial Director

Denmark

North Sea

Skagerrak

TO GREENLAND
TO FAROE ISLANDS

Skagen
Hirtshals
Hjørring
Frederikshavn
Sæby
Brønderslev
Hansholm
Læsø
Thisted
Lim-fjord
Limfjord
Aalborg
Nykøbing
Aalborg Bugt
Kattegat
Lemvig
Skive
Hadsund
Struer
Viborg
Anholt
Holstebro
Jylland
Randers
Grenå
Ringkøbing
Herning
Silkeborg
Århus
Ebeltoft
Samsø
Grindsted
Skanderborg
Horsens
Tisvildeleje
Hornbæk
Skjern
Billund
Vejle
Nykøbing
Helsingør
Frederikssund
Hillerød
Esbjerg
Holsted
Fredericia
Middelfart
Samsøbælt
Kalundborg
Holbæk
Copenhagen
Fanø
Kolding
Odense
Kerteminde
Store-bælt
Jyderup
Roskilde
Sjælland
Amager
Røde
Vojens
Assens
Halsskov
Slagelse
Ringsted
Køge
Køge Bugt
Skærbæk
Haderslev
Lillebælt
Fyn
Nyborg
Korsør
Næstved
St. Heddinge
Tønder
Åbenrå
Als
Fåborg
Langeland
Karrebæksminde
Sønderborg
Svendborg
Tranekær
Vordingborg
Stege
Møn
Ærøskøbing
Troense
Rudkøbing
Nakskov
Nykøbing
Falster
Ærø
Marstal
Maribo
Rødby
Nysted
Lolland
Ostsee

GERMANY

N

0   50 miles
0   75 km

SWEDEN
Baltic Sea
Bornholm
Rønne

TO BORNHOLM

Scandinavia

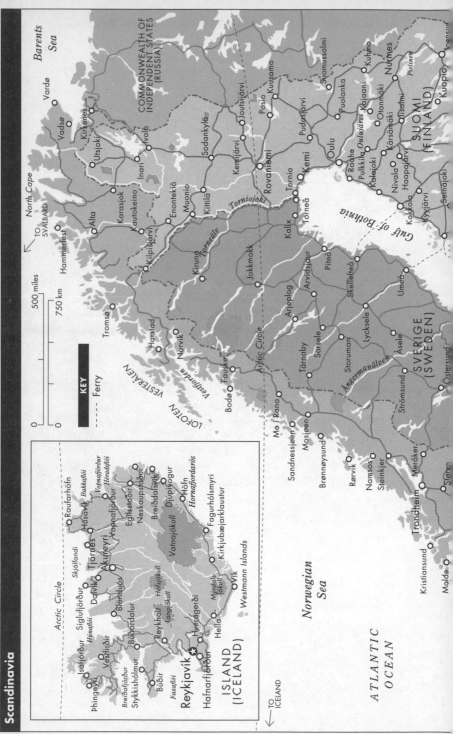

Barents Sea

North Cape

TO SVALBARD

Varde
Vadsø
Kirkenes
Utsjoki
Vardø
Svalb
Hammerfest
Alta
Karasjok
Kautokeino
Inari
Enontekiö
Muonio
Kilpisjärvi
Kittilä
Sodankylä
Ivalo
Posio
Kuusamo
Kemijärvi
Rovaniemi
Kittilä
Tornio
Kemi
Oulu
Raahe
Pulkkila
Kokkola
Kälviä
Kokola

COMMONWEALTH OF INDEPENDENT STATES (RUSSIA)

Suomussalmi
Kuhmo
Nurmes
Pielinen
Puolanka
Kajaani
Otanmäki
Iisalmi
Nivala
Haapajärvi
Kuopio
Seinäjoki
SUOMI (FINLAND)

Torniojoki
Torneälv
Kiruna
Jokkmokk
Kalix
Tornio
Torneå
Gulf of Bothnia

Arctic Circle

Kvikkjokk
Arjeplog
Piteå
Skellefteå
Umeå
Arvidsjaur
Tärnaby
Sorsele
Storuman
Lycksele
Åsele
Ångermanälven
Strömsund
Östersund
Storen
SVERIGE (SWEDEN)

Narvik
Vestfjorden
Harstad
Tromsø
VESTERÅLEN
LOFOTEN
Bodø
Fauske
Mo i Rana
Mosjøen
Sandnessjøen
Brønnøysund
Rørvik
Namsos
Steinkjer
Meråker
Trondheim
Kristiansund
Molde

KEY
--- Ferry
500 miles
750 km

Norwegian Sea

ATLANTIC OCEAN

ISLAND (ICELAND)

TO ICELAND

Reykjavík
Hafnarfjörður
Hv`eragerði
Hella
Vík
Mýrdalsjökull
Westmann Islands
Kirkjubæjarklaustur
Fagurhólsmýri
Höfn
Hornafjarðarós
Djúpivogur
Breiðdalsvík
Neskaupstaður
Egilsstaðir
Vopnafjörður
Héraðsflói
Bakkaflói
Vopnafjörður
Raufarhöfn
Húsavík
Skjálfandi
Tjörnes
Akureyri
Dalvík
Siglufjörður
Hofsjökull
Vatnajökull
Langjökull
Reykholt
Blönduós
Borgardalur
Hnafloi
Vestfirðir
Ísafjörður
Þingeyri
Breiðafjörður
Stykkishólmur
Búðir
Faxaflói

Arctic Circle

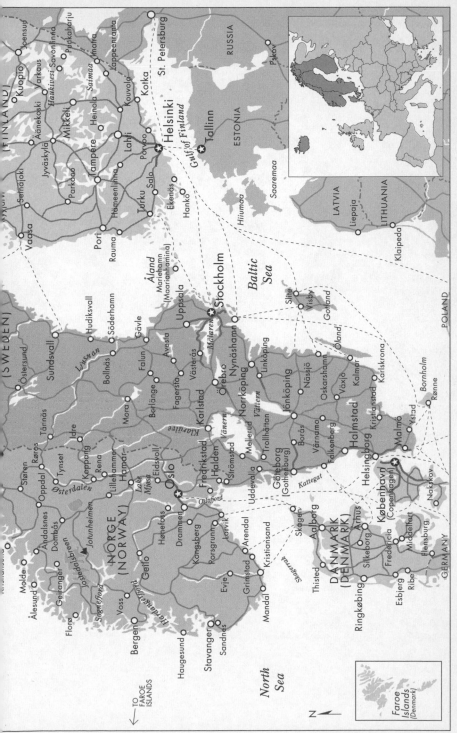

World Time Zones

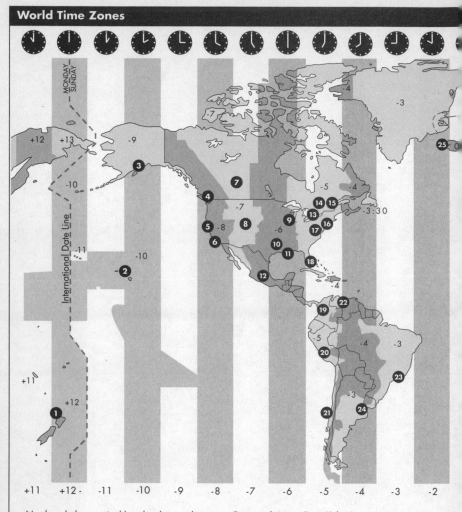

Numbers below vertical bands relate each zone to Greenwich Mean Time (0 hrs.).
Local times frequently differ from these general indications,
as indicated by light-face numbers on map.

Algiers, **29**

Anchorage, **3**

Athens, **41**

Auckland, **1**

Baghdad, **46**

Bangkok, **50**

Beijing, **54**

Berlin, **34**

Bogotá, **19**

Budapest, **37**

Buenos Aires, **24**

Caracas, **22**

Chicago, **9**

Copenhagen, **33**

Dallas, **10**

Delhi, **48**

Denver, **8**

Djakarta, **53**

Dublin, **26**

Edmonton, **7**

Hong Kong, **56**

Honolulu, **2**

Istanbul, **40**

Jerusalem, **42**

Johannesburg, **44**

Lima, **20**

Lisbon, **28**

London (Greenwich), **27**

Los Angeles, **6**

Madrid, **38**

Manila, **57**

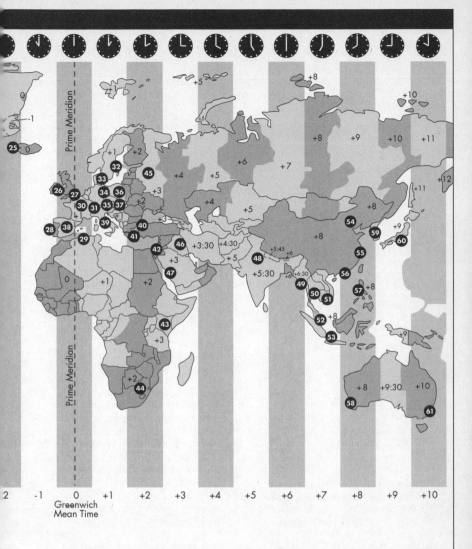

Mecca, **47**

Mexico City, **12**

Miami, **18**

Montréal, **15**

Moscow, **45**

Nairobi, **43**

New Orleans, **11**

New York City, **16**

Ottawa, **14**

Paris, **30**

Perth, **58**

Reykjavík, **25**

Rio de Janeiro, **23**

Rome, **39**

Saigon (Ho Chi Minh City), **51**

San Francisco, **5**

Santiago, **21**

Seoul, **59**

Shanghai, **55**

Singapore, **52**

Stockholm, **32**

Sydney, **61**

Tokyo, **60**

Toronto, **13**

Vancouver, **4**

Vienna, **35**

Warsaw, **36**

Washington, D.C., **17**

Yangon, **49**

Zürich, **31**

SMART TRAVEL TIPS A TO Z

Basic Information on Traveling in Denmark, Savvy Tips to Make Your Trip a Breeze, and Companies and Organizations to Contact

A

AIR TRAVEL

Flights to Copenhagen take 7 hours, 40 minutes from New York; 8 hours, 15 minutes from Chicago; and 9½ hours from Seattle. From London to Copenhagen the flight takes 1 hour, 55 minutes.

MAJOR AIRLINE OR LOW-COST CARRIER?

Most people choose a flight based on price. Yet there are other issues to consider. Major airlines offer the greatest number of departures; smaller airlines—including regional, low-cost and no-frill airlines—usually have a more limited number of flights daily. Major airlines have frequent-flyer partners, which allow you to credit mileage earned on one airline to your account with another. Low-cost airlines offer a definite price advantage and fewer restrictions, such as advance-purchase requirements. Safetywise, low-cost carriers as a group have a good history, but **check the safety record before booking** any low-cost carrier; call the Federal Aviation Administration's Consumer Hotline (☞ Airline Complaints, *below*).

➤ MAJOR AIRLINES: **Delta** (☎ 800/221–1212) (☎ 800/950–5000) has direct service from Atlanta and New York, connecting to 217 cities in North America. **British Airways** (☎ 800/247–9297) offers connecting flights via London from Atlanta, Boston, Chicago, Dallas, Detroit, Los Angeles, Miami, New York, Orlando, Philadelphia, Pittsburgh, San Francisco, Seattle, and Washington, D.C. **Icelandair** (☎ 800/223–5500) makes connecting flights via Reykjavík from Baltimore, Fort Lauderdale, New York, and Orlando. **Scandinavian Airlines (SAS)** (☎ 800/221–2350) makes nonstop flights from Chicago, Newark, and Seattle.

➤ FROM THE UNITED KINGDOM: **British Airways** (✉ 156 Regent St., London W1, ☎ 0181/897–4000) flies nonstop from Heathrow, Gatwick, Birmingham, and Manchester. **Scandinavian Airlines** (SAS)(✉ SAS House, 52–53 Conduit St., London W1R 0AY, ☎ 0171/734–6777) flies nonstop from Heathrow, Manchester, and Glasgow and also from London to Århus. **Mærsk Air** (✉ Terminal House, 52 Grosvenor Gardens, London, SW1, ☎ 0171/333-0066) flies nonstop from Gatwick to Billund and Copenhagen.

GET THE LOWEST FARE

The least-expensive airfares to Denmark are priced for round-trip travel. Major airlines usually require that you **book far in advance and stay at least seven days** and no more than 30 to get the lowest fares. Ask about "ultrasaver" fares, which are the cheapest; they must be booked 90 days in advance and are nonrefundable. A little more expensive are "supersaver" fares, which require only a 30-day advance purchase. Remember that penalties for refunds or scheduling changes are stiffer for international tickets, usually about $150. International flights are also sensitive to the season: **plan to fly in the off season** for the cheapest fares. If your destination or home city has more than one gateway, **compare prices to and from different airports.** Also price flights scheduled for off-peak hours, which may be significantly less expensive.

To save money on flights from the United Kingdom and back, **look into an APEX or Super-PEX ticket.** APEX tickets must be booked in advance and have certain restrictions. Super-PEX tickets can be purchased at the airport on the day of departure—subject to availability.

If you want to economize on the usually expensive intra-Scandinavian travel, **look into the Visit Scandinavia Fare.** One coupon costs about $85; six are about $510, for unlimited air travel in Denmark, Sweden, Norway, and also between Sweden and Finland. It is sold only in the United States and only to non-Scandinavians. Coupons can be used year-round for a maximum of three months and must be purchased in conjunction with transatlantic flights.

DON'T STOP UNLESS YOU MUST

When you book, **look for nonstop flights** and **remember that "direct" flights stop at least once.** International flights on a country's flag carrier are almost always nonstop; U.S. airlines often fly direct. Try to **avoid connecting flights,** which require a change of plane. Two airlines may jointly operate a connecting flight, so ask if your airline operates every segment—you may find that your preferred carrier flies you only part of the way.

USE AN AGENT

Travel agents, especially those who specialize in finding the lowest fares (☞ Discounts & Deals, *below*), can be especially helpful when booking a plane ticket. When you're quoted a price, **ask your agent if the price is likely to get any lower.** Good agents know the seasonal fluctuations of airfares and can usually anticipate a sale or fare war. However, waiting can be risky: The fare could go *up* as seats become scarce, and you may wait so long that your preferred flight sells out. A wait-and-see strategy works best if your plans are flexible, but if you must arrive and depart on certain dates, don't delay.

CHECK WITH CONSOLIDATORS

Consolidators buy tickets for scheduled flights at reduced rates from the airlines then sell them at prices that beat the best fare available directly from the airlines, usually without advance restrictions. Sometimes you can even get your money back if you need to return the ticket. Carefully read the fine print detailing penalties for changes and cancellations, and **confirm your consolidator reservation with the airline.**

➤ CONSOLIDATORS: **United States Air Consolidators Association** (✉ 925 L St., Suite 220, Sacramento, CA 95814, ☎ 916/441–4166, FAX 916/441–3520).

CONSIDER A CHARTER

Charters usually have the lowest fares but are not dependable. Departures are infrequent and seldom on time, flights can be delayed for up to 48 hours or can be canceled for any reason up to 10 days before you're scheduled to leave. Itineraries and prices can change after you've booked your flight, so you must **be very careful to choose a legitimate charter carrier.** Don't commit to a charter operator that doesn't follow proper booking procedures. Be especially careful when buying a charter ticket. Read the fine print regarding refund policies. If you can't pay with a credit card, **make your check payable to a charter carrier's escrow account** (unless you're dealing with a travel agent, in which case his or her check should be made payable to the escrow account). The name of the bank should be in the charter contract.

Airlines routinely overbook planes, knowing that not everyone with a ticket will show up, but sometimes everyone does. When that happens, airlines ask for volunteers to give up their seats. In return these volunteers usually get a certificate for a free flight and are rebooked on the next flight out. If there are not enough volunteers the airline must choose who will be denied boarding. The first to get bumped are passengers who checked in late and those flying on discounted tickets, **so get to the gate and check in as early as possible,** especially during peak periods.

Always **bring a photo ID to the airport.** You may be asked to show it before you are allowed to check in.

ENJOY THE FLIGHT

For more legroom, **request an emergency-aisle seat**; don't, however, sit in the row in front of the emergency aisle or in front of a bulkhead, where seats may not recline.

If you don't like airline food, **ask for special meals when booking.** These can be vegetarian, low-cholesterol, or kosher, for example.

To avoid jet lag try to maintain a normal routine while traveling. At night **get some sleep.** By day **eat light meals, drink water (not alcohol), and move about the cabin** to stretch your legs.

Some carriers have prohibited smoking throughout their systems; others allow smoking only on certain routes or even certain departures from that route, so **contact your carrier regarding its smoking policy.**

COMPLAIN IF NECESSARY

If your baggage goes astray or your flight goes awry, complain right away. Most carriers require that you file a claim immediately.

➤ AIRLINE COMPLAINTS: U.S. Department of Transportation **Aviation Consumer Protection Division** (✉ C-75, Room 4107, Washington, DC 20590, ☎ 202/366–2220). **Federal Aviation Administration (FAA) Consumer Hotline** (☎ 800/322–7873).

AIRPORTS

The major gateway to Denmark is Copenhagen's **Kastrup International Airport,** 10 km (6 mi) from the capital's center.

➤ AIRPORT INFORMATION: **Kastrup International Airport** (☎ 011–45–31/541701).

B

BUS TRAVEL

Traveling by bus or train is easy because **DSB** (☎ 33/14–17–01 or 42/52–92–22) and a few private companies cover the country with a dense network of services, supplemented by buses in remote areas. Bus tickets are usually sold on buses. Children under 5 travel free, and those between 5 and 12 travel for half-price. Ask about discounts for senior citizens and groups of three or more.

C

CAMERAS, CAMCORDERS, & COMPUTERS

Always **keep your film, tape, or computer disks out of the sun.** Carry an extra supply of batteries, and **be prepared to turn on your camera, camcorder, or laptop** to prove to security personnel that the device is real. Always **ask for hand inspection of film,** which becomes clouded after successive exposure to airport x-ray machines, and **keep videotapes and computer disks away from metal detectors.**

➤ PHOTO HELP: **Kodak Information Center** (☎ 800/242–2424). *Kodak Guide to Shooting Great Travel Pictures,* available in bookstores or from Fodor's Travel Publications (☎ 800/533–6478; $16.50 plus $4 shipping).

CUSTOMS

Before departing, **register your foreign-made camera or laptop with U.S. Customs** (☞ Customs & Duties, *below*). If your equipment is U.S.-made, call the consulate of the country you'll be visiting to find out whether the device should be registered with local customs upon arrival.

CAR RENTAL

Major international car rental agencies are represented throughout Denmark. In Copenhagen, most car-rental agencies are located near the Vesterport Station. Rates begin at about $110 a day and $210 a week for an economy car without air conditioning, and with a manual transmission and unlimited mileage.

➤ RENTAL AGENCIES: **Avis** (☎ 800/331–1084, 800/879–2847 in Canada). **Budget** (☎ 800/527–0700, 0800/181181 in the U.K.). **Dollar** (☎ 800/800–4000; 0990/565656 in the U.K., where it is known as Eurodollar). **Europcar** (✉ Copenhagen Airport, ☎ 32/50–30–90). **Hertz** (☎ 800/654–3001, 800/263–0600 in Canada, 0345/555888 in the U.K.). **National InterRent** (☎ 800/227–3876; 01345/222525 in the U.K., where it is known as Europcar InterRent). **Pitzner Auto** (✉ Copenhagen Airport, ☎ 32/50–90–65).

CUT COSTS

To get the best deal, **book through a travel agent who is willing to shop around.**

Also **ask your travel agent about a company's customer-service record.** How has it responded to late plane arrivals and vehicle mishaps? Are there often lines at the rental counter, and, if you're traveling during a holiday period, does a confirmed reservation guarantee you a car?

Be sure to **look into wholesalers,** companies that do not own fleets but rent in bulk from those that do and often offer better rates than traditional car-rental operations. Prices are best during off-peak periods. Rentals booked through wholesalers must be paid for before you leave the United States.

➤ RENTAL WHOLESALERS: **DER Travel Services** (✉ 9501 W. Devon Ave., Rosemont, IL 60018, ☎ 800/782–2424, FAX 800/282–7474 for information or 800/860–9944 for brochures). The **Kemwel Group** (☎ 914/835–5555 or 800/678–0678, FAX 914/835–5126).

NEED INSURANCE?

When driving a rented car you are generally responsible for any damage to or loss of the vehicle. Before you rent, **see what coverage you already have** under the terms of your personal auto- insurance policy and credit cards.

Collision policies that car-rental companies sell for European rentals typically do not cover stolen vehicles. Before you buy additional coverage for theft, find out if your credit card or personal auto insurance will cover the loss.

BEWARE SURCHARGES

Before you pick up a car in one city and leave it in another, **ask about drop-off charges or one-way service fees,** which can be substantial. Note, too, that some rental agencies charge extra if you return the car before the time specified on your contract. To avoid a hefty refueling fee, **fill the tank just before you turn in the car,** but be aware that gas stations near the rental outlet may overcharge.

MEET THE REQUIREMENTS

Ask about age requirements: Several countries require drivers to be over 20 years old, but some car-rental companies require that drivers be at least 25. In Denmark your own driver's license is acceptable for a limited time; check with the country's tourist board before you go. An International Driver's Permit is a good idea; it's available from the American or Canadian automobile association, or, in the United Kingdom, from the Automobile Association or Royal Automobile Club.

CHILDREN & TRAVEL

CHILDREN IN DENMARK

In Denmark children are to be seen *and* heard and are genuinely welcome in most public places.

Be sure to plan ahead and **involve your youngsters** as you outline your trip. When packing, include things to keep them busy en route. On sightseeing days try to schedule activities of special interest to your children. If you are renting a car don't forget to **arrange for a car seat** when you reserve. Most hotels in Denmark allow children under a certain age to stay in their parents' room at no extra charge, but others charge them as extra adults; be sure to **ask about the cutoff age for children's discounts.** Many youth hostels offer special facilities (including multiple-bed rooms and separate kitchens) for families with children. Family hostels also provide an excellent opportunity for children to meet youngsters from other countries. Contact the AYH (☞ Students, *below*).

DISCOUNTS

Children are entitled to discount tickets (often as much as 50% off) on buses, trains, and ferries throughout Scandinavia, as well as reductions on special city cards. Children under 12 pay half-price and children under 2 pay 10% on SAS and Linjeflyg round-trips. The only restriction on this discount is that the family travel together and return to the originating city in Scandinavia at least two days later. With the ScanRail Pass—good for rail journeys throughout Scandinavia—children under 4 (on lap) travel free; those 4–11 pay half-fare and those 12–25 pay 75% of the adult fare.

FLYING

As a general rule, infants under two not occupying a seat fly at greatly reduced fares and occasionally for free. If your children are two or older **ask about children's airfares.**

In general the adult baggage allowance applies to children paying half or more of the adult fare. When booking, **ask about carry-on allowances for those traveling with infants.** In general, for babies charged 10% of the adult fare you are allowed one carry-on bag and a collapsible stroller, which may have to be checked; you may be limited to less if the flight is full.

According to the FAA it's a good idea to use safety seats aloft for children weighing less than 40 pounds. Airlines, however, can set their own policies: U.S. carriers allow FAA-approved models but usually require that you buy a ticket, even if your child would otherwise ride free, since the seats must be strapped into regular seats. Airline rules vary regarding their use, so it's important to **check your airline's policy about using safety seats during takeoff and landing.** Safety seats cannot obstruct any of the other passengers in the row, so get an appropriate seat assignment as early as possible.

When making your reservation, **request children's meals or a free-standing bassinet** if you need them; the latter are available only to those seated at the bulkhead, where there's enough legroom. Remember, however, that bulkhead seats may not have their own overhead bins, and there's no storage space in front of you—a major inconvenience.

GROUP TRAVEL

If you're planning to take your kids on a tour, look for companies that specialize in family travel.

➤ FAMILY-FRIENDLY TOUR OPERATORS: **Families Welcome!** (✉ 92 N. Main St., Ashland, OR 97520, ☎ 541/482–6121 or 800/326–0724, FAX 541/482–0660). **Rascals in Paradise** (✉ 650 5th St., Suite 505, San Francisco, CA 94107, ☎ 415/978–9800 or 800/872–7225, FAX 415/442–0289).

CONSUMER PROTECTION

Whenever possible, **pay with a major credit card** so you can cancel payment if there's a problem, provided that you can provide documentation. This is a good practice whether you're buying travel arrangements before your trip or shopping at your destination.

If you're doing business with a particular company for the first time, **contact your local Better Business Bureau and the attorney general's offices** in your state and the company's home state, as well. Have any complaints been filed?

Finally, if you're buying a package or tour, always **consider travel insurance** that includes default coverage (☞ Insurance, *above*).

➤ LOCAL BBBS: **Council of Better Business Bureaus** (✉ 4200 Wilson Blvd., Suite 800, Arlington, VA 22203, ☎ 703/276–0100, FAX 703/525–8277).

CUSTOMS & DUTIES

ENTERING DENMARK

If you are 21 or older, have purchased goods in a country that is a member of the European Union (EU), and pay that country's value-added tax (VAT) on those goods, you may import duty-free 1½ liters of liquor; 300 cigarettes or 150 cigarillos or 75 cigars or 400 grams of tobacco.

If you are entering Denmark from a non-EU country or if you have purchased your goods on a ferryboat or in an airport not taxed in the EU, you must pay Danish taxes on any amount of alcoholic beverages greater than 1 liter of liquor or 2 liters of strong wine, plus 2 liters of table wine. For tobacco, the limit is 200 cigarettes or 100 cigarillos or 50 cigars or 250 grams of tobacco. You are also allowed 50 grams of perfume. Other articles (including beer) are allowed up to a maximum of DKr1,350.

ENTERING THE U.S.

You may bring home $400 worth of foreign goods duty-free if you've been out of the country for at least 48 hours and haven't already used the $400 allowance or any part of it in the past 30 days.

When shopping, **keep receipts** for all of your purchases. Upon reentering the country, **be ready to show customs officials what you've bought.** If you feel a duty is incorrect, appeal the assessment. If you object to the way your clearance was handled, get the inspector's badge number. In either case, first ask to see a supervisor, then write to the port director at the address listed on your receipt. Send a copy of the receipt and other appropriate documentation. If you still don't get satisfaction you can take your case to customs headquarters in Washington (*see below*).

Travelers 21 and older may bring back 1 liter of alcohol duty-free. In addition, regardless of your age, you are allowed 200 cigarettes and 100 non-Cuban cigars. (At press time, a federal rule restricting tobacco access to persons

18 years and older did not apply to importation.) Antiques, which the U.S. Customs Service defines as objects more than 100 years old, enter duty-free, as do original works of art done entirely by hand, including paintings, drawings, and sculptures.

You may also send packages home duty-free: up to $200 worth of goods for personal use, with a limit of one parcel per addressee per day (and no alcohol or tobacco products or perfume worth more than $5); label the package PERSONAL USE, and attach a list of its contents and their retail value. Do not label the package UNSOLICITED GIFT, or your duty-free exemption will drop to $100. Mailed items do not affect your duty-free allowance on your return.

➤ INFORMATION: **U.S. Customs Service** (Inquiries, ✉ Box 7407, Washington, DC 20044, ☎ 202/927–6724; complaints, Office of Regulations and Rulings, 1301 Constitution Ave. NW, Washington, DC 20229; registration of equipment, ✉ Resource Management, 1301 Constitution Ave. NW, Washington DC, 20229, ☎ 202/927–0540).

ENTERING CANADA

If you've been out of Canada for at least seven days you may bring in C$500 worth of goods duty-free. If you've been away for fewer than seven days but more than 48 hours, the duty-free allowance drops to C$200; if your trip lasts 24–48 hours, the allowance is C$50. You may not pool allowances with family members. Goods claimed under the C$500 exemption may follow you by mail; those claimed under the lesser exemptions must accompany you.

Alcohol and tobacco products may be included in the seven-day and 48-hour exemptions but not in the 24-hour exemption. If you meet the age requirements of the province or territory through which you reenter Canada you may bring in, duty-free, 1.14 liters (40 imperial ounces) of wine or liquor *or* 24 12-ounce cans or bottles of beer or ale. If you are 16 or older you may bring in, duty-free, 200 cigarettes and 50 cigars; these items must accompany you.

You may send an unlimited number of gifts worth up to C$60 each duty-free to Canada. Label the package UNSOLICITED GIFT—VALUE UNDER $60. Alcohol and tobacco are excluded.

➤ INFORMATION: **Revenue Canada** (✉ 2265 St. Laurent Blvd. S, Ottawa, Ontario K1G 4K3, ☎ 613/993–0534, 800/461–9999 in Canada).

ENTERING THE U.K.

If your journey was wholly within European Union (EU) countries you needn't pass through customs when you return to the United Kingdom. If you plan to bring back large quantities of alcohol or tobacco, check on EU limits beforehand.

➤ INFORMATION: **HM Customs and Excise** (✉ Dorset House, Stamford St., London SE1 9NG, ☎ 0171/202–4227).

D

DINING

Although restaurants in Denmark's major cities offer the full range of dining experiences, eating out in any of the smaller towns will probably be limited to traditional local fare, or imported fast-food joints such as McDonald's and Pizza Hut. Local food can be very good, especially in the seafood and game categories, but bear in mind that northern climes beget exceptionally hearty, and heavy, meals. Sausage appears in a thousand forms, likewise potatoes. Some particular northern tastes can seem very different, such as the fondness for pickled and fermented fish—to be sampled carefully at first—and a universal obsession with sweet pastries (☞ Chapter 9), ice cream, and chocolate. Other novelties for the visitor might be the use of fruit in main dishes and soups, or sour milk on breakfast cereal, or preserved fish paste as a spread for crackers, or the prevalence of crackers and complete absence of sliced bread. The Swedish *smörgåsbord* and its Danish cousins are often the traveling diner's best bet, since they include fresh fish and vegetables alongside meat and starches; they are also among the lower-priced menu choices.

Restaurant meals are a big-ticket item throughout Denmark, but there are ways to keep the cost of eating down.

Take full advantage of the large, buffet breakfast usually included in the cost of a hotel room. At lunch, look for the "menu" that offers a set two- or three-course meal for a set price, or limit yourself to a hearty appetizer. At dinner, pay careful attention to the price of wine and drinks, since the high tax on alcohol raises these costs considerably. For more information on affordable eating, *see* Costs *in* Money, *below.*

DISABILITIES & ACCESSIBILITY

ACCESS IN DENMARK

Facilities for travelers with disabilities in Denmark are generally good, and most of the major tourist offices offer special booklets and brochures on travel and accommodations.

LODGING

The **Best Western** chain (☎ 800/528–1234) offers properties with wheelchair-accessible rooms just outside Copenhagen. If wheelchair-accessible rooms are not available, ground-floor rooms are provided.

TIPS AND HINTS

When discussing accessibility with an operator or reservationist, **ask hard questions.** Are there any stairs, inside *or* out? Are there grab bars next to the toilet *and* in the shower/tub? How wide is the doorway to the room? To the bathroom? For the most extensive facilities meeting the latest legal specifications, **opt for newer accommodations,** which are more likely to have been designed with access in mind. Older buildings or ships may offer more limited facilities. Be sure to **discuss your needs before booking.**

➤ COMPLAINTS: **Disability Rights Section** (✉ U.S. Department of Justice, Box 66738, Washington, DC 20035–6738, ☎ 202/514–0301 or 800/514–0301, ✆ 202/307–1198, TTY 202/514–0383 or 800/514–0383) for general complaints. **Aviation Consumer Protection Division** (☞ Air Travel, *above*) for airline-related problems. **Civil Rights Office** (✉ U.S. Department of Transportation, Departmental Office of Civil Rights, S-30, 400 7th St. SW, Room 10215, Washington, DC, 20590, ☎ 202/366–4648) for problems with surface transportation.

TRAVEL AGENCIES & TOUR OPERATORS

The Americans with Disabilities Act requires that travel firms serve the needs of all travelers. That said, you should note that some agencies and operators specialize in making travel arrangements for individuals and groups with disabilities.

➤ TRAVELERS WITH MOBILITY PROBLEMS: **Access Adventures** (✉ 206 Chestnut Ridge Rd., Rochester, NY 14624, ☎ 716/889–9096), run by a former physical-rehabilitation counselor. **Hinsdale Travel Service** (✉ 201 E. Ogden Ave., Suite 100, Hinsdale, IL 60521, ☎ 630/325–1335), a travel agency that benefits from the advice of wheelchair traveler Janice Perkins. **Wheelchair Journeys** (✉ 16979 Redmond Way, Redmond, WA 98052, ☎ 425/885–2210 or 800/313–4751), for general travel arrangements.

DISCOUNTS & DEALS

Be a smart shopper and **compare all your options before making a choice.** A plane ticket bought with a promotional coupon may not be cheaper than the least expensive fare from a discount ticket agency. For high-price travel purchases, such as packages or tours, keep in mind that what you get is just as important as what you save. Just because something is cheap doesn't mean it's a bargain.

LOOK IN YOUR WALLET

When you use your credit card to make travel purchases you may get free travel-accident insurance, collision-damage insurance, and medical or legal assistance, depending on the card and the bank that issued it. American Express, MasterCard, and Visa provide one or more of these services, so **get a copy of your credit card's travel-benefits policy.** If you are a member of the American Automobile Association (AAA) or an oil-company-sponsored road-assistance plan, always **ask hotel or car-rental reservationists about auto-club discounts.** Some clubs offer additional discounts on tours, cruises, or admission to attractions. And don't forget that auto-club membership entitles you to free maps and trip-planning services.

DIAL FOR DOLLARS

To save money, **look into "1-800" discount reservations services,** which use their buying power to get a better price on hotels, airline tickets, even car rentals. When booking a room, always **call the hotel's local toll-free number** (if one is available) rather than the central reservations number—you'll often get a better price. Always ask about special packages or corporate rates.

When shopping for the best deal on hotels and car rentals **look for guaranteed exchange rates,** which protect you against a falling dollar. With your rate locked in you won't pay more even if the price goes up in the local currency.

➤ AIRLINE TICKETS: ☎ **800/FLY–4–LESS.**

➤ HOTEL ROOMS: **Travel Interlink** (☎ 800/888–5898).

SAVE ON COMBOS

Packages and guided tours can both save you money, but don't confuse the two. When you buy a package your travel remains independent, just as though you had planned and booked the trip yourself. Fly/drive packages, which combine airfare and car rental, are often a good deal. If you **buy a rail/drive pass** you'll save on train tickets and car rentals. All Eurail- and Europass holders get a discount on Eurostar fares through the Channel Tunnel.

JOIN A CLUB?

Many companies sell discounts in the form of travel clubs and coupon books, but these cost money. You must use participating advertisers to get a deal, and only after you recoup the initial membership cost or book price do you begin to save. If you plan to use the club or coupons frequently you may save considerably. Before signing up, find out what discounts you get for free.

➤ DISCOUNT CLUBS: **Entertainment Travel Editions** (✉ 2125 Butterfield Rd., Troy, MI 48084, ☎ 800/445–4137; $23–$48, depending on destination). **Great American Traveler** (✉ Box 27965, Salt Lake City, UT 84127, ☎ 800/548–2812; $49.95 per year). **Moment's Notice Discount Travel Club** (✉ 7301 New Utrecht Ave., Brooklyn, NY 11204, ☎ 718/234–6295; $25 per year, single or family). **Privilege Card International** (✉ 237 E. Front St., Youngstown, OH 44503, ☎ 330/746–5211 or 800/236–9732; $74.95 per year). **Sears's Mature Outlook** (✉ Box 9390, Des Moines, IA 50306, ☎ 800/336–6330; $14.95 per year). **Travelers Advantage** (✉ CUC Travel Service, 3033 S. Parker Rd., Suite 1000, Aurora, CO 80014, ☎ 800/548–1116 or 800/648–4037; $49 per year, single or family). **Worldwide Discount Travel Club** (✉ 1674 Meridian Ave., Miami Beach, FL 33139, ☎ 305/534–2082; $50 per year family, $40 single).

DRIVING

Excellent, well-marked roads make driving a great way to explore—but beware that gasoline costs about DKr6 per liter of lead-free gas, roughly four times the typical U.S. price. Ferry costs are steep, and reservations are vital. Tolls on some major roads add to the expense, as do the high fees for city parking; tickets for illegal parking are painfully costly.

In case you're driving to Denmark, the only part of the country that is connected to the European continent is Jylland, via the E45 highway from Germany. The E20 highway then leads to Middelfart on Fyn and east to Knudshoved. From there a ferry crosses to Korsør on Sjælland and E20 leads east to Copenhagen.

Another option is to take the two-hour car ferry from Århus directly to Kalundborg in western Sjælland. From there, Route 23 leads to Copenhagen. Make reservations for the ferry in advance through the **Scanlines** (☎ 33/15–15–15). (*Note:* During the busy summer months, passengers without reservations for their vehicles can wait hours.)

The **Storebæltsbro Bridge,** connecting Fyn and Sjælland via the E20 highway, has greatly reduced the travel time between the islands.

EMERGENCY ASSISTANCE

Before leaving home, **consult your insurance company.** Members of organizations affiliated with Alliance International de Tourisme (AIT) can get technical and legal advice from the **Danish Motoring Organization**

(FDM, ✉ Firskovvej 32, 2800 Lyngby, ☎ 45/93–08– 00), open 10–4 weekdays. All highways have emergency phones, and you can call the rental company for help. If you cannot drive your car to a garage for repairs, the rescue corps **Falck** (☎ 33/14–22–22) can help anywhere, anytime. In most cases they do charge for assistance.

PARKING

You can usually park on the right-hand side of the road, though not on main roads and highways. Signs reading PARKERING/STANDSNING FORBUNDT mean no parking or stopping, though you are allowed a three-minute grace period for loading and unloading. In town, parking disks are used where there are no automatic ticket-vending machines. Get disks from gas stations, post offices, police stations, or tourist offices, and set them to show your time of arrival. For most downtown parking, you must buy a ticket from an automatic vending machine and display it on the dash. Parking costs about DKr10 or more per hour.

RULES OF THE ROAD

To drive in Denmark you need a valid driver's license, and if you're using your own car, it must have a certificate of registration and national plates. A triangular hazard-warning sign is compulsory in every car and is provided with rentals. No matter where you sit in a car, **you must wear a seat belt, and cars must have low beams on at all times.** Motorcyclists must wear helmets and use low-beam lights as well.

Drive on the right and give way to traffic—*especially to bicyclists*—on the right. A red-and-white YIELD sign or a line of white triangles across the road means you must yield to traffic on the road you are entering. Do not turn right on red unless there is a green arrow indicating that this is allowed. Speed limits are 50 kph (30 mph) in built-up areas; 100 kph (60 mph) on highways; and 80 kph (50 mph) on other roads. If you are towing a trailer, you must not exceed 70 kph (40 mph). Speeding is treated severely, even if no damage is caused. Americans and foreign tourists must pay fines on the spot.

Be aware that there are relatively low legal blood-alcohol limits and tough penalties for driving while intoxicated in Denmark. Penalties include suspension of the driver's license and fines or imprisonment and are enforced by random police roadblocks in urban areas on weekends. In addition, an accident involving a driver with an illegal blood-alcohol level usually voids all insurance agreements, so the driver becomes responsible for his own medical bills and damage to the cars.

➤ AUTO CLUBS: In the U.S., **American Automobile Association** (☎ 800/564–6222). In the U.K., **Automobile Association** (AA, ☎ 0990/500–600), **Royal Automobile Club** (RAC, membership ☎ 0990/722–722; insurance 0345/121–345).

E

ELECTRICITY

To use your U.S.-purchased electric-powered equipment, **bring a converter and adapter.** The electrical current in Denmark is 220 volts, 50 cycles alternating current (AC); wall outlets take Continental-type plugs, with two round prongs.

If your appliances are dual-voltage, you'll need only an adapter. Don't use 110-volt outlets, marked FOR SHAVERS ONLY, for high-wattage appliances such as blow-dryers. Most laptops operate equally well on 110 and 220 volts and so require only an adapter.

EMERGENCIES

The general emergency number with service 24 hours throughout Denmark is 112.

F

FERRIES

Taking a ferry isn't only fun, it's often necessary. Many companies arrange package trips, some offering a rental car and hotel accommodations as part of the deal.

Ferry crossings often last overnight. The trip between Copenhagen and Oslo, for example, takes approximately 16 hours, most lines leaving at about 5 PM and arriving about 9 the next morning. The shortest ferry route runs between Helsingør, Denmark, and Helsingborg, Sweden; it takes only 25 minutes.

DISCOUNT PASSES

The ScanRail Pass, for travel anywhere within Scandinavia (Denmark, Sweden, Norway, and Finland), and the Interail and EurailPasses are valid on some ferry crossings. Call the **DSB** Travel Office (☎ 33/14–17–01 or 42/52–92–22) for information.

➤ FERRY LINES: The main ferry operators running within Scandinavian waters are **Color Line** (✉ Box 30, DK–9850 Hirsthals, Denmark, ☎ 45/99–56–19–66, FAX 45/98–94–50–92; Hjortneskaia, Box 1422 Vika, N–0115 Oslo, Norway, ☎ 47/22–94–44–00, FAX 47/22–83–07–71; c/o Bergen Line, Inc., 505 5th Ave., New York, NY 10017, ☎ 800/323–7436, FAX 212/983–1275; Tyne Commission Quay, North Shields NE29 6EA, Newcastle, England, ☎ 0191/296–1313, FAX 091/296–1540), and **Scand-Lines** (✉ Box 1, DK–3000 Helsingør, Denmark, ☎ 45/49–26–26–83, FAX 45/49–26–11–24; Knutpunkten 44, S–252 78 Helsingborg, Sweden, ☎ 46/42–186100, FAX 46/42–187410).

The chief operator between England and many points within Scandinavia is **DFDS/Scandinavian Seaways** (✉ Sankt Annae Plads 30, DK–1295 Copenhagen, Denmark, ☎ 45/33–42–30–00, FAX 45/33–42–30–69; DFDS Travel Centre, 15 Hanover St., London W1R 9HG, ☎ 0171/409–6060, FAX 0171/409–6035; DFDS Seaways USA Inc., 6555 NW 9th Ave., Suite 207, Fort Lauderdale, FL 33309, ☎ 800/533–3755, FAX 305/491–7958; Box 8895, Scandiahamnen, S–402 72 Göteborg, Sweden, ☎ 46/8–650650), with ships connecting Harwich and Newcastle to Göteborg and Amsterdam.

Scandinavian Seaways Ferries (DFDS) (✉ Scandinavia House, Parkeston Quay, Harwich, Essex CO12 4QG, England, ☎ 01255/24–02–40; in Denmark, ☎ 33/11–22–55) sail from Harwich to Esbjerg (20 hours) on Jylland's west coast and from Newcastle to Esbjerg (21 hours). Schedules in both summer and winter are very irregular. There are many discounts, including 20% for senior citizens and the disabled, and 50% for children between the ages of 4 and 16.

Connections from Denmark to Norway and Sweden are available through DFDS and the **Stena Line** (✉ Trafikhamnen, DK–9900 Frederikshavn, Denmark, ☎ 45/96–20–02–00, FAX 45/96–20–02–81; Jernbanetorget 2, N–0154 Oslo 1, Norway, ☎ 47/23–17–90–00, FAX 47/22–41–44–40; Scandinavia AB, S–405 19 Göteborg, Sweden, ☎ 46/31–775–0000, FAX 46/31–858595).

Connections to the Faroe Islands from Norway and Denmark are available through the **Smyril Line** (DFDS— ☞ *above*—or J. Bronksgoøta 37, Box 370, FR–110 Tórshavn, Faroe Islands, ☎ 298/15–900, FAX 298/15–707; Bergen, Norway, ☎ 47/55–32–09–70, FAX 47/55–96–02–72).

Travel by car often necessitates travel by ferry. Some well-known vehicle and passenger ferries run between Dragør, Denmark (just south of Copenhagen), and Limhamn, Sweden (just south of Malmö); between Helsingør, Denmark, and Helsingborg, Sweden; and between Copenhagen and Göteborg, Sweden. On the Dragør/Limhamn ferry (ScandLines), taking a car one-way costs SKr395 (about $60 or £39). An easy trip runs between Copenhagen and Göteborg on **Stena Line** (in Sweden, ☎ 031/75–00–00). The Helsingør/Helsingborg ferry (Scand-Lines also) takes only 25 minutes; taking a car along one-way costs SKr330 (about $50 or £33). Fares for round-trip are cheaper, and on weekends the Öresund Runt pass (for crossing between Dragoør and Limhamn one way and Helsingborg and Helsingoør the other way) costs only SKr495 (about $75 or £49).

G

GAY & LESBIAN TRAVEL

➤ GAY- AND LESBIAN-FRIENDLY TRAVEL AGENCIES: **Advance Damron** (✉ 1 Greenway Plaza, Suite 800, Houston, TX 77046, ☎ 713/850–1140 or 800/695–0880, FAX 713/888–1010). **Club Travel** (✉ 8739 Santa Monica Blvd., West Hollywood, CA 90069, ☎ 310/358–2200 or 800/429–8747, FAX 310/358–2222). **Islanders/Kennedy Travel** (✉ 183 W. 10th St., New York, NY 10014, ☎ 212/242–3222 or 800/988–1181, FAX 212/929–8530). **Now Voyager** (✉ 4406 18th St., San Francisco,

CA 94114, ☎ 415/626–1169 or 800/255–6951, FAX 415/626–8626). Yellowbrick Road (✉ 1500 W. Balmoral Ave., Chicago, IL 60640, ☎ 773/561–1800 or 800/642–2488, FAX 773/561–4497). Skylink Women's Travel (✉ 3577 Moorland Ave., Santa Rosa, CA 95407, ☎ 707/585–8355 or 800/225–5759, FAX 707/584–5637), serving lesbian travelers.

H

HEALTH

MEDICAL PLANS

No one plans to get sick while traveling, but it happens, so **consider signing up with a medical-assistance company.** Members get doctor referrals, emergency evacuation or repatriation, 24-hour telephone hot lines for medical consultation, cash for emergencies, and other personal and legal assistance. Coverage varies by plan, so **review the benefits carefully.**

➤ MEDICAL-ASSISTANCE COMPANIES: **International SOS Assistance** (✉ Box 11568, Philadelphia, PA 19116, ☎ 215/244–1500 or 800/523–8930; ✉ 1255 University St., Suite 420, Montréal, Québec H3B 3B6, ☎ 514/874–7674 or 800/363–0263; ✉ 7 Old Lodge Pl., St. Margarets, Twickenham TW1 1RQ, England, ☎ 0181/744–0033). **MEDEX Assistance Corporation** (✉ Box 5375, Timonium, MD 21094-5375, ☎ 410/453–6300 or 800/537–2029). **Traveler's Emergency Network** (✉ 3100 Tower Blvd., Suite 1000B, Durham, NC 27707, ☎ 919/490–6055 or 800/275–4836, FAX 919/493–8262). **TravMed** (✉ Box 5375, Timonium, MD 21094, ☎ 410/453–6380 or 800/732–5309). **Worldwide Assistance Services** (✉ 1133 15th St. NW, Suite 400, Washington, DC 20005, ☎ 202/331–1609 or 800/821–2828, FAX 202/828–5896).

I

INSURANCE

Travel insurance is the best way to **protect yourself against financial loss.** The most useful policies are trip-cancellation-and-interruption, default, medical, and comprehensive insurance.

Without insurance you will lose all or most of your money if you cancel

your trip, regardless of the reason. It's essential that you **buy trip-cancellation-and-interruption insurance,** particularly if your airline ticket, cruise, or package tour is nonrefundable and cannot be changed. When considering how much coverage you need, look for a policy that will cover the cost of your trip plus the nondiscounted price of a one-way airline ticket, should you need to return home early. Also **consider default or bankruptcy insurance,** which protects you against a supplier's failure to deliver.

Medicare generally does not cover health-care costs outside the United States, nor do many privately issued policies. If your own policy does not cover you outside the United States, **consider buying supplemental medical coverage.** Remember that travel health insurance is different from a medical-assistance plan (☞ Health, *above*).

Citizens of the United Kingdom can buy an annual travel-insurance policy valid for most vacations during the year in which it's purchased. If you are pregnant or have a preexisting medical condition, make sure you're covered.

If you have purchased an expensive vacation, particularly one that involves travel abroad, comprehensive insurance is a must. **Look for comprehensive policies that include trip-delay insurance,** which will protect you in the event that weather problems cause you to miss your flight, tour, or cruise. A few insurers sell waivers for preexisting medical conditions. Companies that offer both features include Access America, Carefree Travel, Travel Insured International, and Travel Guard (☞ *below*).

Always **buy travel insurance directly from the insurance company**; if you buy it from a travel agency or tour operator that goes out of business you probably will not be covered for the agency or operator's default, a major risk. Before you make any purchase, **review your existing health and home-owner's policies** to find out whether they cover expenses incurred while traveling.

➤ TRAVEL INSURERS: In the U.S., **Access America** (✉ 6600 W. Broad

St., Richmond, VA 23230, ☏ 804/285–3300 or 800/284–8300), **Carefree Travel Insurance** (✉ Box 9366, 100 Garden City Plaza, Garden City, NY 11530, ☏ 516/294–0220 or 800/323–3149), **Near Travel Services** (✉ Box 1339, Calumet City, IL 60409, ☏ 708/868–6700 or 800/654–6700), **Travel Guard International** (✉ 1145 Clark St., Stevens Point, WI 54481, ☏ 715/345–0505 or 800/826–1300), **Travel Insured International** (✉ Box 280568, East Hartford, CT 06128–0568, ☏ 860/528–7663 or 800/243–3174), **Travelex Insurance Services** (✉ 11717 Burt St., Suite 202, Omaha, NE 68154-1500, ☏ 402/445–8637 or 800/228–9792, FAX 800/867–9531), **Wallach & Company** (✉ 107 W. Federal St., Box 480, Middleburg, VA 20118, ☏ 540/687–3166 or 800/237–6615). In Canada, **Mutual of Omaha** (✉ Travel Division, 500 University Ave., Toronto, Ontario M5G 1V8, ☏ 416/598–4083, 800/268–8825 in Canada). In the U.K., **Association of British Insurers** (✉ 51 Gresham St., London EC2V 7HQ, ☏ 0171/600–3333).

L

LANGUAGE

Despite the fact that four of the five Scandinavian tongues are in the Germanic family of languages, it is a myth that someone who speaks German can understand Danish. Fortunately, English is widely spoken in Scandinavia. German is the most common third language. Outside major cities, English becomes rarer, and it's a good idea to **take along a dictionary or phrase book.** Even here, however, anyone under the age of 50 is likely to have studied English in school.

Characters special to these three languages are the Danish "ø" and the Swedish "ö," pronounced a bit like a very short "er", similar to the French "eu"; "æ" or "ä," which sounds like the "a" in "ape" but with a glottal stop, or the "a" in "cat," depending on the region, and the "å" (also written "aa"), which sounds like the "o" in "ghost." The important thing about these characters isn't that you pronounce them correctly—foreigners usually can't—but that you know to look for them in the phone book at the very end. Mr. Søren Åstrup, for example, will be found after "Z." Æ or Ä and Ø or Ö follow.

LODGING

In the larger cities, lodging ranges from first-class business hotels run by SAS, Sheraton, and Scandic to good-quality tourist-class hotels, such as RESO, Best Western, Scandic Budget, and Sweden Hotels, to a wide variety of single-entrepreneur hotels. In the countryside, look for independently run inns and motels. In Denmark they're called *kroer.*

Two things about hotels usually surprise North Americans: the relatively limited dimensions of Scandinavian beds and the generous size of Scandinavian breakfasts. Scandinavian double beds are often about 60 inches wide or slightly less, close in size to the U.S. queen size. King-size beds (72 inches wide) are difficult to find and, if available, require special reservations.

Scandinavian breakfasts resemble what many people would call lunch, usually including breads, cheeses, marmalade, hams, lunch meats, eggs, juice, cereal, milk, and coffee. Generally, the farther north you go, the larger the breakfasts become. As time goes on, an increasing number of hotels are eliminating breakfast from their room rates; even if it is not included, breakfast is usually well worth its price.

Danes generally prefer a shower to a bath, so **if you particularly want a bath, ask for it,** but be prepared to pay more. Also, many older hotels, particularly the country inns and independently run smaller hotels in the cities, do not have private bathrooms. Ask ahead if this is important to you.

Older hotels may have some rooms described as "double," which in fact have one double bed plus one foldout sofa big enough for two people. This arrangement is occasionally called a combi-room but is being phased out.

CAMPING

If you plan to camp in one of Denmark's 500-plus approved campsites, you'll need an International Camping Carnet or Danish Camping Pass (available at any campsite and valid for one year). For details on camping and discounts for groups and families, contact **Campingrådet** (✉ Hesseløg. 16, DK–2100 Copenhagen Ø, ☎ 39/27–88–44).

DISCOUNTS

Before you leave home, **ask your travel agent about discounts** (☞ Travel Agencies, *below*), including summer hotel checks for Best Western, Scandic, and Inter Nor hotels, and enormous year-round rebates at SAS hotels for travelers over 65. Many places offer summer reductions to compensate for the slowdown in business travel and conferences. All EuroClass (business class) passengers can get discounts of at least 10% at SAS hotels when they book through SAS.

Denmark offers Inn Checks, or prepaid hotel vouchers, for accommodations ranging from first-class hotels to country cottages. These vouchers, which must be purchased from travel agents or from the Danish Tourist Board before departure, are sold individually and in packets for as many nights as needed and offer savings of up to 50%. For further information about Scandinavian hotel vouchers, contact the Danish Tourist Board (☞ Visitor Information, *below*).

FARM VACATIONS

There's a minimum stay of three nights for most farm stays. Bed-and-breakfast costs DKr150; half-board, around DKr245. Lunch and dinner can often be purchased for DKr25 to DKr35, and full board can be arranged. Children under 11 get 50% (for the youngest, you can save by booking directly through the farm). Contact **Ferie på Landet** (Holiday in the Country, ✉ Ceresvej 2, DK 8410 Rønde, Jylland, ☎ 70/10–41–90) for details.

INNS

Contact **Dansk Kroferie** (✉ Vejlevej 16, DK–8700 Horsens, ☎ 75/64–87–00) to order a free catalog of B&B inns, but choose carefully: the organization includes some chain hotels that would be hard-pressed to demonstrate a modicum of inn-related charm. The price of an inn covers one overnight stay in a room with bath, breakfast included. Note that some establishments tack an additional DKr125 surcharge onto the price of a double. You can save money by investing in **Inn Checks,** valid at 84 inns. Each check costs DKr585 per couple. **Family checks** (DKr665–DKr745) are also available. Contact the Danish Tourist Board (☞ Visitor Information, *below*) for the checks.

RENTALS

A simple house with room for four will cost from DKr2,500 per week and up. Contact **DanCenter** (✉ Falkoner Allé 7, DK–2000 Frederiksberg, ☎ 31/19–09–00).

RESERVATIONS

Make reservations whenever possible, especially in resort areas near the coasts. Even countryside inns, which usually have space, are sometimes packed with vacationing Europeans.

Ask about high and low seasons when making reservations, since some hotels lower prices during tourist season, whereas others raise them during the same period.

The very friendly staff at the **hotel booking desk** (☎ 33/12–28–80) in the main tourist office (✉ Bernstorffsg. 1, DK–1577 Copenhagen V, ☎ 33/11–13–25) can help find rooms in hotels, hostels, and private homes, or even at campsites. Prices range from budget upward. Prebooking in private homes and hotels must be done two months in advance, but last-minute (as in same-day) hotel rooms can also be found and will save you 50% off the normal price.

YOUTH AND FAMILY HOSTELS

If you have a Hosteling International–American Youth Hostels card (obtainable before you leave home, ☎ 202/783–6161 in Washington, D.C.), the average cost is DKr70 to DKr85 per person. Without the card, there's a surcharge of DKr25. The hostels fill up quickly in summer, so make your reservations early. Most hostels are particularly sympathetic to students and will usually find them at least a place on the floor. Bring your own linens or sleep sheet, though these can usually be rented at the hostel. Sleeping bags are not allowed. Contact **Danhostel Danmarks Vandrehjem** (✉ Vesterbrog. 39, DK–1620, Copenhagen V, ☎ 31/31–36–12, FAX 31/31–36–26). It charges for information, but you can get a free brochure, *Camping/Youth and Family Hostels,* from the Danish Tourist Board.

M
MAIL

POSTAL RATES

Airmail letters and postcards to the United States cost DKr5.25 for 20 grams. Letters and postcards to the United Kingdom and EU countries cost DKr4. You can buy stamps at post offices or from shops selling postcards.

RECEIVING MAIL

You can arrange to have your mail sent general delivery, marked *poste restante,* to any post office, hotel, or inn. The address for the main post office in Copenhagen is Tietgensgade 37, DK–1704 KBH. If you do not have an address, **American Express** (✉ Amagertorv 18, DK–1461 KBH K, ☎ 33/12–23–01) will also receive and hold cardholders' mail.

MONEY

The monetary unit in Denmark is the krone (DKr), divided into 100 øre. New 50, 100, 200, 500 and 1,000 kroner notes, featuring Great Danes like authoress Karen Blixen and physicist Niels Bohr, are to be issued in the years up to the millennium, as the old notes are phased out.

In this book currency is abbreviated DKr (Danish kroner). In Denmark you may see prices indicated with Kr only, and you may see exchange rates in banks quoted for DKK.

ATMS

Before leaving home, **make sure that your credit cards have been programmed for ATM use in Denmark.** Note that Discover is accepted mostly in the United States. Local bank cards often do not work overseas or may access only your checking account; **ask your bank about a MasterCard/Cirrus or Visa debit card,** which works like a bank card but can be used at any ATM displaying a MasterCard/Cirrus or Visa logo. These cards, too, may tap only your checking account; check with your bank about their policy.

➤ ATM LOCATIONS: **Cirrus** (☎ 800/424–7787). A list of **Plus** locations is available at your local bank.

COSTS

Denmark's economy is stable, and inflation remains reasonably low.

Although lower than Norway's and Sweden's, the Danish cost of living is nonetheless high. Prices are highest in Copenhagen, lower elsewhere in the country. Some sample prices: cup of coffee, DKr14–DKr20; bottle of beer, DKr15–DKr30; soda, DKr10–DKr15; ham sandwich, DKr25–DKr40; 1-mi taxi ride, DKr35–DKr50, depending on traffic.

Sales tax is high, but you can get some refunds by shopping at tax-free stores (☞ VAT, *below*). The **Copenhagen Card** can save you money on transportation and admission costs. It offers unlimited travel on buses and suburban trains (S-trains), admission to more than 70 museums and sites in Copenhagen and around Sjælland, and a reduction on the ferry crossing to Sweden. You can buy the card, which costs DKr140 (24 hours), DKr255 (48 hours), or DKr320 (72 hours) and is half-price for children, at tourist offices and hotels and from travel agents.

You can **reduce the cost of food by planning.** Breakfast is often included in your hotel bill; if not, you may wish to buy fruit, sweet rolls, and a beverage for a picnic breakfast. Electrical devices for hot coffee or tea should be bought abroad, though, to conform to the local current. **Opt for a restaurant lunch instead of dinner,** since the latter tends to be significantly more expensive. When ordering water, specify tap water if that is what you want, as the term "water" can refer to soft drinks and bottled water, which are also expensive.

Denmark takes a less restrictive approach to alcohol than most of Scandinavia, with liquor and beer available in the smallest of grocery stores, open weekdays and Saturday morning, but prices are high. (When you visit relatives in Scandinavia, a bottle of liquor or fine wine bought duty-free on the trip over is often a much-appreciated gift.)

CURRENCY EXCHANGE

At press time, the krone stood at 6.93 to the dollar, 11.38 to the pound sterling, and 4.73 to the Canadian dollar.

For the most favorable rates, **change money at banks.** Although fees charged for ATM transactions may be higher abroad than at home, Cirrus and Plus exchange rates are excellent, because they are based on wholesale rates offered only by major banks. You won't do as well at exchange booths in airports or rail and bus stations, in hotels, in restaurants, or in stores, although you may find their hours more convenient. To avoid lines at airport exchange booths, **get a small amount of local currency before you leave home.**

➤ EXCHANGE SERVICES: **International Currency Express** (☎ 888/842–0880 on the East Coast or 888/278–6628 on the West Coast for telephone orders). **Thomas Cook Currency Services** (☎ 800/287–7362 for telephone orders and retail locations).

TIPPING

The egalitarian Danes do not expect to be tipped. Service is included in bills for hotels, bars, and restaurants. Taxi drivers round up the fare to the next krone but expect no tip. The exception is hotel porters, who receive about DKr5 per bag.

TRAVELER'S CHECKS

Whether or not to buy traveler's checks depends on where you are headed. **Take cash if your trip includes rural areas** and small towns, traveler's checks to cities. If your checks are lost or stolen, they can usually be replaced within 24 hours. To ensure a speedy refund, buy your checks yourself (don't ask someone else to make the purchase). When making a claim for stolen or lost checks, the person who bought the checks should make the call.

⊙ OPENING AND CLOSING TIMES

MUSEUMS

A number of Copenhagen's museums hold confounding hours, so always call first to confirm. As a rule, however, most museums are open 10 to 3 or 11 to 4 and are closed on Monday. In winter, opening hours are shorter, and some museums close for the season. Check the local papers or ask at tourist offices for current schedules.

SHOPS

Though many Danish stores are expanding their hours, sometimes even staying open on Sundays, most shops still keep the traditional hours: weekdays 10 to 5:30, until 7 on Thursday and Friday, until 1 or 2 on Saturday—though the larger department stores stay open until 5. Everything except bakeries, kiosks, flower shops, and a handful of grocers are closed on Sunday, and most bakeries take Monday off. The first and last Saturday of the month are Long Saturdays, when even the smaller shops, especially in large cities, stay open until 4 or 5. Grocery stores stay open until 8 PM on weekdays, and kiosks until much later.

BANKS

Banks in Copenhagen are open weekdays 9:30 to 4 and Thursdays until 6. Several *bureaux de change*, including the ones at Copenhagen's central station and airport, stay open until 10 PM. Outside Copenhagen, banking hours vary.

OUTDOOR ACTIVITIES AND SPORTS

BIKING

Bicycles can be sent as baggage between most train stations and can also be carried onto most trains and ferries; contact **DSB** (☎ 33/14–17–01) for information. All cabs must be able to take bikes and are equipped with racks (they add a modest fee).

Most towns have rentals, but check with local tourism offices for referrals. For more information, contact the **Danish Cyclist Federation** (✉ Rømersg. 7, DK–1362 KBH K, ☎ 33/32–31–21). The Danish Tourist Board also publishes bicycle maps and brochures.

Copenhagen-based **BikeDenmark** (✉ Åboulevarden 1, ☎ 35/36–41- -00) combines the flexibility of individual tours with the security of an organized outing. Choose from seven preplanned 5- to 10-day tours, which include bikes, maps, two fine meals per day, hotel accommodations, and hotel-to-hotel baggage transfers.

➤ UNITED STATES TOUR COMPANIES: **Borton Oversees** (✉ 5516 Lyndale Ave. S, Minneapolis, MN 55419, ☎ 800/843–0602). **Nordique Tours**

(✉ 5250 W. Century Blvd., Suite 626, Los Angeles, CA 90045, ☎ 800/995–7997). **Scanam World Tours** (✉ 933 Rte. 23, Pompton Plains, NJ 07444, ☎ 800/545–2204). **Gerhard's Bicycle Odysseys** (✉ Box 757, Portland Oregon, 97207, ☎ 503/223- 2402.

FISHING AND ANGLING

Licenses are required for fishing along the coasts; requirements vary from one area to another for fishing in lakes, streams, and the ocean. Licenses generally cost around DKr100 and can be purchased from any post office. Remember—it is illegal to fish within 1,650 ft of the mouth of a stream.

P

PACKING FOR DENMARK

Bring a folding umbrella and a lightweight raincoat, as it is common for the sky to be clear at 9 AM, rainy at 11 AM, and clear again in time for lunch. **Pack casual clothes,** as Danes tend to dress more casually than their Continental brethren. If you have trouble sleeping when it is light or are sensitive to strong sun, **bring an eye mask and dark sunglasses;** the sun rises as early as 4 AM in some areas, and the far-northern latitude causes it to slant at angles unseen elsewhere on the globe. **Bring bug repellent** if you plan to venture away from the capital cities; large mosquitoes can be a real nuisance on summer evenings in Denmark as well as in the far-northern reaches of Norway and Sweden.

Bring an extra pair of eyeglasses or contact lenses in your carry-on luggage, and if you have a health problem, **pack enough medication** to last the entire trip or have your doctor write you a prescription using the drug's generic name, because brand names vary from country to country. It's important that you **don't put prescription drugs or valuables in luggage to be checked**: it might go astray. To avoid problems with customs officials, carry medications in the original packaging. Also, don't forget the addresses of offices that handle refunds of lost traveler's checks.

LUGGAGE

In general, you are entitled to check two bags on flights within the United States and on international flights leaving the United States. A third piece may be brought on board, but it must fit easily under the seat in front of you or in the overhead compartment.

If you are flying between two foreign destinations, note that baggage allowances may be determined not by piece but by weight—generally 88 pounds (40 kilograms) in first class, 66 pounds (30 kilograms) in business class, and 44 pounds (20 kilograms) in economy. If your flight between two cities abroad *connects* with your transatlantic or transpacific flight, the piece method still applies.

Airline liability for baggage is limited to $1,250 per person on flights within the United States. On international flights it amounts to $9.07 per pound or $20 per kilogram for checked baggage (roughly $640 per 70-pound bag) and $400 per passenger for unchecked baggage. Insurance for losses exceeding these amounts can be bought from the airline at check-in for about $10 per $1,000 of coverage; note that this coverage excludes a rather extensive list of items, which is shown on your airline ticket.

Before departure, **itemize your bags' contents** and their worth, and label the bags with your name, address, and phone number. (If you use your home address, cover it so that potential thieves can't see it readily.) Inside each bag, **pack a copy of your itinerary.** At check-in, **make sure that each bag is correctly tagged** with the destination airport's three-letter code. If your bags arrive damaged or fail to arrive at all, file a written report with the airline before leaving the airport.

PASSPORTS & VISAS

Once your travel plans are confirmed, **check the expiration date of your passport.** It's also a good idea to **make photocopies of the data page**; leave one copy with someone at home and keep another with you, separated from your passport. If you lose your passport, promptly call the nearest embassy or consulate and the local police; having a copy of the data page can speed replacement.

U.S. CITIZENS

All U.S. citizens, even infants, need only a valid passport to enter Denmark for stays of up to three months.

➤ INFORMATION: **Office of Passport Services** (☎ 202/647–0518).

CANADIANS

You need only a valid passport to enter Denmark for stays of up to three months.

➤ INFORMATION: **Passport Office** (☎ 819/994–3500 or 800/567–6868).

U.K. CITIZENS

Citizens of the United Kingdom need only a valid passport to enter Denmark for stays of up to three months.

➤ INFORMATION: **London Passport Office** (☎ 0990/21010) for fees and documentation requirements and to request an emergency passport.

S

SENIOR-CITIZEN TRAVEL

To qualify for age-related discounts, **mention your senior-citizen status up front** when booking hotel reservations (not when checking out) and before you're seated in restaurants (not when paying the bill). Note that discounts may be limited to certain menus, days, or hours. When renting a car, **ask about promotional car-rental discounts,** which can be cheaper than senior-citizen rates.

➤ EDUCATIONAL TRAVEL PROGRAMS: **Elderhostel** (✉ 75 Federal St., 3rd floor, Boston, MA 02110, ☎ 617/426–8056). **Interhostel** (✉ University of New Hampshire, 6 Garrison Ave., Durham, NH 03824, ☎ 603/862–1147 or 800/733–9753, FAX 603/862–1113).

SHOPPING

Prices in Denmark are never low, but quality is high, and specialties are sometimes less expensive here than elsewhere. Danish Lego blocks are just one of the items to look for. Keep an eye out for sales, called *udsalg* in Danish.

STUDENTS

To save money, **look into deals available through student-oriented travel agencies.** To qualify you'll need a bona fide student ID card. Members of international student groups are also eligible.

➤ STUDENT IDs AND SERVICES: **Council on International Educational Exchange** (✉ CIEE, 205 E. 42nd St., 14th floor, New York, NY 10017, ☎ 212/822–2600 or 888/268–6245, FAX 212/822–2699), for mail orders only, in the United States. **Travel Cuts** (✉ 187 College St., Toronto, Ontario M5T 1P7, ☎ 416/979–2406 or 800/667–2887) in Canada.

➤ HOSTELING: **Hostelling International—American Youth Hostels** (✉ 733 15th St. NW, Suite 840, Washington, DC 20005, ☎ 202/783–6161, FAX 202/783–6171). **Hostelling International—Canada** (✉ 400-205 Catherine St., Ottawa, Ontario K2P 1C3, ☎ 613/237–7884, FAX 613/237–7868). **Youth Hostel Association of England and Wales** (✉ Trevelyan House, 8 St. Stephen's Hill, St. Albans, Hertfordshire AL1 2DY, ☎ 01727/855215 or 01727/845047, FAX 01727/844126). Membership in the U.S., $25; in Canada, C$26.75; in the U.K., £9.30).

➤ STUDENT TOURS: **AESU Travel** (✉ 2 Hamill Rd., Suite 248, Baltimore, MD 21210-1807, ☎ 410/323–4416 or 800/638–7640, FAX 410/323–4498).

T

TAXES

VALUE-ADDED TAX (V.A.T.)

All hotel, restaurant, and departure taxes and VAT (what the Danes call *moms*) are automatically included in prices. VAT is 25%. One way to beat high prices is to **take advantage of tax-free shopping.** Throughout Denmark, you can make major purchases free of tax if you have a foreign passport. The more than 1,500 shops that participate in the tax-free scheme have a white TAX FREE sticker on their windows. Ask about tax-free shopping when you make a purchase for DKr300 (about $45, or £32) or more; the refund for non-EU tourists is 18% for purchases over Dkr300. At the shop, you'll be asked to fill out a form and show your passport. You'll receive a special export receipt with your purchase—**hold on to this.** Keep your parcels sealed and unused and take them out of the country within 30 days of purchase. Occasionally, customs authorities do ask to see purchases, so **pack them where they will be accessible.** When you leave, you can obtain a refund of the tax in cash (in kroner or dollars) or on a major credit-card from a airport or ferry customs desk, or, upon arriving home, you can send your receipts to an office in the country of purchase to receive your refund by mail. Be aware that limits for EU tourists are higher than for those coming from outside the EU.

TELEPHONES

The country code for Denmark is 45.

Telephone exchanges throughout Denmark were changed over the past couple of years. If you hear a recorded message or three loud beeps, chances are the number you are trying to reach has been changed. Directory assistance (**KTAS**)(☎ 118) can always find current numbers.

CALLING HOME

Before you go, **find out the local access codes** for your destinations. AT&T, MCI, and Sprint long-distance services make calling home relatively convenient, but you may find the local access number blocked in many hotel rooms. First ask the hotel operator to connect you. If the hotel operator balks, ask for an international operator, or dial the international operator yourself. One way to improve your odds of getting connected to your long-distance carrier is to travel with more than one company's calling card (a hotel may block Sprint, for example, but not MCI). If all else fails, call your phone company collect in the United States or call from a pay phone in the hotel lobby.

➤ To Obtain Access Codes: **AT&T USADirect** (☎ 800/874–4000). **MCI Call USA** (☎ 800/444–4444). **Sprint Express** (☎ 800/793–1153).

➤ Local Access Codes: **AT&T USADirect** (☎ 800/100100). **MCI Call USA** (☎ 800/1022). **Sprint Express** (☎ 800/10877).

DIRECTORY ASSISTANCE AND OPERATOR INFORMATION

Most operators speak English. For national directory assistance (KTAS), dial ☎ 118; for an international operator, dial ☎ 113; for a directory-assisted international call, dial ☎ 115. To reach an AT&T direct operator in the United States, for collect, person-to-person, or credit-card calls, dial ☎ 80–01–0010.

INTERNATIONAL CALLS

Dial ☎ 00, then the country code (1 for the United States and Canada, 44 for Great Britain), the area code, and the number. It's very expensive to telephone or fax from hotels, although the regional phone companies offer a discount after 7:30 PM. It's less expensive to make calls from either the Copenhagen main rail station or the airports.

LOCAL CALLS

Phones accept 1-, 5-, 10-, and 20-kroner coins. Pick up the receiver, dial the number, always including the area code, and wait until the party answers; then deposit the coins. You have roughly a minute per krone, so you can make another call on the same payment if your time has not run out. When it does, you will hear a beep and your call will be disconnected unless you deposit another coin. Dial the eight-digit number for calls anywhere within the country. For calls to the Faroe Islands (☎ 298) and Greenland (☎ 299), dial ☎ 00, then the three-digit code, then the five-digit number.

TOUR OPERATORS

Buying a prepackaged tour or independent vacation can make your trip to Denmark less expensive and more hassle-free. Because everything is prearranged you'll spend less time planning.

Operators that handle several hundred thousand travelers per year can use their purchasing power to give you a good price. Their high volume may also indicate financial stability. But some small companies provide more personalized service; because they tend to specialize, they may also be more knowledgeable about a given area.

A GOOD DEAL?

The more your package or tour includes, the better you can predict the ultimate cost of your vacation. Make sure you know exactly what is covered, and **beware of hidden costs.**

THE GOLD GUIDE / SMART TRAVEL TIPS

Are taxes, tips, and service charges included? Transfers and baggage handling? Entertainment and excursions? These can add up.

If the package or tour you are considering is priced lower than in your wildest dreams, **be skeptical.** Also, **make sure your travel agent knows the accommodations** and other services. Ask about the hotel's location, room size, beds, and whether it has a pool, room service, or programs for children, if you care about these. Has your agent been there in person or sent others you can contact?

BUYER BEWARE

Each year consumers are stranded or lose their money when tour operators—even very large ones with excellent reputations—go out of business. So **check out the operator.** Find out how long the company has been in business, and ask several agents about its reputation. **Don't book unless the firm has a consumer-protection program.**

Members of the National Tour Association and United States Tour Operators Association are required to set aside funds to cover your payments and travel arrangements in case the company defaults. Nonmembers may carry insurance instead. Look for the details, and for the name of an underwriter with a solid reputation, in the operator's brochure. Note: When it comes to tour operators, **don't trust escrow accounts.** Although the Department of Transportation watches over charter-flight operators, no regulatory body prevents tour operators from raiding the till. You may want to protect yourself by buying travel insurance that includes a tour-operator default provision. For more information, *see* Consumer Protection, *above.*

It's also a good idea to choose a company that participates in the American Society of Travel Agent's Tour Operator Program (TOP). This gives you a forum if there are any disputes between you and your tour operator; ASTA will act as mediator.

➤ Tour-Operator Recommendations: **American Society of Travel Agents** (☞ Travel Agencies, *below*). **National Tour Association** (⊠ NTA, 546 E. Main St., Lexington, KY

40508, ☎ 606/226–4444 or 800/755–8687). **United States Tour Operators Association** (⊠ USTOA, 342 Madison Ave., Suite 1522, New York, NY 10173, ☎ 212/599–6599, FAX 212/599–6744).

USING AN AGENT

Travel agents are excellent resources. In fact, large operators accept bookings made only through travel agents. But it's a good idea to **collect brochures from several agencies,** because some agents' suggestions may be influenced by relationships with tour and package firms that reward them for volume sales. If you have a special interest, **find an agent with expertise in that area**; ASTA (☞ Travel Agencies, *below*) has a database of specialists worldwide. Do some homework on your own, too: Local tourism boards can provide information about lesser-known and small-niche operators, some of which may sell only direct.

SINGLE TRAVELERS

Prices for packages and tours are usually quoted per person, based on two sharing a room. If traveling solo, you may be required to pay the full double-occupancy rate. Some operators eliminate this surcharge if you agree to be matched with a roommate of the same sex, even if one is not found by departure time.

GROUP TOURS

Among companies that sell tours to Denmark, the following are nationally known, have a proven reputation, and offer plenty of options. The classifications used below represent different price categories, and you'll probably encounter these terms when talking to a travel agent or tour operator. The key difference is usually in accommodations, which run from budget to better, and better-yet to best.

➤ Super-deluxe: **Abercrombie & Kent** (⊠ 1520 Kensington Rd., Oak Brook, IL 60521-2141, ☎ 630/954–2944 or 800/323–7308, FAX 630/954–3324). **Travcoa** (⊠ Box 2630, 2350 S.E. Bristol St., Newport Beach, CA 92660, ☎ 714/476–2800 or 800/992–2003, FAX 714/476–2538).

➤ Deluxe: **Globus** (⊠ 5301 S. Federal Circle, Littleton, CO 80123-2980, ☎ 303/797–2800 or 800/221–0090, FAX 303/347–2080). **Maupin-**

tour (✉ 1515 St. Andrews Dr.,
Lawrence, KS 66047, ☎ 913/843–
1211 or 800/255–4266, FAX 913/843–
8351). **Tauck Tours** (✉ Box 5027,
276 Post Rd. W, Westport, CT
06881-5027, ☎ 203/226–6911 or
800/468–2825, FAX 203/221–6828).

➤ FIRST-CLASS: **Bennett Tours** (✉
270 Madison Ave., New York, NY
10016-0658, ☎ 212/532–5060 or
800/221–2420, FAX 212/779–8944).
Brendan Tours (✉ 15137 Califa St.,
Van Nuys, CA 91411, ☎ 818/785–
9696 or 800/421–8446, FAX 818/902–
9876). **Brekke Tours** (✉ 802 N. 43rd
St., Ste. D, Grand Forks, ND 58203,
☎ 701/772–8999 or 800/437—5302,
FAX 701/780–9352). **Caravan Tours**
(✉ 401 N. Michigan Ave., Chicago,
IL 60611, ☎ 312/321–9800 or 800/
227–2826, FAX 312/321–9845). **Col-
lette Tours** (✉ 162 Middle St., Paw-
tucket, RI 02860, ☎ 401/728–3805
or 800/832–4656, FAX 401/728–1380).
Finnair (☎ 800/950–5000). **KITT
Holidays** (✉ 2 Appletree Sq., #150,
8011 34th Ave. S, Minneapolis, MN
55425, ☎ 612/854–8005 or 800/
262—8728, FAX 612/854–6948).
Scantours (✉ 1535 6th St., #205,
Santa Monica, CA 90401-2533,
☎ 310/451–0911 or 800/223–7226,
FAX 310/395–2013). **Scan Travel
Center** (✉ 66 Edgewood Ave., Larch-
mont, NY 10538, ☎ 803/671–6758
or 800/759–7226). **Trafalgar Tours**
(✉ 11 E. 26th St., New York, NY
10010, ☎ 212/689–8977 or 800/
854–0103, FAX 800/457–6644).

➤ BUDGET: **Cosmos** (☞ Globus,
above). **Trafalgar** (☞ *above*).

PACKAGES

Like group tours, independent vacation packages are available from
major tour operators and airlines. The
companies listed below offer vacation
packages in a broad price range.

➤ AIR/HOTEL/SIGHTSEEING: **Delta
Dream Vacations** (☎ 800/872–7786,
FAX 954/357–4687). **DER Tours** (✉
9501 W. Devon St., Rosemont, IL
60018, ☎ 800/937–1235, FAX 800/
282–7474; FAX 800/860–9944, for
brochures). **Icelandair** (☎ 800/757–
3876).

➤ FLY/DRIVE: **Delta Dream Vacations**
(☞ *above*).

THEME TRIPS

➤ ADVENTURE: **Borton Overseas** (✉
1621 E. 79th St., Bloomington, MN
55425, ☎ 612/883–0704 or 800/
843–0602, FAX 612/883–0221). **Scandinavian Special Interest Network**
(✉ Box 313, Sparta, NJ 07871, ☎
201/729–8961, FAX 201/729–6565).

➤ BICYCLING: **Euro-Bike Tours** (✉
Box 990, De Kalb, IL 60115, ☎ 800/
321–6060, FAX 815/758–8851).

➤ CRUISING: **Bergen Line** (✉ 405 Park
Ave., New York, NY 10022, ☎ 212/
319–1300 or 800/323–7436, FAX 212/
319–1390). **EuroCruises** (✉ 303 W.
13th St., New York, NY 10014, ☎
212/691–2099 or 800/688—3876).
**Swan Hellenic/Classical Cruises &
Tours** (✉ 132 E. 70th St., New York,
NY 10021, ☎ 800/252–7745, FAX 212/
774–1545).

➤ CUSTOMIZED PACKAGES: **Scandinavian Special Interest Network** (☞
Adventure, *above*).

➤ FISHING: **Scandinavian Special
Interest Network** (☞ Adventure,
above).

➤ GENEALOGY: **Scan Travel Center**
(☞ Groups, *above*).

➤ MUSIC: **Dailey-Thorp Travel** (✉
330 W. 58th St., #610, New York,
NY 10019-1817, ☎ 212/307–1555
or 800/998–4677, FAX 212/974–1420).

TRAIN TRAVEL

DSB and a few private companies
cover the country with a dense
network of services, supplemented
by buses in remote areas. Hourly
intercity trains connect the main
towns in Jylland and Fyn with
Copenhagen and Sjælland, using
high-speed diesels, called IC-3, on
the most important stretches. All
these trains make one-hour ferry
crossings of the Great Belt, the
waterway separating Fyn and Sjælland. You can reserve seats on intercity trains, and you *must* have a
reservation if you plan to cross the
Great Belt. Buy tickets at stations.
The ScanRail Pass and the Interail
and Eurailpasses are also valid on all
DSB trains. Call the **DSB** Travel
Office (☎ 33/14–17–01 or 42/52–
92–22) for additional information.

Trains within Europe are well connected to Denmark, with Copenhagen serving as the main hub; however, it's often little cheaper than flying, especially if you make your arrangements from the United States. Scanrail Passes offer discounts on train, ferry, and car transportation in Denmark, Finland, Sweden, and Norway (☞ *below*). EurailPasses, purchased only in the United States, are accepted by the Danish State Railways and on some ferries operated by DSB (☞ *below*).

FROM THE UNITED KINGDOM

From London, the crossing takes 23 hours, including ferry. **British Rail European Travel Center** (✉ Victoria Station, London, ☎ 0171/834–2345). **Eurotrain** (✉ 52 Grosvenor Gardens, London SW1, ☎ 0171/730–3402). **Wasteels** (✉ 121 Wilton Rd., London SW1, ☎ 0171/834–7066).

DISCOUNT PASSES

The **ScanRail** pass, which affords unlimited train travel throughout Denmark, Finland, Norway, and Sweden and restricted ferry passage in and beyond Scandinavia, comes in various denominations: 5 days of travel within 15 days ($222 first class, $176 second class); 10 days within a month ($354 first class, $284 second class); or 1 month ($516 first class, $414 second class). For info on the ScanRail'n Drive Pass, *see* Train Travel *in* the Gold Guide). In the United States, call Rail Europe (☎ 800/848–7245) or **DER** (☎ 800/782–2424). You may want to wait to buy the pass until you get to Scandinavia; unlike the EurailPass, which is cheaper in the United States, the ScanRail Pass is cheaper in Scandinavia. Double-check prices before you leave home. No matter where you get it though, various discounts are offered to holders of the pass by hotel chains and other organizations; ask DER, Rail Europe, or your travel agent for details.

Travelers over 60 can buy a **SeniorRail Card** for DKr150 (about $27) . It gives 30% discounts on train travel in 21 European countries for a whole year from purchase.

Denmark is one of 17 countries in which you can **use EurailPasses,** which provide unlimited first-class rail travel, in all of the participating countries, for the duration of the pass. If you plan to rack up the miles, get a standard pass. These are available for 15 days ($522), 21 days ($678), one month ($838), two months ($1,188), and three months ($1,468).

In addition to standard EurailPasses, **ask about special rail-pass plans.** Among these are the Eurail Youthpass (for those under age 26), the Eurail Saverpass (which gives a discount for two or more people traveling together), a Eurail Flexipass (which allows a certain number of travel days within a set period), the Euraildrive Pass, and the Europass Drive (which combines travel by train and rental car).

Whichever pass you choose, remember that you must **purchase your pass before you leave** for Europe.

Many travelers assume that rail passes guarantee them seats on the trains they wish to ride. Not so. You need to **book seats ahead even if you are using a rail pass**; seat reservations are required on some European trains, particularly high-speed trains, and are a good idea on trains that may be crowded—particularly in summer on popular routes. You will also need a reservation if you purchase sleeping accommodations.

➤ RAIL PASSES: Danish rail passes are sold by travel agents as well as **Rail Europe** (✉ 226–230 Westchester Ave., White Plains, NY 10604, ☎ 914/682–5172 or 800/438–7245; 2087 Dundas East, Suite 105, Mississauga, Ontario L4X 1M2, ☎ 416/602–4195).

Eurail and EuroPasses are available through travel agents and **Rail Europe** (✉ 226-230 Westchester Ave., White Plains, NY 10604, ☎ 914/682–5172 or 800/438–7245; 2087 Dundas East, Suite 105, Mississauga, Ontario L4X 1M2, ☎ 416/602–4195), **DER Tours** (✉ Box 1606, Des Plaines, IL 60017, ☎ 800/782–2424, ℻ 800/282–7474), or **CIT Tours Corp.** (✉ 342 Madison Ave., Suite 207, New York, NY 10173, ☎ 212/697–2100 or 800/248–8687, or 800/248–7245 in western U.S.).

TRAVEL AGENCIES

A good travel agent puts your needs first. Look for an agency that has been in business at least five years, emphasizes customer service, and has someone on staff who specializes in your destination. In addition, **make sure the agency belongs to the American Society of Travel Agents** (ASTA). If your travel agency is also acting as your tour operator, *see* Buyer Beware in Tour Operators, *above*).

➤ LOCAL AGENT REFERRALS: **American Society of Travel Agents** (ASTA, ☎ 800/965–2782 24-hr hot line, FAX 703/684–8319). **Alliance of Canadian Travel Associations** (✉ Suite 201, 1729 Bank St., Ottawa, Ontario K1V 7Z5, ☎ 613/521–0474, FAX 613/521–0805). **Association of British Travel Agents** (✉ 55–57 Newman St., London W1P 4AH, ☎ 0171/637–2444, FAX 0171/637–0713).

TRAVEL GEAR

Travel catalogs specialize in useful items, such as compact alarm clocks and travel irons, that can **save space when packing.** They also offer dual-voltage appliances, currency converters, and foreign-language phrase books.

➤ MAIL-ORDER CATALOGS: **Magellan's** (☎ 800/962–4943, FAX 805/568–5406). **Orvis Travel** (☎ 800/541–3541, FAX 540/343–7053). **Travel-Smith** (☎ 800/950–1600, FAX 800/950–1656).

U

U.S. GOVERNMENT

The U.S. government can be an excellent source of inexpensive travel information. When planning your trip, **find out what government materials are available.**

➤ ADVISORIES: **U.S. Department of State** (✉ Overseas Citizens Services Office, Room 4811 N.S., Washington, DC 20520); enclose a self-addresses, stamped envelope. Interactive hot line (☎ 202/647–5225, FAX 202/647–3000). Computer bulletin board (☎ 301/946–4400).

➤ PAMPHLETS: **Consumer Information Center** (✉ Consumer Information Catalogue, Pueblo, CO 81009, ☎ 719/948–3334) for a free catalog that includes travel titles.

VISITOR INFORMATION

Before you go, call or write to the tourist board for general information. From the U.K., contact the individual countries' tourist boards.

➤ DANISH TOURIST BOARD: U.S. and Canada: (✉ Box 4649, Grand Central Station, New York, NY 10163–4649, ☎ 212/885–9700, FAX 212/885–9710). United Kingdom: **Danish Tourist Board** (✉ 55 Sloane St., London SW1 X9SY, ☎ 0171/259–5959).

➤ IN DENMARK: Danmarks Turistråd (✉ Danish Tourist Board, Bernstorffsg. 1, DK–1577 Copenhagen V, ☎ 33/11–13–25).

W

WHEN TO GO

The tourist season peaks in June, July, and August, when daytime temperatures are often in the 70s (21°C to 26°C) and sometimes rise into the 80s (27°C to 32°C). In general, the weather is not overly warm, and a brisk breeze and brief rainstorms are possible anytime. Nights can be chilly, even in summer.

Visit in summer if you want to experience the delightfully long summer days. In June, the sun rises in Copenhagen at 4 AM and sets at 11 PM and daylight lasts even longer farther north, making it possible to extend your sightseeing into the balmy evenings. Many attractions extend their hours during the summer, and many shut down altogether when summer ends. Fall, spring, and even winter are pleasant, despite the area's reputation for gloom. The days become shorter quickly, but the sun casts a golden light one does not see farther south. On dark days, fires and candlelight will warm you indoors.

The Gulf Stream warms Denmark, making winters there similar to those in London.

THE GOLD GUIDE / SMART TRAVEL TIPS

CLIMATE

COPENHAGEN

Jan.	36F	2C	May	61F	16C	Sept.	64F	18C
	28	− 2		46	8		52	11
Feb.	36F	2C	June	66F	19C	Oct.	54F	12C
	27	− 3		52	11		45	7
Mar.	41F	5C	July	72F	22C	Nov.	45F	7C
	30	− 1		57	14		37	3
Apr.	52F	11C	Aug.	70F	21C	Dec.	39F	4C
	37	3		57	14		34	1

➤ FORECASTS: **Weather Channel Connection** (☎ 900/932–8437), 95¢ per minute from a Touch-Tone phone.

1 Destination: Denmark

FAIRY TALES AND FJORDS

THE KINGDOM OF DENMARK dapples the Baltic Sea in an archipelago of some 450 islands and the crescent of one peninsula. Measuring 43,069 square km (17,028 square mi) and with a population of 5 million, it is the geographical link between Scandinavia and Europe. Half-timber villages and tidy agriculture rub shoulders with provincial towns and a handful of cities, where pedestrians set the pace, not traffic. Mothers safely park baby carriages outside bakeries while outdoor cafés fill with cappuccino-sippers, and lanky Danes pedal to work in lanes thick with bicycle traffic. Clearly this is a land where the process of life is the greatest reward.

While in Denmark, visitors pinch themselves in disbelief and make long lists of resolutions to emulate the natives. The Danes' lifestyle is certainly enviable, not yet the pressure-cooked life of some other Western countries. Long one of the world's most liberal countries, Denmark has a highly developed social-welfare system. Hefty taxes are the subject of grumbles and jokes, but Danes remain proud of their state-funded medical and educational systems and high standard of living. They enjoy monthlong vacations, 7½-hour workdays, and overall security.

Educated, patriotic, and keenly aware of their tiny international stance, most Danes travel extensively and have a balanced perspective of their nation's benefits and shortfalls. As in many other provincial states, egalitarianism is often a constraint for the ambitious. In Denmark, the *Jante* law, which refers to a literary principle penned in the early 20th century by Axel Sandemose, essentially means "Don't think you're anything special"—and works as an insidious cultural barrier to talent and aspiration. On the other hand, free education and state support give refugees, immigrants, and the underprivileged an opportunity to begin new, often prosperous lives.

The history of the little country stretches back 250,000 years, when Jylland was

inhabited by nomadic hunters, but it wasn't until AD 500 that a tribe from Sweden, called the Danes, migrated south and christened the land Denmark. The Viking expansion that followed was based on the country's strategic position in the north. Struggles for control of the North Sea with England and western Europe, for the Skagerrak (the strait between Denmark and Norway) with Norway and Sweden, and for the Baltic Sea with Germany, Poland, and Russia ensued. With high-speed ships and fine-tuned warriors, intrepid navies navigated to Europe and Canada, invading and often pillaging, until, under King Knud (Canute) the Great (995–1035), they captured England by 1018.

After the British conquest, Viking supremacy declined as feudal Europe learned to defend itself. Internally, the pagan way of life was threatened by the expansion of Christianity, introduced under Harald Bluetooth, who in AD 980 "baptized" the country, essentially to avoid war with Germany. For the next several hundred years, the country tried to maintain its Baltic power with the influence of the German Hanseatic League. Under the leadership of Valdemar IV (1340–1375), Sweden, Norway, Iceland, Greenland, and the Faroe Islands became a part of Denmark. Sweden broke away by the mid-15th century and battled Denmark for much of the next several hundred years, whereas Norway remained under Danish rule until 1814, Iceland until 1943. Greenland and the Faroe Islands are still self-governing Danish provinces.

Denmark prospered again in the 16th century, thanks to the Sound Dues, a levy charged to ships crossing the Øresund, the slender waterway between Denmark and Sweden. Under King Christian IV, a construction boom crowned the land with what remain architectural gems today, but his fantasy spires and castles, compounded with the Thirty Years' War in the 17th century, led to state bankruptcy.

By the 18th century, absolute monarchy had given way to representative democracy, and culture flourished. Then—in a fatal mistake—Denmark sided with France and refused to surrender its navy to the English during the Napoleonic Wars. In a less than valiant episode of British history, Lord Nelson turned his famous blind eye to the destruction and bombed Copenhagen to bits. The defeated King Frederik VI handed Norway to Sweden. Denmark's days of glory were over.

Though Denmark was unaligned during World War II, the Nazis invaded in 1940. Against them, the Danes used the only weapons they had: a cold shoulder and massive underground resistance. After the war, Denmark focused inward, refining its welfare system and concentrating on its main industries of agriculture, shipping, and financial and technical services. It is an outspoken member of the European Union (EU), championing environmental responsibility and supporting development in emerging economies.

Copenhagen fidgets with its modern identity as both a Scandinavian–European link and cozy capital. The center of Danish politics, culture, and finance, it copes through balance and a sense of humor with a taste for the absurd. Stroll the streets and you'll pass classic architecture painted in candy colors, businessmen clad in jeans and T-shirts.

Sjælland's surrounding countryside is not to be missed. Less than an hour away, fields and half-timber cottages checker the land. Roskilde, to the east, has a 12th-century cathedral, and in the north, the Kronborg Castle of *Hamlet* fame crowns Helsingør. Beaches, some chic, some deserted, are powdered with fine white sand.

Fyn rightly earned its storybook reputation by making cuteness a local passion. The city of Odense, Hans Christian Andersen's birthplace, is cobbled with crooked old streets and Lilliputian cottages. Jylland's landscape is the most severe, with Ice Age–chiseled fjords and hills, sheepishly called mountains by the Danes. In the cities of Århus and Aalborg you'll find museums and nightlife rivaling Copenhagen's.

The best way to discover Denmark is to strike up a conversation with an affable and hospitable Dane. Hyggelig defies definition but comes close to meaning a cozy and charming hospitality. A summertime beach picnic can be as hyggelig as tea on a cold winter's night. The only requirement is the company of a Dane.

— By Karina Porcelli

NEW AND NOTEWORTHY

In early 1998, Prime Minister Poul Nyrup Rasmussen, leader of the Social Democrat party, called for new elections, held March 11. In an even election, decided by just over one mandate, the equivalent of 150 votes, his party was able to maintain power by forming a middle-of-the-road coalition government with the Social Liberals. The ballots were so evenly cast across the country that the deciding votes came in from the Faroe Islands and Greenland.

In 1998, Roskilde celebrates its 1,000-year anniversary. Established in 998 by Harald Bluetooth, it served as the country's first capital and center for trade, art, science, and religion. Concerts, performances, and exhibits will run all year, and on June 23, Midsummer Eve will be celebrated with a huge fireworks display over the fjord. On September 5th, a cultural blowout will keep shops, cinemas, museums, and libraries open late into the night.

The biennial Golden Days in Copenhagen, held September 4–20 in 1998, celebrates the artistic flowering of the city between 1800 and 1850, highlighting the works of author Hans Christian Andersen, philosopher Søren Kierkegaard, sculptor Bertil Thorvaldsen, and painter Kristoffer Eckersberg. Exhibitions, concerts, ballet performances, poetry, literature readings, and walking tours top the list of enlightening events.

The Storebæltsbro (Great Belt) rail and automobile link between Fyn and Sjælland is scheduled for completion in June 1998. Construction of the bridge connecting Copenhagen and Malmö, Sweden, is underway, with completion estimated for the year 2000.

Plans to streamline travel between Copenhagen Airport and the city center with a new highway and an extension of the city train system are in the works. By 2005 the Copenhagen Airport will be improved by a cool $1 billion addition, showing off a swank Danish-designed refurbishment: linked international and domestic terminals, a new train terminal with check-in facilities, and an east terminal primarily for SAS and its partner airlines, notably Lufthansa. The total number of gates will increase from 35 to 80.

WHAT'S WHERE

The Kingdom of Denmark dapples the Baltic Sea in an archipelago of some 450 islands and the arc of one peninsula. Measuring 43,069 square km (16,628 square mi), with a population of 5 million, it is the geographical link between Scandinavia and Europe.

The island of Sjælland, the largest of the Danish isles, is the most popular tourist destination. Here you'll find **Copenhagen**, Scandinavia's largest city (population 1.5 million), Denmark's capital, and the seat of the oldest kingdom in the world. If there's such as a thing as a cozy city, this is it: bicycles spin alongside cars in the narrow streets, and a handful of skyscrapers are tucked away amid cafés, museums, and quaint old homes. To the north of the city are royal castles (including Helsingør's Kronberg of *Hamlet* fame) and ritzy beach towns. To the west, Roskilde holds relics of medieval Denmark. And to the west and south, rural towns and farms edge up to beach communities and fine white beaches, often surrounded by forests.

Fyn, the smaller of the country's two main islands, is the site of Denmark's third-largest city, Odense, the birthplace of Hans Christian Andersen. It's no wonder this area inspired many fairy tales: 1,120 km (700 mi) of coastline and lush stretches of vegetable and flower gardens are punctuated by manor houses, beech glades, castles, swan ponds, and thatched houses.

Jylland, Denmark's western peninsula, shares its southern border with Germany. At the northern tip lies Skagen, a luminous, dune-covered point, and just below it are Århus and Aalborg, respectively Denmark's second- and fourth-largest cities. The heart of the peninsula, mostly lakeland and beech forests, is dotted with castles and parklands and is home to the famed Legoland. Along the east coast, deep fjords are rimmed by forests. The south holds marshlands, gabled houses, and Ribe, Denmark's oldest town.

Finally, there's the island of **Bornholm,** 177 km (110 mi) southeast of Sjælland, with a temperate climate that distinguishes it from the rest of Denmark. Bornholm's natural beauty and winsomely rustic towns have earned it the title of Pearl of the Baltic.

Norse ruins and icebergs, Ice Age–gouged mountains and jagged fjords punctuate **Greenland,** an island—the world's largest—straddling the Arctic Circle, four hours northwest by plane from Denmark. Even though travel within Greenland is limited to helicopter, coastal boat, and dogsled, the number of tourists here is growing at an enormous rate, fivefold since 1993.

Situated 1,300 km (812 mi) northwest of Denmark, the 18 **Faroe Islands** lift up out of the North Atlantic in an extended knuckle of a volcanic archipelago marked by azure skies and rugged, mossy mountains. Clinging to the hillsides are villages dotted with colorful thatched houses, their inhabitants maintaining a civilized life of fishing, fish farming, shepherding—and more recently, tourism.

PLEASURES AND PASTIMES

Beaches

In this country of islands, coastline, and water, beaches come in many breeds. In Sjælland, a series of chic strands stretches along Strandvejen—the old beach road—pinned down by a string of lovely old seaside towns; here is where young people go to strut and preen. Fyn's gentle, golden beaches are less a showplace than a quiet getaway for a largely northern European crowd. Windswept Jylland has the country's most expansive and dramatic beaches—at its tip you can even see the line in the waves where the Kattegat meets the Skaggerak Sea.

Biking

Without a doubt, Denmark is one of the best places for biking. More than half of the population pedals along city streets that effectively coordinate public transportation and cycle traffic and country paths laced through Jylland and the island of Bornholm.

Boating and Sailing

Well-marked channels and nearby anchorages make sailing and boating easy and popular along the 7,300-km (4,500-mi) coastline. Waters range from the open seas of the Kattegat and the Baltic to Smålandshavet (between Sjælland, Lolland, and Falster) and the calm Limsfjord in Jylland. The country's calm streams are navigable for canoes and kayaks. In Copenhagen, the historic harbors of Christianshavn and Nyhavn and scores of marinas bristling with crisp, white sails are lined with old wooden houseboats, motorboats, yachts, and their colorful crews. And it's not only the well-heeled taking up this pastime: tousle-haired parents and babes, partying youths, and leathery pensioners tend to their boats and picnics, lending a festive, community spirit to the marinas.

Danish Design

Danish design has earned an international reputation for form and function. The best sales take place after Christmas until February, when you can snatch up glassware, stainless steel, pottery, ceramics, and fur for good prices. Danish antiques and silver are also much cheaper here than in the United States. For major purchases—Bang & Olufsen products, for example—check prices stateside first so you can spot a good price.

Dining

From the hearty meals of Denmark's fishing heritage to the inspired creations of a new generation of chefs, Danish cuisine combines the best of tradition and novelty. Though the country has long looked to the French as a beacon of gastronomy, chefs have proudly returned to the Danish table, emphasizing fresh, local ingredients. Sample fresh fish and seafood from the Baltic, beef and pork from Jylland, and more exotic delicacies, such as reindeer, caribou, seal meat, and whale from Greenland. Denmark's famed dairy products—sweet butter and milk among them—as well as a burgeoning organic foods industry, all contribute to the freshness of the modern Danish kitchen.

Lunchtime is reserved for *smørrebrød*. You'll find the best, most traditional sampling of these open-face sandwiches in modest family-run restaurants that focus on generous portions—though never excessive—and artful presentation. If you fix your gaze on tender mounds of roast beef topped with pickles or baby shrimp marching across a slice of French bread, you are experiencing a slice of authentic Danish culture. Another specialty is *wienerbrød,* a confection far superior to anything billed as "Danish pastry" elsewhere. All Scandinavian countries have versions of the cold table, but Danes claim that theirs, *det store kolde bord,* is the original and the best.

On the liquid refreshment front, slowly the ubiquitous Carlsberg and Tuborg are facing international competition. You can't do better than to stick with the Danish brands, which happily complement the traditional fare better than high-priced wine. If you go for the harder stuff, try the famous *snaps,* the aquavit traditionally savored with cold food.

CATEGORY	COPENHAGEN*	OTHER AREAS*
$$$$	over DKr400	over DKr350
$$$	DKr200–DKr400	DKr200–DKr350
$$	DKr120–DKr200	DKr100–DKr200
$	under DKr120	under DKr100

Prices are per person for a three-course meal, including taxes and service charge and excluding wine.

Lodging

Accommodations in Denmark range from spare to resplendent. Luxury hotels in the city or countryside offer rooms of a high standard, and in a manor-house hotel you may find yourself sleeping in a four-poster bed. Even inexpensive hotels are well designed with good materials and good, firm beds—and the country's 100 youth and family hostels and 500-plus campgrounds are among the world's finest. Usually for all of July, conference hotels often lower prices and offer weekend specials.

Farmhouses and *kroer* (old stagecoach inns) offer a terrific alternative to more traditional hotels. Perhaps the best way to see how the Danes live and work, farm stays allow you to share meals with the family and maybe even help with the chores. If you prefer a more independent setup, consider renting a summer home in the countryside.

CATEGORY	COPENHAGEN*	OTHER AREAS*
$$$$	over DKr1,100	over DKr850
$$$	DKr800– DKr1,100	DKr650– DKr850
$$	DKr670–DKr800	DKr450– DKr650
$	under DKr670	under DKr450

Prices are for two people in a double room and include service and taxes and usually breakfast.

FODOR'S CHOICE

Dining

★ **Kong Hans, Copenhagen.** Franco-Danish-Asian inspired dishes, from foie gras with raspberry-vinegar sauce to warm oysters with salmon roe, is served in a subterranean space with whitewashed walls and vaulted ceilings. $$$$

★ **Restaurant Le St. Jacques, Copenhagen.** Though the chef and owners come from some of the finest restaurants in town, this unassuming little place manages a casual, friendly ambience—and some of the most creative seasonal cuisine around. $$

Lodging

★ **D'Angleterre, Copenhagen.** This grande dame has hosted everyone from royalty to rock stars. $$$$

★ **Skovshoved, Copenhagen.** Licensed since 1660, this lovely art- filled inn is nestled amid fishing cottages on the harbor, 8 km (5 mi) from the city. $$$

★ **Vandrehjem (youth hostels), anywhere in Denmark.** More than 100 excellent youth hostels welcome travelers of all ages. $

Castles and Churches

★ **Christianborg Slot, Copenhagen.** The queen still receives guests in this 12th-century castle.

★ **Kronborg Slot, Helsingør, Sjælland.** William Shakespeare never saw this fantastic castle, but that didn't stop him from using it as the setting for *Hamlet*.

★ **Rosenborg Slot, Copenhagen.** The only castle that is still passed down from monarch to monarch, Rosenborg Slot is home to the crown jewels.

Museums

★ **Louisiana, Copenhagen.** A half-hour drive from the city, this world-class modern art collection displays the likes of Warhol and Picasso.

★ **Nationalmuseet, Copenhagen.** Brilliantly restored and regarded as one of the best national museums in Europe, this institution curates exhibits chronicling Danish cultural history.

Special Moments

★ Walking through Tivoli at dusk (☞ Chapter 9)

★ Watching a bonfire on Skt. Hansaften, the longest day of the year

FESTIVALS AND SEASONAL EVENTS

SPRING

MAR.➤ The **Ice Sculpture Festival** takes place in Nuuk, Greenland; the **Nuuk Marathon** draws a hardy crowd of runners.

APR.➤ In Greenland, the **Arctic Circle Race** begins in Kangangerlussuaq and ends in Sisimiut.

APR. 16➤ The **Queen's Birthday** is celebrated with the royal guard in full ceremonial dress as the royal family appears before the public on the balcony of Amalienborg.

MAY➤ **Copenhagen Carnival** includes boat parades in Nyhavn and costumed revelers in the streets.

SUMMER

MAY–AUG.➤ **Tivoli** in Copenhagen twinkles with rides, concerts, and entertainment.

MAY–SEPT.➤ **Legoland,** a park constructed of 35 million Lego blocks, is open in Billund, Jylland.

JUNE➤ The **Around Fyn Regatta** starts in Kerteminde. The **Round Zealand Regatta,** one of the largest yachting events in the world, starts and ends in Helsingør. The **Aalborg Jazz Festival** fills the city with four days of indoor and outdoor concerts, many of them free. The **Viking Festival** in Frederikssund includes open-air performances of a Viking play. On **Midsummer's Night,** Danes celebrate the longest day of the year with bonfires and picnics.

JUNE 21➤ **Greenland National Day** celebrates the anniversary of Home Rule.

JUNE–JULY➤ The **Roskilde Festival,** the largest rock concert in northern Europe, attracts dozens of bands and 75,000 fans.

JULY➤ The **Copenhagen Jazz Festival** gathers international and Scandinavian jazz greats for a week of concerts, many of them free.

JULY 4➤ The **Fourth of July** celebration in Rebild Park, near Aalborg, sets off the only American Independence Day festivities outside the United States.

MID-JULY➤ The **Århus Jazz Festival** gathers European and other world-renowned names, with indoor and outdoor concerts.

AUG.➤ Between the 7th and 10th, the **Cutty Sark Tall Ship Race** brings more than 100 ships to the Copenhagen harbor.

MID-AUG.➤ The annual **Copenhagen Water Festival** celebrates the city's ties to the sea with concerts, exhibits, and plenty of outdoor activities.

AUTUMN

SEPT.➤ The **Århus Festival,** Denmark's most comprehensive fête, fills the city with concerts, sports, and theater.

WINTER

NEW YEAR'S EVE➤ Fireworks at the Town Hall Square are set off by local revelers.

2 Copenhagen

OPENHAGEN—KØBENHAVN IN DANISH—has no
glittering skylines, few killer views, and only a handful of meager skyscrapers. Bicycles glide alongside
manageable traffic at a pace that's utterly human. The early morning
air in the pedestrian streets of the city's core, Strøget, is redolent of
freshly baked bread and soap-scrubbed storefronts. If there's such a
thing as a cozy city, this is it.

Extremely livable and relatively calm, Copenhagen is not a microcosm
of Denmark, but rather a cosmopolitan city with an identity of its own.
Denmark's political, cultural, and financial capital is inhabited by 1.5
million Danes, a fifth of the population, as well as a growing immigrant community. Filled with museums, restaurants, cafés, and lively
nightlife, it has its greatest resource in its spirited inhabitants. The imaginative, unconventional, and affable Copenhageners exude an egalitarian philosophy that embraces nearly all lifestyles and leanings.

The town was a fishing colony until 1157, when Valdemar the Great
gave it to Bishop Absalon, who built a castle on what is now Christianborg. It grew as a center on the Baltic trade route and became known
as *købmændenes havn* (merchants' harbor) and eventually København. In the 15th century it became the royal residence and the capital of Norway and Sweden. A hundred years later, Christian IV, a
Renaissance king obsessed with fine architecture, began a building boom
that crowned the city with towers and castles, many of which still exist.
They are almost all that remain of the city's 800-year history; much
of Copenhagen was destroyed by two major fires in the 18th century
and by Lord Nelson's bombings during the Napoleonic Wars.

Despite a tumultuous history, Copenhagen survives as the liveliest
Scandinavian capital. With its backdrop of copper towers and crooked
rooftops, the venerable city is humored by playful street musicians and
performers, soothed by one of the highest standards of living in the
world, and spangled by the thousand lights and gardens of Tivoli.

EXPLORING COPENHAGEN

The sites in Copenhagen rarely jump out at you; its elegant spires and
tangle of cobbled one-way streets are best sought out on foot, and lingered over. Excellent bus and train systems can come to the rescue of
weary legs. It is not divided into single-purpose districts; people work,
play, shop, and live throughout the central core of this multilayered,
densely-populated capital.

Be it sea or canal, Copenhagen is surrounded by water. A network of
bridges and drawbridges connects the two main islands—Sjælland
and Amager—that Copenhagen is built on. The seafaring atmosphere
is indelible, especially around Nyhavn and Christianshavn.

You might wonder why so many Copenhagen sites, especially churches,
keep such peculiar, and often short, hours. It's a good idea to call and
confirm opening times, especially in fall and winter.

Rådhus Pladsen, Christiansborg Slot, and Strøget

In 1728, and again in 1795, fires broke out in central Copenhagen with
devastating effect. Disaster struck again in 1801, when Lord Nelson
bombed the city—*after* the Danes had surrendered and *after* he was
ordered to stop, he feigned ignorance and turned his famed blind eye
to the command. These events still shape modern Copenhagen, which

was rebuilt with wide, curved-corner streets—making it easier for fire trucks to turn—and large, four-sided apartment buildings centered with courtyards.

Arguably the liveliest area of the city, central Copenhagen is packed with shops, restaurants, businesses, and apartment buildings, as well as the crowning architectural achievements of Christian IV—all of it aswarm with Danes and visitors. Copenhagen's central spine consists of the five consecutive pedestrian strands known as Strøget and the surrounding tangle of roads and courtyards—less than a mile square in total. Across the capital's main harbor is the smaller, 17th-century Christianshavn. In the early 1600s, this area was mostly a series of shallows between land, which were eventually dammed. Today Christianshavn's colorful boats and postcard maritime character make it one of the toniest parts of town.

A Good Walk

The city's heart is the Rådhus Pladsen, home to the Baroque-style **Rådhus** ① and its clock tower. On the right side of the square is the landmark **Lurblæserne** ②. Off the square's northeastern corner is Frederiksberggade, the first of the five pedestrian streets that make up **Strøget** ③, Copenhagen's shopping district. Walk past the cafés and trendy boutiques to the double square of Gammeltorv and Nytorv.

Down Rådhusstræde toward Frederiksholms Kanal, the **Nationalmuseet** ④ contains an amazing collection of Viking artifacts. Cross Frederiksholms Kanal to Christiansborg Slotsplads, a small atoll divided by the canal and dominated by the burly **Christiansborg Slot** ⑤. North of the castle is **Thorvaldsen Museum** ⑥, devoted to the works of one of Denmark's most important sculptors, Bertel Thorvaldsen. On the south end of Slotsholmen is the three-story Romanesque-style **Kongelige Bibliotek** ⑦ (closed for renovations through late 1998), edged by carefully tended gardens and tree-lined avenues. Back on the south face of Christiansborg are the **Teatermuseum** ⑧ and the **Kongelige Stald** ⑨.

On the street that bears its name is the **Tøjhusmuseet** ⑩, and a few steps away is the architecturally marvelous **Børsen** ⑪ and the **Holmens Kirken** ⑫. To the east is **Christianshavn,** connected to Slotsholmen by the drawbridge Knippelsbro. Farther north, the former shipyard of Holmen is marked by expansive venues and several departments of the Københavns Universitet.

From nearly anywhere in the area, you can see the green-and-gold spire of **Vor Frelsers Kirken** ⑬. Across the Knippels Torvegade Bridge, under a mile down Børgsgade through Højbroplads, is Amagertorv, one of Strøget's five streets. On the left is **W. Ø. Larsens Tobakmuseet** ⑭, and farther down the street and to the left is the 18th-century **Helligånds Kirken** ⑮. On Strøget's Østergade, the massive spire of **Nikolaj Kirken** ⑯ looks many sizes too large for the tiny cobbled streets below.

TIMING

The walk itself takes about two hours. Typically, Christiansborg Slot and its ruins and the Nationalmuseet both take at least an hour and a half to see—even more for Viking fans. Expect to spend more than an hour if you want to see a film at the Omnimax Theater at the Tycho Brahe Planetarium. The hundreds of shops along Strøget are enticing, so plan extra shopping and café time—at least as much as your wallet can spare. Note that many sites in this walk are closed Sunday or Monday, and some have odd hours; always call ahead.

Sights to See

⑪ **Børsen** (Stock Exchange). Believed to be the oldest stock exchange still in use, this masterpiece of fantasy and architecture is topped by a spire of three intertwined dragons' tails—said to have been twisted by its builder, King Christian IV. Built between 1619 and 1640, it was originally used as a sort of medieval mall, filled with shopping stalls. With its steep roofs, tiny windows, and gables, the treasured building is used only for special occasions. ⊠ *Christiansborg Slotspl.* ⊙ *Not open to the public.*

★ ⑤ **Christiansborg Slot** (Christiansborg Castle). Surrounded by canals on three sides, the massive granite castle is where the queen officially receives guests. From 1441 until the fire of 1795, it was used as the royal residence. Even though the first two castles on the site were burned, Christiansborg remains an impressive Baroque compound, even by European standards: there's the **Folketinget** (Parliament House); the **Kongelige Repræsantationlokaler** (Royal Reception Chambers), where you'll be asked to don slippers to protect the floors; and the **Højesteret** (Supreme Court), on the site of the city's first fortress and built by Bishop Absalon in 1167. The guards at the entrance are knowledgeable and friendly; call them first to double-check the complicated opening hours.

While the castle was being rebuilt at the turn of the century, the Nationalmuseet (☞ *below*) excavated the **ruins** beneath it. This dark, subterranean maze contains fascinating models and architectural relics.

Wander around **Højbro Plads** and the delightful row of houses that border the northern edge of Slotsholmen. The quays were long Copenhagen's fish market, but today a lone early-morning fisherwoman hawking fresh fish, marinated herring, and eel is the sole fish monger you'll see carrying on the tradition. ⊠ *Christiansborg. Ruins,* ☎ *33/92–64–92. Folketinget,* ☎ *33/37–55–00.* ▣ *Ruins DKr15; reception chambers DKr28; Folketinget free.* ⊙ *Ruins: May–Sept., daily 9:30–3:30; Oct.–Apr., Tues., Thurs, and weekends 9:30–3:30. Reception chambers (guided tours only): May and Sept., Tues.–Sun., English tours at 11 and 3; June–Aug., Tues.–Sun., tours at 11, 1, and 3; Oct.–Dec. and Feb.–Apr., Tues., Thurs., and Sun., tours at 11 and 3. Folketinget: May–Sept., Mon.–Sat., tours hourly (except noon) 10–4; Oct.–Apr., Tues., Thurs., and Sat., tours hourly (except noon) 10–4.*

Christianshavn. This tangle of cobbled avenues, antique street lamps, and Left Bank charm makes up one of the oldest neighborhoods in the city. Even the old system of earthworks—the best preserved of Copenhagen's original fortification walls—still exists. In the 17th century, King Christian IV offered what were patches of partially flooded land for free, and with additional tax benefits; in return, takers would have to fill them in and construct sturdy buildings for trade, commerce, housing for the shipbuilding workers, and defense against sea attacks. Gentrified today, the area harbors restaurants, cafés, and boutiques, and its ramparts are edged with green areas and walking paths, making it the perfect neighborhood for an afternoon or evening amble.

OFF THE BEATEN PATH

CHRISTIANIA – If you are nostalgic for the '60s counterculture, head to this anarchists' commune on Christianshavn. Founded in 1971, when students occupied army barracks, it is now a peaceful community of nonconformists who run a number of businesses, including a bike shop, bakery, rock club, and communal bathhouse. Wall cartoons preach drugs and peace, but the inhabitants are less fond of cameras—picture-taking is forbidden. ⊠ *Prinsesseg. and Badsmandsstr.*

HOLMEN – Previously isolated (indeed closed) from central Copenhagen, this former shipyard just north of Christianshavn produced ships and ammunition until a few years ago. It was formally opened as the sight of the 1995 United Nations Summit on Human Development and played an im-

12

Amalienborg, **21**
Børsen, **11**
Botanisk Have, **33**
Carlsberg Bryggeri, **41**
Charlottenborg, **19**
Christiansborg Slot, **5**
Den Lille Havfrue, **26**
Frihedsmuseet, **24**
Gefion
Springvandet, **27**
Helligånds Kirken, **15**
Hirschsprungske
Samling, **35**
Hølmens Kirken, **12**
Kastellet, **25**
Københavns
Bymuseum, **40**
Københavns
Synagoge, **30**
Københavns
Universitet, **29**
Kongelige Bibliotek, **7**
Kongelige Stald, **9**
Kongelige Teater, **18**
Kongens Nytorv, **17**
Kunstindus-
trimuseet, **23**
Lurblæserne, **2**
Marmorkirken, **22**
Nationalmuseet, **4**
Nikolaj Kirken, **16**
Ny Carlsberg
Glyptotek, **37**
Nyhavn, **20**
Rådhus, **1**
Rosenborg Slot, **32**
Rundetårn, **31**
Statens Museum for
Kunst, **34**
Strøget, **3**
Teatermuseum, **8**
Thorvaldsen
Museum, **6**
Tivoli, **36**
Tøjhusmuseet, **10**
Tycho Brahe
Planetarium, **38**
Vesterbro, **39**
Vor Frelsers Kirken, **13**
Vor Frue Kirken, **28**
W. Ø. Larsens
Tobakmuseet, **14**

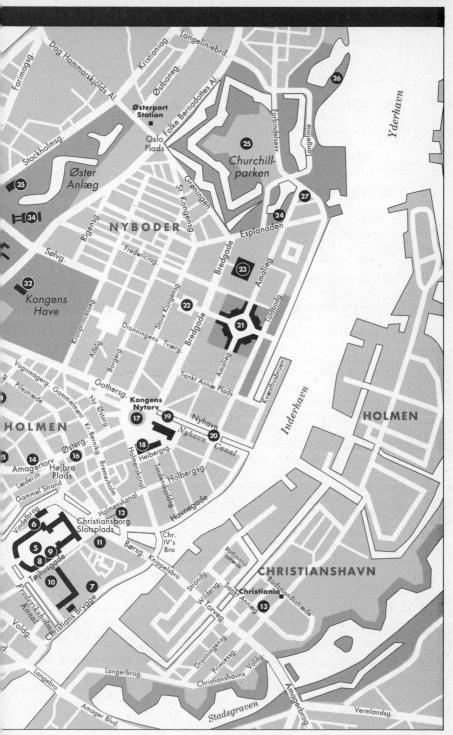

portant role as a cultural area during Copenhagen's 1996 reign as the Cultural Capital of Europe. Today, among its several cultural venues is the city's biggest performance space, the Torpedo Hall, where torpedoes were actually produced. You'll also find the Danish Art Academy's Architecture School, the National Theater School, the Rhythmic Music Conservatory, and the Danish Film School, which all host special activities.

⑮ **Helligånds Kirken** (Church of the Holy Ghost). This 18th-century church was founded as an abbey of the Holy Ghost and is still one of the city's oldest places of worship. Its choir contains a font by the sculptor Thorvaldsen, and more modern art is found in the large exhibition room—once a hospital—that faces Strøget. ⊠ *Niels Hemmingseng. 5, Amagertorv section,* ☎ *33/12–95–55.* ⊡ *Free.* ⊙ *Weekdays noon–4.*

⑫ **Holmens Kirken** (Islet's Church). Two of the country's most revered naval heroes are buried here: Niels Juel crushed the Swedish fleet at Køge in 1677. Peder Tordenskjold defeated Charles XII of Sweden during the Great Northern War in the early 18th century. ⊠ *Holmens Kanal,* ☎ *33/13–61–78.* ⊡ *Free.* ⊙ *May 15–Sept. 15, weekdays 9–2, Sat. 9–noon; Sept. 16–May 14, Mon.–Sat. 9–noon.*

❼ **Kongelige Bibliotek** (Royal Library). Closed for renovation until sometime in late 1998, the Royal Library ordinarily houses the country's largest collection of books, newspapers, and manuscripts. Among the more than 2 million volumes are accounts of Viking journeys to America and Greenland and original manuscripts by Hans Christian Andersen and Karen Blixen (a.k.a. Isak Dinesen). If you happen to be in the area anyway and are craving a literary encounter, ramble around the statue of philosopher Søren Kierkegaard (1813–55), formal gardens, and tree-lined avenues surrounding the scholarly building. When it reopens, the library will be expanded with a new, massive granite annex between the current building and the waterfront. ⊠ *Christians Brygge 8,* ☎ *33/93–01–11.* ⊙ *Closed until late 1998; call for hrs when reopened.*

☚ ❾ **Kongelige Stald** (Royal Stables). Between 9 and noon, time stands still while riders elegantly clad in breeches and jackets exercise the horses. The vehicles, including coaches and carriages, and harnesses on display have been used by the Danish monarchy from 1778 to the present. ⊠ *Christiansborg Ridebane 12,* ☎ *33/40–10–10.* ⊡ *DKr10.* ⊙ *May–Oct., Fri.–Sun. 2–4; Nov.–Apr., weekends 2–4.*

❷ **Lurblæserne** (Lur Blower Column). Topped by two Vikings blowing an ancient trumpet called a *lur,* this column displays a good deal of artistic license—the lur dates from the Bronze Age, 1500 BC, whereas the Vikings lived a mere 1,000 years ago. City tours often start at this important landmark. ⊠ *East side of Rådhus Pl.*

★ ☚ ❹ **Nationalmuseet** (National Museum). This brilliantly restored 18th-century royal residence, peaked by massive overhead windows, has housed what is regarded as one of the best national museums in Europe since the 1930s. Extensive collections chronicle Danish cultural history from prehistoric to modern times—included is one of the largest collections of Stone Age tools in the world—and Egyptian, Greek, and Roman antiquities are on display. The children's museum, with a Viking ship, castles from the Middle Ages, and other touchable exhibits, closes one hour before the rest of the museum. ⊠ *Ny Vesterg. 10,* ☎ *33/13–44–11.* ⊡ *DKr30.* ⊙ *Tues.–Sun. 10–5.*

⑯ **Nikolaj Kirken** (Nicholas Church). Though the green spire of the imposing church—named for the patron saint of seafarers—appears as old as the surrounding medieval streets, it is actually relatively young. The current building was finished in 1914; the previous structure, which dated from the 13th century, was destroyed by the 1728 fire. Today the church is an art gallery and exhibition center that often shows more experimental work. ⊠ *Nikolaj Pl.,* ☎ *33/93–16–26.* 🖾 *Varies according to special exhibitions.* ⊘ *Daily noon—5.*

NEED A BREAK? **Café Nikolaj** (⊠ Nikolajpl., ☎ 33/93–16–26), inside Nikolaj Kirken, is a reliable, inexpensive café with good Danish pastries and light meals. It's open noon to 3 for lunch and until 5 for cakes and drinks.

❶ Rådhus (City Hall). Completed in 1905, the mock-Renaissance building dominates **Rådhus Pladsen** (City Hall Square), the hub of Copenhagen's commercial district. Architect Martin Nyrop's creation was popular from the start, perhaps because he envisioned that it should give "gaiety to everyday life and spontaneous pleasure to all . . ."; accordingly, a statue of Copenhagen's 12th-century founder, Bishop Absalon, sits atop the main entrance.

Besides being an important ceremonial meeting place for Danish VIPs, the intricately decorated Rådhus contains the first **World Clock.** The multidialed, superaccurate astronomical timepiece has a 570,000-year calendar and took inventor Jens Olsen 27 years to complete before it was put into action in 1955. If you're feeling energetic, take a guided tour up the 350-ft bell tower for the panoramic, but not particularly inspiring, view.

The modern glass and gray-steel **bus terminal** flanking the square's northwest side has French granite floors, pear-tree-wood shelving, and underground marble bathrooms. The $2.8 million creation proved so architecturally contentious—more for its placement than for its design—that there was serious discussion of moving it.

Look up to see one of the city's most charming bronze sculptures, created by the Danish artist E. Utzon Frank in 1936. Diagonally across Rådhus Pladsen, atop a corner office building you'll see a **neon thermometer** and a **gilded barometer.** On sunny days there's a golden sculpture of a girl on a bicycle; come rain, a girl with an umbrella appears. ⊠ *Rådhus Pl.,* ☎ *33/66–25–82.* 🖾 *Tours DKr20, tower DKr10.* ⊘ *Weekdays 9:30–3. Tours in English, weekdays at 3, Sat. at 10. Tower tours Mon.–Sat. at noon; additionally June–Sept. at 10 and 2. Call to confirm hrs.*

★ **❸ Strøget.** Though it is referred to as one street, the city's pedestrian spine, pronounced *Stroy-et,* is actually a series of five streets: Frederiksberggade, Nygade, Vimmelskaftet, Amagertorv, and Østergade. By mid-morning, particularly on Saturday, it is congested with people, baby strollers, and street performers. Past swank and trendy, and sometimes flashy and trashy, boutiques of **Frederiksberggade** is the double square of **Gammeltorv** (Old Square) and **Nytorv** (New Square), in summer often crowded with street vendors selling cheap jewelry.

In 1728 and again in 1795, much of Strøget was heavily damaged by fire. When rebuilding, the city fathers straightened and widened the streets. Today, you can still see buildings from this reconstruction period, as well as a few that survived the fires.

In addition to shopping, you'll enjoy Strøget for strolling, as hundreds do. Outside the posh fur and porcelain shops and bustling cafés and restaurants, the sidewalks have a festive street-fair atmosphere.

❽ Teatermuseum (Theater Museum). After you brush up on theater and ballet history, wander around the boxes, stage, and dressing rooms of the **Royal Court Theater** of 1766, which King Christian VII had built as the first court theater in Scandinavia. ⊠ *Christiansborg Ridebane 18,* ☎ *33/11–51–76.* 🎫 *DKr20.* ⊙ *Wed. 2–4, Sun. noon–4.*

❻ Thorvaldsen Museum. The 19th-century artist Bertel Thorvaldsen (1770–1844) is buried at the center of this museum in a simple, ivy-covered tomb. Greatly influenced by the statues and reliefs of classical antiquity, he is recognized as one of the world's greatest neoclassical artists and completed many commissions all over Europe. The museum, once a coachhouse to Christiansborg, now houses Thorvaldsen's interpretations of classical and mythological figures, and an extensive collection of paintings and drawings by other artists that Thorvaldsen assembled while living—for most of his life—in Rome. The outside frieze by Jørgen Sonne depicts the sculptor's triumphant return to Copenhagen after years abroad. ⊠ *Porthusg. 2, Slotsholmen,* ☎ *33/32–15–32.* 🎫 *Free.* ⊙ *Tues.–Sun. 10–5.*

❿ Tøjhusmuseet (Royal Danish Arsenal Museum). This Renaissance structure—built by King Christian IV and one of central Copenhagen's oldest—contains impressive displays of uniforms, weapons, and armor in an arched hall 600 ft long. ⊠ *Tøjhusg. 3,* ☎ *33/11–60–37.* 🎫 *DKr20.* ⊙ *Tues.–Sun. 10–4.*

⓭ Vor Frelsers Kirken (The Church of Our Savior). Dominating the area around Christianshavn is the green-and-gold tower of this church, a Gothic structure built in 1696. Local legend has it that the staircase encircling it was built curling the wrong way around, and that when its architect reached the top and realized what he'd done, he jumped. At press time, a renovation was possible (but not yet scheduled) for 1999 or earlier. ⊠ *Skt. Annæg. 29,* ☎ *31/57–27–98.* 🎫 *Tower DKr20.* ⊙ *Mid-Mar.–May and Sept.–Oct., Mon.–Sat. 9–3:30, Sun., 9–1:30 and 3–4:30; June–Aug., Mon.–Sat. 9–4:30, Sun. 1:30–4:30; Nov., Mon.–Sat. 10–2, Sun. 11:30–1:30. Tower closed Dec.–mid-Mar. and during inclement weather.*

⓮ W. Ø. Larsens Tobakmuseet (W. O. Larsens Tobacco Museum). Looking like a storefront window from the outside, the Tobacco Museum in fact has a full-fledged collection of pipes made in every conceivable shape from every possible material. Look for the tiny pipe that's no bigger than an embroidery needle. There are also paintings, drawings, and an amazing collection of smoking implements. ⊠ *Amagertorv 9,* ☎ *33/12–20–50.* 🎫 *Free.* ⊙ *Mon.–Thurs., 10–6, Fri. 10–7, Sat. 10–4.*

Around Amalienborg and Sites North

North of Kongens Nytorv, the city becomes a fidgety grid of parks and wider boulevards pointing northwest across the canal toward upscale Østerbro—wreathed by manors commissioned by wealthy merchants and bluebloods. In the mid-1700s, King Frederik V donated parcels of this land to anyone who agreed to build from the work of architect Niels Eigtved, who also designed the Kongelige Teater. The jewel of this crown remains Amalienborg and its Rococo mansions.

A Good Walk

At the end of Strøget, **Kongens Nytorv** ⑰ is flanked on its south side by the **Kongelige Teater** ⑱, and backed by **Charlottenborg** ⑲, which contains the Danish Academy of Fine Art (call to see if an exhibition has opened the castle to the public). The street leading southeast from Kongens Nytorv is **Nyhavn** ⑳, a onetime sailors' haunt and now a popular waterfront hub. From the south end of the harbor (north end of Havnegade) depart high-speed craft to Malmö, Sweden; on the other north side, Kvævthusbroen—at the end of Skt. Annæ Plads (☞ *below*)—is the quay for boats to Oslo, Norway, and Bornholm, Denmark.

West of the harbor front is the grand square called Skt. Annæ Plads. Perpendicular to the square is Amaliegade, its wooden colonnade bordering the cobbled square of **Amalienborg** ㉑, the royal residence with a pleasant garden on its harbor side. Steps west from the square is Bredgade, where the Baroque **Marmorkirken** ㉒ flaunts its Norwegian marble structure. Farther north on Bredgade is the Rococo **Kunstindustrimuseet** ㉓. Back on Bredgade (you can also take the more colorful, café-lined Store Kongensgade, just west), turn right onto Esplanaden and you'll see the enormously informative **Frihedsmuseet** ㉔. At the Churchillparken's entrance stands the English church, St. Albans. In the park's center, the **Kastellet** ㉕ serves as a reminder of the city's grim military history. At its eastern perimeter is Langelinie, a waterfront promenade with a view of Denmark's best-known pinup, **Den Lille Havfrue**㉖. Wending your way back toward Esplanaden and the town center, you'll pass the **Gefion Springvandet** ㉗.

TIMING

This walk amid parks, gardens, canals, and building exteriors should take a full day. If it's nice, linger in the parks, especially along Kastellet and Amalienhaven, and plan on a long lunch at Nyhavn. The Kunstindustrimuseet merits about an hour, more if you plan on perusing the design books in the museum's well-stocked library. The Frihedsmuseet may require more time: its evocative portrait of Danish life during World War II intrigues even the most history-weary teens. Avoid taking this tour Monday, when some sites are closed.

Sights to See

㉑ **Amalienborg** (Amalia's Castle). The four identical Rococo buildings occupying this square have housed the royals since 1784. The Christian VIII palace across from the Queen's residence houses the **Amalienborg Museum,** which displays the second division of the Royal Collection (the first is at Rosenborg Slot, ☞ *below*) and chronicles royal lifestyles between 1863 and 1947. Here you can view the study of King Christian IX (1818–1906) and the drawing room of his wife, Queen Louise. Rooms are packed with family gifts and regal baubles ranging from tacky knickknacks to Fabergé treasures, including a nephrite and ruby table clock, and a small costume collection.

In the square's center is a magnificent equestrian statue of King Frederik V by the French sculptor Jacques François Joseph Saly. It reputedly cost as much as all the buildings combined. Every day at noon, the Royal Guard and band march from Rosenborg Slot through the city for the changing of the guard. At noon on Queen Margrethe's birthday, April 16, crowds of Danes gather to cheer their monarch, who stands and waves from her balcony. On Amalienborg's harbor side are the trees, gardens, and fountains of **Amalienhaven.** ⊠ *Amalienborg Castle,* ☎ *33/12–21–86.* ☐ *DKr35.* ☉ *May–mid-Oct., daily 11–4; mid-Oct.–Apr., Tues.–Sun. 11–4.*

㉙ **Charlottenborg** (Charlotte's Castle). This Dutch Baroque–style castle was built by Frederik III's half brother in 1670. Since 1754 the garden-flanked property has housed the faculty and students of the Danish Academy of Fine Art. It is open only during exhibits, usually in winter. ⊠ *Nyhavn 2,* ☎ *33/13–40–22.* ☐ *DKr20.* ☉ *Closed to public, except for exhibitions. Exhibition hrs daily 10–5, Wed. until 7.*

㉖ **Den Lille Havfrue** (*The Little Mermaid*). On the Langelinie promenade, this somewhat overrated 1913 statue commemorates Hans Christian Andersen's lovelorn creation, and is the subject of hundreds of travel posters. Donated to the city by Carl Jacobsen, the son of the founder of Carlsberg Breweries, the innocent waif has also been the subject of some cruel practical jokes, including decapitation and the loss of an arm, but she is currently in one piece. Especially on a sunny Sunday, the Langelinie promenade is thronged with Danes and visitors making their pilgrimage to see the statue.

★ ㉔ **Frihedsmuseet** (Resistance Museum). Evocative, sometimes moving displays commemorate the heroic Danish resistance movement, which saved 7,000 Jews from the Nazis by hiding them and then smuggling them to Sweden. The homemade tank outside was used to spread the news of the Nazi surrender after World War II. ⊠ *Churchillparken,* ☎ *33/13–77–14.* ⊡ *Free.* ◷ *May–Sept. 15, Tues.–Sat. 10–4, Sun. 10– 5; Sept. 16–Apr., Tues.–Sat. 11–3, Sun. 11–4.*

㉗ **Gefion Springvandet** (Gefion Fountain). Not far from *The Little Mermaid,* yet another dramatic myth is illustrated. The goddess Gefion was promised as much of Sweden as she could carve in a night. The story goes that she changed her sons to oxen and created the island of Sjælland. ⊠ *East of Frihedsmuseet.*

㉕ **Kastellet** (Citadel). At Churchill Park's entrance stands the spired English church, **St. Albans.** From there, walk north on the main path and you'll reach the Citadel. The structure's smooth, peaceful walking paths, marina, and greenery belie its fierce past as a city fortification. Built in the aftermath of the Swedish siege of the city on February 10, 1659, the double moats were among the improvements made to the city's defense. The Citadel served as the city's main fortress into the 18th century; in a grim reversal during World War II, the Germans used it as their headquarters during their occupation. ⊠ *Center of Churchill Park.* ⊡ *Free.* ◷ *Daily 6 AM–sunset.*

⑱ **Kongelige Teater** (Danish Royal Theater). The stoic, pillared and gallery-fronted theater is the country's preeminent venue for music, opera, ballet, and theater. The Danish Royal Ballet, its repertoire ranging from classical to modern works, performs here.

The current building was opened in 1874, though the annex, known as the **Nesting Box,** was not inaugurated until 1931. Statues of Danish poet Adam Oehlenschläger and author Ludvig Holberg—whose works remain the core of Danish theater—flank the facade. Born in Bergen, Norway, in 1684, Holberg came to Denmark as a student and stayed. Often compared to Molière, he wrote 32 of his comedies in a "poetic frenzy" between 1722 and 1728, and, legend has it, he complained of interminable headaches the entire time. He published the works himself, made an enormous fortune, and invested in real estate. Perhaps the theater is taking his cue: an annex designed by Norwegian architect Sverre Fehn is being constructed on the eastern side of the theater. With an estimated budget of roughly $115 million and a completion date of 2001, the pale concrete, marble, and oak structure will transform Tordenskjoldsgade into a covered shopping promenade. ⊠ *Tordenskjoldsg. 3,* ☎ *33/14–10–02.* ◷ *Not open for tours.*

★ ⑰ **Kongens Nytorv** (King's New Square). A mounted statue of Christian V dominates the square. Crafted in 1688 by the French sculptor Lamoureux, he is conspicuously depicted as a Roman emperor. Every year, at the end of June, graduating high-school students arrive in horse-drawn carriages and dance beneath the furrowed brow of the sober statue.

NEED A BREAK?   Dozens of restaurants and cafés line Nyhavn. Among the best is **Cap Horn** (⊠ Nyhavn 21, ☎ 33/12–85–04) for moderately priced, hearty, light Danish treats served in a cozy, art-filled dining room that looks like a ship's galley. Try the fried plaice, swimming in a sea of parsley butter with boiled potatoes.

㉓ **Kunstindustrimuseet** (Museum of Decorative Art). Originally built in the 18th century as a royal hospital, the fine Rococo-style museum houses a large selection of European and Asian crafts. You'll also find ceramics, silverware, tapestries, and special exhibitions usually focusing on contemporary design. The museum's excellent library is stocked with design books and magazines, and there's also a small café. ⊠ *Bredg. 68,* ☎ *33/14–94–52.* ▣ *DKr35 (additional fee for some special exhibits).* ◷ *Permanent collection, Tues.–Sun. 1–4; changing exhibits, Tues.–Sat. 10–4, Sun. 1–4.*

㉒ **Marmorkirken** (Marble Church). Officially the Frederikskirke, the ponderous Baroque sanctuary of precious Norwegian marble was begun in 1749 and lay unfinished from 1770 to 1874 due to budget restraints. It was finally completed and consecrated in 1894. Around the exterior are 16 statues of various religious leaders from Moses to Luther, and below them stand sculptures of outstanding Danish ministers and bishops. The hardy can scale 273 steps to the outdoor balcony. Walk past the exotic gilded onion domes of the **Russiske Ortodoks Kirke** (Russian Orthodox Church). ⊠ *Bredg.,* ☎ *33/15–37–63.* ▣ *Free; balcony, DKr20.* ◷ *Mon., Tues., Thurs., Fri. 11–2, Wed 11–6, Sat. 11–4, Sun. noon–4.*

Nyboder. Tour the neat, mustard-colored enclave of Nyboder, a perfectly laid-out compound of flat, long, former sailors' homes built by Christian IV. Like Nyhavn, this salty sailors' area was seedy and boisterous at the beginning of the 1970s, but today has become one of Copenhagen's more fashionable neighborhoods. ⊠ *West of Store Kongensg. and east of Rigensg.*

★ ⑳ **Nyhavn** (New Harbor). This harbor-front neighborhood was built 300 years ago to attract traffic and commerce to the city center. Until 1970, the area was a favorite haunt of sailors. Though restaurants, boutiques, and antiques stores now outnumber tattoo parlors, many old buildings have been well preserved and have retained the harbor's authentic 18th-century maritime atmosphere; you can even see a fleet of old-time sailing ships from the quay. Hans Christian Andersen lived at various times in the Nyhavn houses at numbers 18, 20, and 67.

Down Vesterbrogade and Nørrebro

To the southwest of the city are the vibrant working-class and immigrant neighborhoods of Vesterbro, where you'll find a good selection of inexpensive ethnic restaurants and shops. You'll find more cafés, restaurants, clubs, and shops on Nørrebrogade and Skt. Hans Torv.

By the 1880s, many of the buildings that now line Vesterbro and Nørrebro were being hastily thrown up as housing for area laborers. Many of these flats—typically decorated with a row of pedimented windows and a portal entrance—have been renovated through a massive urban renewal program. But to this day, many share hall toilets, have no showers, and are heated only by kerosene ovens.

A Good Walk

Take the train from Østerport Station, off of Oslo Plads, to Nørreport Station on Nørrevoldgade and walk down Fiolstræde to **Vor Frue Kirken** ㉘, its very tall copper spire and four shorter ones crowning the area. Backtracking north on Fiolstræde you'll come to the main building of **Københavns Universitet** ㉙; on the corner of Krystalgade is the **Københavns Synagoge** ㉚.

Fiolstræde ends at the Nørreport train station. Perpendicular to Nørrevoldgade is Frederiksborggade, which leads northwest to the neighborhood of Nørrebro; to the south after the Kultorvet, or Coal Square,

Frederiksborggade turns into the pedestrian street Købmagergade. From anywhere in the area, you can see the stout **Rundetårn** ③: it stands as one of Copenhagen's most beloved landmarks, with an observatory open fall and winter evenings. Straight down from the Rundetårn on Landemærket, Gothersgade gives way to **Rosenborg Slot** ③, its Dutch Renaissance design standing out against the vivid green of the well-tended Kongens Have. For a heavier dose of plants and living things, head across Øster Voldgade to the 25-acre **Botanisk Have** ③.

Leave the garden's north exit to reach the **Statens Museum for Kunst** ③ (closed for reconstruction through late 1998), notable for exceptional Matisse works. An adjacent building houses the **Hirschsprungske Samling** ③, with 19th-century Danish art.

Back at the Nørreport station, you can catch a train back to Copenhagen's main station, Hovedbanegården. When you exit on Vesterbrogade, take a right and you'll see the city's best-known attraction, **Tivoli** ③. At the southern end of the gardens, on Hans Christian Andersen Boulevard, the neoclassical **Ny Carlsberg Glyptotek** ③ contains one of the most impressive collections of antiquities and sculpture in northern Europe. Tucked between Sankt Jørgens Sø, or St. Jørgens Lake, and the main arteries of Vestersøgade and Gammel Kongevej is the **Tycho Brahe Planetarium** ③, with an Omnimax Theater.

Continue down Vesterbrogade into **Vesterbro** ③, Copenhagen's own Lower East Side of New York. Parallel to the south is **Istedgade,** Copenhagen's half-hearted red-light district.

Farther west down Vesterbrogade is **Københavns Bymuseum** ④, its entrance flanked by a miniature model of medieval Copenhagen. Beer enthusiasts and zymurgy fanatics can head south on Enghavevej and take a right on Ny Carlsbergvej for a tour of **Carlsberg Bryggeri** ④.

TIMING

All of the sites on this tour are relatively close together and can be seen in one day. Tivoli offers charms throughout the day; visit in the late afternoon, and stay until midnight, when colored electrical bulbs and fireworks illuminate the park. Note that some sites below close Monday or Tuesday; call ahead.

Sights to See

③ **Botanisk Have** (Botanical Garden). Trees, flowers, ponds, sculptures, and a spectacular *Palmehuset* (Palm House) of tropical and subtropical plants blanket the garden's 25-plus acres. There's also an observatory and a geological museum. Take time to explore the gardens and watch the pensioners feed the birds. Some have been coming here so long that the birds actually alight on their fingers. ⊠ *Gothersg. 128,* ☎ *35/32–22–40.* ⊡ *Free.* ☉ *Gardens Apr.–mid-Sept., daily 8:30–6; mid-Sept.–Mar., daily 8:30–4. Palm House daily 10–3.*

OFF THE
BEATEN PATH **ARBEJDERMUSEET –** The Workers Museum chronicles the working class from 1870 to the present, with evocative life-size "day-in-the-life-of" exhibits, including reconstructions of a city street and tram and an original apartment once belonging to a brewery worker, his wife, and eight children. Changing exhibits focusing on Danish as well as international issues are often excellent. The museum also has a 19th-century-style restaurant serving old-fashioned Danish specialties and a '50s-style coffee shop. ⊠ *Rømersg. 22,* ☎ *33/13–01–52.* ⊡ *DKr25.* ☉ *July–Oct., daily 10–5; Nov.–June, Tues.–Fri., 10–3, weekends 11–4.*

④ **Carlsberg Bryggeri** (Carlsberg Brewery). Four giant Bornholm granite elephants guard the entrance to this world-famous brewery; a tour of the draft horse stalls and **Carlsberg Museum** meets at this gate. At the end, you're rewarded with a few minutes to quaff a beer. ⊠ *Ny Carlsbergvej 140,* ☎ *33/27–13–14.* ⊙ *Tours weekdays at 11 and 2 or by arrangement for groups.*

③⑤ **Hirschsprungske Samling** (Hirschsprung Collection). This Danish art collection showcases works from the country's golden age—especially the late-19th-century paintings of the Skagen School. Their luminous works capture the play of light and water so characteristic of the Danish countryside. ⊠ *Stockholmsg. 20,* ☎ *31/42–03–36.* ⊠ *DKr20.* ⊙ *Mon. and Thurs.–Sun. 11–4, Wed. 11–9.*

Istedgade. In Copenhagen's half-hearted red-light district, mom-and-pop kiosks and ethnic restaurants stand side by side with seedy porn shops and shady outfits aiming to satisfy all proclivities. Though it is relatively safe, you may want to avoid the area for a late-night stroll. ⊠ *Street south and parallel to Vesterbrogade, west of Tivoli.*

④⓪ **Københavns Bymuseum** (Copenhagen City Museum). For a surprisingly evocative collection detailing Copenhagen's history, head to this 17th-century building in the heart of Vesterbro. Outside is a meticulously maintained model of medieval Copenhagen; inside there is also a memorial room for philosopher Søren Kierkegaard, the father of existentialism. ⊠ *Vesterbrog. 59,* ☎ *31/21–07–72.* ⊠ *Free.* ⊙ *May–Sept., Tues.–Sun. 10–4; Oct.–Apr., Tues.–Sun. 1–4.*

③⓪ **Københavns Synagoge** (Copenhagen Synagogue). This synagogue was designed by the contemporary architect Gustav Friedrich Hetsch, who borrowed from the Doric and Egyptian styles in creating the arklike structure. ⊠ *Krystalg. 12.* ⊙ *Daily services 4:15.*

②⑨ **Københavns Universitet** (Copenhagen University). Denmark's leading school for higher learning was constructed in the 19th century on the site of the medieval bishops' palace. ⊠ *Nørreg. 10,* ☎ *35/32–26–26.*

NEED A BREAK? The nearby **Sømods Bolcher** (⊠ Nørreg. 36, ☎ 33/12–60–46) is a must for children and candy lovers: its old-fashioned hard candy is pulled and cut by hand.

★ ③⑦ **Ny Carlsberg Glyptotek** (New Carlsberg Museum). Among Copenhagen's most important museums—thanks to its exquisite antiquities and Gauguins and Rodins—the neoclassical New Carlsberg Museum was donated in 1888 by Carl Jacobsen, son of the founder of the Carlsberg Brewery. Surrounding its lush indoor garden, a series of nooks and chambers houses works by Degas and other Impressionists, plus an extensive assemblage of Egyptian, Greek, Roman, and French sculpture, not to mention the best collection of Etruscan art outside Italy and Europe's finest collection of Roman portraits. ⊠ *Dantes Pl. 7,* ☎ *33/41–81–41.* ⊠ *DKr15, free Wed. and Sun.* ⊙ *May–Aug., Tues.–Sun. 10–4; Sept.–Apr., Tues.–Sat. noon–3, Sun. 10–4.*

★ ③② **Rosenborg Slot** (Rosenborg Castle). This Dutch Renaissance castle contains ballrooms, halls, and reception chambers, but for all of its grandeur, there's an intimacy that makes you think the king might return any minute. Thousands of objects are displayed, including beer glasses, gilded clocks, golden swords, family portraits, a pearl-studded saddle, and gem-encrusted tables; an adjacent treasury contains the royal jewels. The castle's setting is equally welcoming: it's smack in the middle of the **Kongens Have** (King's Garden), amid lawns, park benches, and shady walking paths.

King Christian IV built the Rosenborg Castle as a summer residence but loved it so much that he ended up living and dying there. In 1849, when the absolute monarchy was abolished, the royal castles became state property, except for Rosenborg, which is still passed down from monarch to monarch. Once a year, during the fall holiday, the castle stays open until midnight, and visitors are invited to explore its darkened interior with bicycle lights. ⊠ *Øster Voldg. 4A,* ☎ *33/15–32–86.* ▨ *DKr40.* ☉ *May–mid-Oct., daily 11–3; mid-Oct.–mid-Dec. and Jan.–Apr., Tues., Fri., and Sun. 11–2.*

★ ㉛ **Rundetårn** (Round Tower). Instead of climbing the stout Round Tower's stairs, visitors scale a smooth, 600-ft spiral ramp on which—legend has it—Peter the Great of Russia rode a horse alongside his wife, Catherine, who took a carriage. From its top, you enjoy a panoramic view of the twisted streets and crooked roofs of Copenhagen. The unusual building was constructed as an observatory in 1642 by Christian IV and is still maintained as the oldest such structure in Europe.

The art gallery features changing exhibits, and occasional concerts are held within its massive stone walls. An observatory and telescope are open to the public evenings mid-October through March, and an astronomer is on hand to answer questions. ⊠ *Købmagerg. 52A,* ☎ *33/93–66–60.* ▨ *DKr15.* ☉ *June–Aug., Mon.–Sat. 10–8, Sun. noon–8; Sept.–May, Mon.–Sat. 10–5, Sun. noon–5. Observatory and telescope mid-Oct.–Mar., Tues.–Wed. 7 PM–10 PM.*

㉞ **Statens Museum for Kunst** (National Art Gallery). Works from the golden age to modern Danish art, plus examples of Rubens, Dürer, and the Impressionists, comprise the gallery collection. A sculpture garden filled with classical, modern, and whimsical pieces flanks the building. The museum is closed until sometime in late 1998 for major reconstruction and expansion. ⊠ *Sølvg. 48–50,* ☎ *33/91–21–26.* ☉ *Closed through late 1998; call for hours when reopened.*

★ ℭ ㊱ **Tivoli.** Copenhagen's best-known attraction, conveniently next to its main train station, attracts an astounding number of visitors: 4 million people from May to September. Tivoli is more sophisticated than a mere funfair; among its attractions are a pantomime theater, open-air stage, elegant restaurants (24 in all), and frequent classical, jazz, and rock concerts. Fantastic flower exhibits color the lush gardens and float on the swan-filled ponds.

On Wednesday and Saturday night, elaborate fireworks are set off, and every day the Tivoli Guard, a youth version of the Queen's Royal Guard, performs. Try to see Tivoli at least once by night, when 100,000 colored lanterns illuminate the Chinese pagoda and the main fountain. The park was established in the 1840s, when Danish architect George Carstensen persuaded a worried King Christian VIII to let him build an amusement park on the edge of the city's fortifications, rationalizing that "when people amuse themselves, they forget politics." Call to double-check prices, which include family discounts at various times during the day. ⊠ *Vesterbrog. 3,* ☎ *33/15–10–01.* ▨ *Mon.–Sat. 10–1, DKr30; 1–9:30, DKr44; 9:30–midnight, DKr20; Sun. 11–9:30, DKr30; 9:30–midnight, DKr20.* ☉ *Late-Apr.–mid-Sept., daily 10 AM–midnight.*

ℭ ㊳ **Tycho Brahe Planetarium.** This modern, cylindrical planetarium, which appears to be sliced at an angle, features astronomy exhibits. The **Omnimax Theater** takes you on visual odysseys as varied as journeys through space and sea, the stages of the Rolling Stones, or Kuwaiti fires from the Persian Gulf War. These films are not recommended for children under seven. ⊠ *Gammel Kongevej 10,* ☎ *33/12–12–24.* ▨

DKr65. ⊙ *Show times vary. Open Mon., Wed., and Fri.–Sun. 10:30–9, Tues. 9:45–9, Thurs. 9:30–9.*

③⑨ Vesterbro. Copenhagen's equivalent of New York's Lower East Side is populated by immigrants, students, and union workers, it's a great place to find ethnic groceries, discount shops, and cheap international restaurants. ⊠ *At the southern end of Vesterbrogade.*

②⑧ Vor Frue Kirken (Church of Our Lady). Copenhagen's cathedral since 1924 occupies a site that has drawn worshipers since the 13th century, when Bishop Absalon built a chapel here. Today's church is actually a reconstruction: the original church was destroyed during the Napoleonic Wars. Five towers top the neoclassical structure. Inside you can see Thorvaldsen's marble sculptures depicting Christ and the 12 Apostles, and Moses and David, cast of bronze. ⊠ *Nørreg., Frue Pl.,* ☎ *33/15–10–78.* ⊡ *Free.* ⊙ *Apr.–Aug., Mon.–Sat. 8–5, Sun. noon–4; Sept.–Mar., Mon.–Sat. 8–5, Sun. noon–1.*

OFF THE
BEATEN PATH

ZOOLOGISKE HAVE – Kids love the Zoological Gardens, home to more than 2,000 animals. In the small petting zoo and playground live cows, horses, rabbits, goats, and hens. The indoor rain forest is abuzz with butterflies, sloths, alligators, and other tropical creatures. Sea lions, lions, and elephants are fed in the early afternoon. ⊠ *Roskildevej 32,* ☎ *36/30–25–55.* ⊡ *DKr55.* ⊙ *June–Aug., daily 9–6; Sept.–Oct. and Apr.–May, daily 9–5; Nov.–Mar., Tues.–Sun. 11–5.*

DINING

In the more than 2,000 restaurants in Copenhagen, traditional Danish fare spans all price categories: you can order a light lunch of traditional smørrebrød, munch alfresco from a street-side pølser (sausage) cart, or dine out on Limfjord oysters and local plaice. Even the most upscale restaurants have moderate-price fixed menus. Though few Danish restaurants require reservations, it's best to call ahead to avoid a wait. The city's more affordable ethnic restaurants are concentrated in Vesterbro, Nørrebro, and the side streets off Strøget. And for less-expensive, savory noshes in stylish digs, consider lingering at a café (☞ Cafés *in* Nightlife and the Arts, *below*).

Rådhus Pladsen, Christiansborg Slot, and Strøget

$$$$ ✕ **Gyldne Fortun's Fiskekældere.** Among the city's finest seafood restaurants, this "fish cellar" is brightly decorated with seashell-shaded halogen lamps and aquariums. Across the street from Christiansborg, it is popular with politicians as well as businesspeople. Try the fillets of Scandinavian sole poached in white wine, stuffed with salmon mousseline, glazed with hollandaise, and served with prawns. ⊠ *Ved Stranden 18,* ☎ *33/12–20–11. Reservations essential. AE, DC, MC, V. No lunch weekends.*

$$$$ ✕ **Kong Hans.** Five centuries ago this was a Nordic vineyard; now it's
★ one of Scandinavia's finest restaurants. Chef Thomas Rode Andersen's French-Danish-Asian–inspired dishes employ the freshest local ingredients and are served in a mysterious subterranean space with white-washed walls and vaulted ceilings. Try the foie gras with raspberry-vinegar sauce or the warm oysters with salmon roe. Jackets are recommended. ⊠ *Vingårdstr. 6,* ☎ *33/11–68–68. AE, DC, MC, V. Closed July. No lunch.*

$$$$ ✕ **Krogs.** This elegant canal-front restaurant has developed a loyal cliente-
★ le—both foreign and local. Pale-green walls are simply adorned with

## 24

Dining

Copenhagen
Corner, **27**
El Meson, **8**
Els, **11**
Flyvefisken, **21**
Gyldne Fortun's
Fiskekældere, **23**
Havfruen, **17**
Ida Davidsen, **7**
Kasmir, **2**
Kommandanten, **10**
Kong Hans, **25**
Krogs, **24**
L'Alsace, **14**
Pakhuskælderen, **26**
Peder Oxe, **13**
Quattro Fontane, **1**
Restaurant Le
St. Jacques, **5**
Riz Raz, **22**
Skt. Gertrudes
Kloster, **6**
Victor, **15**
Wiinblad, **16**

Lodging

Ascot, **19**
Cab–Inn
Scandinavia, **3**
Copenhagen
Admiral, **18**
Copenhagen
Danhostel, **32**
D'Angleterre, **16**
Kong Frederik, **20**
Missionhotellet
Nebo, **30**
Neptun, **12**
Nyhavn 71, **26**
Phoenix, **9**
Plaza, **29**
SAS Scandinavia, **31**
Skovshoved, **4**
Triton, **28**

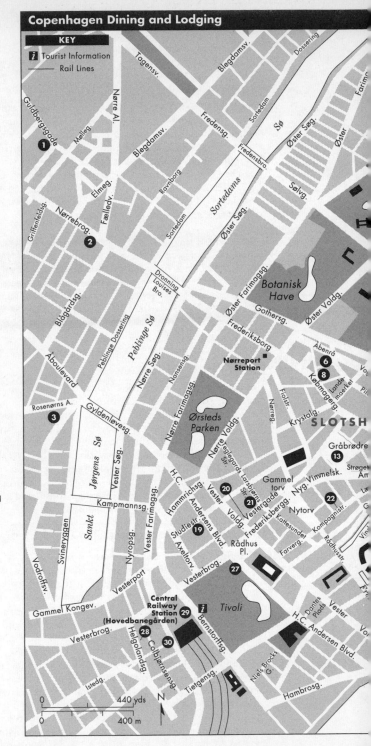

Copenhagen Dining and Lodging

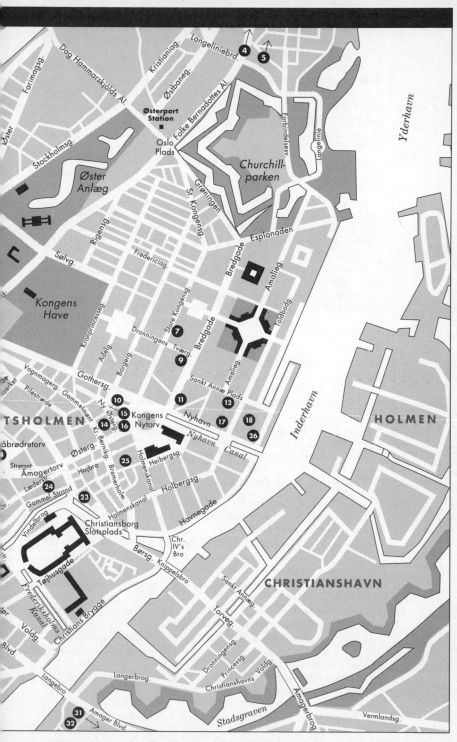

paintings of old Copenhagen to create an understated ambience. The menu includes such specialties as pan-grilled lobster flavored with vanilla oil. Jackets are recommended. ⊠ *Gammel Strand 38,* ☎ *33/ 15–89–15. Reservations essential. AE, DC, MC, V.*

$$ ✕ **Copenhagen Corner.** Diners here are treated to a superb view of the Rådhus Pladsen, as well as to terrific smørrebrød, both of which compensate for the often harried staff. Specialties include fried veal with bouillon gravy and fried potatoes; entrecôte in garlic and bordelaise sauce paired with creamed potatoes; and a herring plate with three types of spiced, marinated herring and boiled potatoes. ⊠ *Rådhus Pl.,* ☎ *33/91–45–45. AE, DC, MC, V.*

$$ ✕ **Peder Oxe.** On a 17th-century square, this lively, countrified bistro has rustic tables and 15th-century Portuguese tiles. All entrées—among them grilled steaks and fish and the best fancy burgers in town–come with an excellent self-service salad bar replete with whole tomatoes, feta cheese, and fresh greens. Damask-covered tables are set with heavy cutlery and opened bottles of hearty Pyrénées wine. A clever call-light for the waitress is above each table. ⊠ *Gråbrødretorv 11,* ☎ *33/11– 00–77. D, MC, V.*

$ ✕ **Flyvefisken.** Silvery stenciled fish swim along blue-and-yellow walls in this funky Thai eatery. Spicy concoctions include chicken with cashew nuts, and herring shark in basil sauce. The less-expensive health-food café in the basement serves excellent food to a steady stream of students and hipsters. ⊠ *Lars Bjørnstr. 18,* ☎ *33/14–95– 15. DC, MC, V. Closed Sun.*

$ ✕ **Riz Raz.** On a corner off Strøget, this Middle Eastern restaurant hops
★ with young locals, families, couples, and anyone who appreciates good value and spicy fare. The inexpensive all-you-can-eat buffet is heaped with lentils, tomatoes, potatoes, olives, hummus, warm pita bread, *kufte* (Middle Eastern meatballs), yogurt and cucumbers, pickled vegetables, bean salads, and occasionally pizza. Don't be put off by the hordes— just join them, either in the restaurant's endless labyrinth of dining rooms or in the jam-packed summertime patio. ⊠ *Kompagnistr. 20,* ☎ *33/ 15–05–75. Reservations essential. DC, MC, V.*

Around Amalienborg and North

$$$ ✕ **Els.** When it opened in 1853, the intimate Els was the place to be seen before the theater, and the painted Muses on the walls still watch diners rush to make an eight o'clock curtain. Antique wooden columns complement the period furniture, which includes tables inlaid with Royal Copenhagen tile work. Chef Pierre Gravelund changes his nouvelle French-Danish four-course menu every two weeks, always incorporating game, fish, and market produce. Jackets are recommended. ⊠ *Store Strandestr. 3,* ☎ *33/14–13–41. AE, DC, MC, V.*

$$$ ✕ **Kommandanten.** Fancifully decorated by master florist Tage Andersen
★ with brushed iron and copper furniture, down pillows, and foliage-flanked lights, this is among the city's most chic dinner spots, attracting well-heeled businesspeople and local celebrities—as well as two Michelin stars. The adventuresome international fare includes rabbit with bouillon-cooked lentils, herbs, and bacon, and marinated salmon with oysters and parsley. Jackets are recommended. ⊠ *Ny Adelg. 7,* ☎ *33/12–09–90. AE, DC, MC, V. Closed Sun. No lunch Sat.*

$$$ ✕ **L'Alsace.** Set in the cobbled courtyard of Pistolstræde and hung with
★ paintings by Danish surrealist Wilhelm Freddie, this restaurant is peaceful and quiet, attracting such diverse diners as Queen Margrethe, Elton John, and Pope Paul II. The hand-drawn menu lists oysters from Brittany, terrine de foie gras, and *choucroûte à la Strasbourgeoise* (a hearty mélange of cold cabbage, homemade sausage, and pork). Try

the superb fresh-fruit tarts and cakes for dessert, and ask to sit in the patio overlooking the courtyard. ⊠ *Ny Østerg. 9,* ☎ *33/14–57–43. AE, DC, MC, V. Closed Sun.*

$$$ ✕ **Pakhuskælderen.** Part of the Nyhavn 71 hotel, this intimate restaurant attracts a mix of business and holiday guests. The three- or four-course chef's menu may feature a main course of beef fillet in a shallot sauce served with organic potatoes or baked catfish with lobster sauce and saffron rice. The Danish lunch special usually includes a herring starter, followed by a light plate, drink, and dessert. The restaurant's thick white walls and raw timbers lend it a mood of antiquity. ⊠ *Nyhavn 71,* ☎ *33/11–85–85. Reservations essential. AE, DC, MC, V. Closed July. No lunch.*

$$$ ✕ **Wiinblad.** This restaurant doubles as a gallery inspired by the work of contemporary Danish artist Bjørn Wiinblad. Almost everything— tiles, wall partitions, plaques, candlesticks, vases, and even some tables—has been made by the great Dane, and the effect is bright, cheerful, and very elegant. The eatery offers an ample breakfast buffet, lunch, tea, and grilled specialties for dinner. Try the pickled herring with new potatoes and topped with sour cream, or the breast of duck in cranberry cream sauce. It's in the D'Angleterre hotel (☞ Lodging, *below*). ⊠ *D'Angleterre, Kongens Nytorv 34,* ☎ *33/12–80–95. AE, DC, MC, V.*

$$ ✕ **Havfruen.** A life-size wooden mermaid swings from the ceiling in this small, rustic fish restaurant in Nyhavn. Natives love the cozy, maritime-bistro air and come for the daily changing French and Danish menu, heavy on cream sauces, fresh salmon, turbot, and cod. ⊠ *Nyhavn 39,* ☎ *33/11–11–38. DC, MC, V.*

$$ ✕ **Ida Davidsen.** Five generations old, this world-renowned lunch spot is synonymous with smørrebrød. Dimly lit, with worn wooden tables and news clippings of famous visitors, it's usually packed. Creative sandwiches include the H. C. Andersen, with liver pâté, bacon, and tomatoes, and the airplane clipper—steak tartare shaped like a plane and topped with caviar, smoked salmon, and egg yolk. You'll also enjoy a terrific smoked duck that Ida's husband, Adam, smokes himself and serves alongside a horseradish-spiked cabbage salad. ⊠ *Store Kongensg. 70,* ☎ *33/91–36–55. Reservations essential. DC, MC, V. Closed weekends and July. No dinner.*

$$ ✕ **Restaurant Le St. Jacques.** This tiny restaurant barely accommo-
★ dates a dozen tables, but as soon as the sun shines, diners spill out of its icon-filled dining room to sit at tables facing busy Østerbrogade. The chef and owners come from some of the finest restaurants in town, but claim they started this place to slow down the pace and enjoy the company of their customers. The fare changes according to what is available at the market, but expect fabulous concoctions—smoked salmon with crushed eggplant, Canadian scallops with leeks and salmon roe in a beurre blanc sauce, sole with basil sauce and reduced balsamic glaze, and a savory *poussin* (young, small chicken) with sweetbreads scooped into phyllo pastry atop a bed of polenta and lentils. Close tables and chitchat with the owners give this a true café atmosphere. ⊠ *Skt. Jacobs Pl. 1,* ☎ *31/42–77–07. Reservations essential. DC, MC, V.*

$$ ✕ **Victor.** Excellent people-watching and good bistro fare are the calling cards at this French-style corner café. It's best during weekend lunches, when young and old gather for such specialties as rib roast, homemade pâté, and smoked-salmon and cheese platters. Come here for one of the best brunches in town. Be warned, however, that the formal restaurant in the back of the space is quite expensive—order from the front café side for a less expensive meal. ⊠ *Ny Østerg. 8,* ☎ *33/13–36–13. AE, DC, MC, V.*

Down Vesterbrogade and Nørrebro

$$$$ ✕ **Skt. Gertrudes Kloster.** The history of this medieval monastery goes back 700 years, and from the beginning its vaulted stone interiors have welcomed tradesmen and wayfarers. The dining room is bedecked with hundreds of icons, and the only light is provided by 2,000 candles. The French menu is extensive, with such specials as fresh fillet of halibut steamed in oyster sauce and l'Alsace duck breast in a sherry vinaigrette. A jacket and tie are recommended. ✉ *32 Hauser Pl.,* ☎ *33/14–66–30. Reservations essential. AE, DC, MC, V. No lunch.*

$$ ✕ **El Meson.** At Copenhagen's best Spanish restaurant, you are seated at smoothly worn wooden tables in a dimly lit dining room hung with earthen crockery. The wait staff is knowledgeable and serves generous portions of beef spiced with spearmint, lamb with honey sauce, or paella Valenciano—a mixture of rice, chicken, ham, shrimp, lobster, squid, green beans, and peas—for two. ✉ *Hausers Pl. 12 (behind Kultorvet),* ☎ *33/11–91–31. AE, DC, MC, V. Closed Sun. No lunch.*

$ ✕ **Kasmir.** This quiet, carpet-shrouded Indian restaurant is a favorite with locals, who come for the unusual vegetarian and fish menu. Specialties include tandoori-baked salmon, a hearty lentil soup, and the basic side dishes—such as *bhajis* (fried vegetables in tomato sauce), *raita* (yogurt and cucumbers), and nan, the thick round bread. ✉ *Nørrebrog. 35,* ☎ *35/37–54–71. AE, MC, V.*

$ ✕ **Quattro Fontane.** On a corner west of the lakes, one of Copenhagen's best Italian restaurants is a busy, noisy, two-story affair, packed tight with marble-topped tables and a steady flow of young Danes. Served by chatty Italian waiters, the homemade food includes cheese or beef ravioli or cannelloni, linguine with clam sauce, and thick pizza. ✉ *Guldbergsg. 3,* ☎ *31/39–39–31. No credit cards.*

LODGING

Copenhagen is well served by a wide range of hotels, overall among Europe's most expensive. The hotels around the seedy red-light district of Istedgade—which looks more dangerous than it is—are the least expensive. In summer, reservations are recommended, but should you arrive without one, try the hotel-booking desk in the tourist office. They can give you a same-day, last-minute price (if available) for about DKr200–DKr250 for a single hotel room. This service will also find rooms in private homes, with rates starting at about DKr160 for a single. Young travelers should head for **Huset** (✉ Rådhusstr. 13, ☎ 33/15–65–18) to get lodging information. Breakfast is included in the room rate and rooms have bath or shower at the following hotels unless otherwise noted.

Rådhus Pladsen, Christiansborg Slot, and Strøget

$$$$ 🏨 **SAS Scandinavia.** Near the airport, this is one of northern Europe's largest hotels and Copenhagen's token skyscraper. An immense lobby, with cool, recessed lighting and streamlined furniture, gives access to the city's first (and only) casino. Guest rooms are large and somewhat institutional but offer every modern convenience, making this a good choice if you prefer convenience over character. Breakfast is not included in the rates. ✉ *Amager Boulevarden 70, DK–2300 KBH S,* ☎ *33/11–24–23,* 𝔽𝔸𝕏 *31/57–01–93. 542 rooms, 52 suites. 4 restaurants, bar, room service, indoor pool, health club, casino, concierge, meeting rooms, free parking. AE, DC, MC, V.*

$$$ 🏨 **Kong Frederik.** North of Rådhus Pladsen and a two-minute walk from Strøget, this intimate hotel has the same British style as its sister

hotel, the D'Angleterre (☞ *below*). The difference is the sun-drenched Queen's Restaurant, where a hearty morning buffet is served (not included in rates) in addition to lunch and dinner. The rooms are elegant, with Asian vases, mauve carpets, and blue bedspreads. Ask for a top room for tower views. ⊠ *Vester Voldg. 25, DK–1552 KBH V,* ☎ *33/12–59–02,* ℻ *33/93–59–01. 110 rooms, 13 suites. Restaurant, bar, room service, meeting rooms, free parking. AE, MC, V.*

$$ 🏨 **Ascot.** This charming downtown hotel's two outstanding features are a wrought-iron staircase and an excellent breakfast buffet. The lobby is classic, with marble and columns, but the guest rooms and apartments are comfy, with modern furniture and bright colors; some have kitchenettes. ⊠ *Studiestr. 61, DK–1554 KBH V,* ☎ *33/12–60–00,* ℻ *33/14–60–40. 143 rooms, 30 apartments. Restaurant, bar, exercise room, meeting rooms, free parking. AE, DC, MC, V.*

$ 🏨 **Copenhagen Danhostel.** This simple lodging is 4½ km (3 mi) outside out of town, close to the airport. The hostel is spread over nine interconnecting buildings, all laid out on one floor. International Youth Hostel members—including student backpackers as well as families—use the communal kitchen or buy breakfast and dinner from the restaurant. The hostel is also wheelchair-accessible. Before 5 PM on weekdays, take Bus 46 from the main station directly to the hostel. After 5, from Rådhus Pladsen or the main station, take Bus 10 to Mozartplads, and change to Bus 37. Ask the driver to signal your stop. ⊠ *Vejlands All 200, DK–2300 KBH S,* ☎ *32/52–29–08,* ℻ *32/52–27–08. 64 rooms with 2 beds, 80 family rooms with 5 beds, 4 large communal bathrooms. Restaurant. No credit cards.*

Around Amalienborg and North

$$$$ 🏨 **D'Angleterre.** The grande dame of Copenhagen welcomes royalty
★ and rock stars in palatial surroundings: an imposing New Georgian facade leads into an English-style sitting room. Standard guest rooms are furnished in pastels, with overstuffed chairs and modern and antique furniture. The spit-and-polish staff accommodates every wish. Breakfast is not included in the rates. ⊠ *Kongens Nytorv 34, DK–1050 KBH K,* ☎ *33/12–00–95,* ℻ *33/12–11–18. 130 rooms, 28 suites. 2 restaurants, bar, room service, indoor pool, nightclub, concierge, meeting rooms, parking (fee). AE, DC, MC, V.*

$$$$ 🏨 **Nyhavn 71.** In a 200-year-old warehouse, this quiet and slightly fraying hotel is a good choice for privacy-seekers. It overlooks the old ships of Nyhavn, and its nautical interiors have been preserved with their original thick plaster walls and exposed brick. The rooms are tiny but cozy, with warm woolen spreads, dark woods, soft leather furniture, and crisscrossing timbers, but at least some of this may be changing as the hotel is renovated throughout the late '90s. The staff promises, however, that the rooms will remain elegantly cozy. Breakfast is not included. ⊠ *Nyhavn 71, DK–1051 KBH K,* ☎ *33/11–85–85,* ℻ *33/ 93–15–85. 82 rooms, 6 suites. Restaurant, bar, room service, concierge, meeting rooms, free parking. AE, DC, MC, V.*

$$$ 🏨 **Neptun.** This elegant, central hotel was bought years ago with the intention of making it the bohemian gathering place of Copenhagen, but proprietress Bente Noyens has also made it practical. The lobby and lounge are light, with slender furnishings and peach tones. Guest rooms have a tasteful modern decor; they vary greatly in size within the same price category, so specify a larger room when booking. Next door is a regional Danish restaurant. ⊠ *Skt. Annæ Pl. 14–20, DK– 1250 KBH K,* ☎ *33/13–89–00,* ℻ *33/14–12–50. (In the U.S., call Best Western, 800/528–1234.) 133 rooms, 13 suites. Restaurant, room service, meeting rooms, free parking. AE, DC, MC, V.*

$$$ ⊞ **Phoenix.** This luxury hotel has automatic glass doors, crystal chandeliers, and gilt touches everywhere. The staff is multilingual and adept at accommodating both a business and tourist clientele. The suites and business-class rooms are adorned with faux antiques and 18-carat-gold bathroom fixtures, whereas the standard rooms are very small, measuring barely 9 by 15 ft. It's so convenient to central-city attractions that the hotel gets a certain amount of street noise; light sleepers should ask for rooms above the second floor. ⊠ *Bredg. 37, DK–1260 KBH K,* ☎ *33/95–95–00,* 𝔽𝔸𝕏 *33/33–98–33. 212 rooms, 7 suites. Restaurant, pub (closed Sun.), meeting room. AE, DC, MC, V.*

$$$ ⊞ **Skovshoved.** This delightful, art-filled inn is 8 km (5 mi) north of
★   town, near a few old fishing cottages beside the yacht harbor. Licensed since 1660, it has retained its provincial charm. Its larger rooms overlook the sea, smaller ones rim the courtyard; all have both modern and antique furnishings. ⊠ *Strandvejen 267, DK–2920 Charlottelund,* ☎ *31/64–00–28,* 𝔽𝔸𝕏 *31/64–06–72. 20 rooms. Restaurant, bar, meeting room. AE, DC, MC, V.*

$$ ⊞ **Copenhagen Admiral.** A five-minute stroll from Nyhavn, overlooking old Copenhagen and Amalienborg, the monolithic Admiral was once a grain warehouse but now affords travelers no-nonsense accommodations. With massive stone walls—broken by rows of tiny windows—it's one of the less expensive top hotels, cutting frills and prices. Its guest rooms are spare, with jutting beams and modern prints. ⊠ *Toldbodg. 24–28, DK–1253 KBH K,* ☎ *33/11–82–82,* 𝔽𝔸𝕏 *33/32–55– 42. 365 rooms, 52 suites. Restaurant, bar, sauna, nightclub, meeting rooms, free parking. AE, DC, MC, V.*

Down Vesterbrogade and Nørrebro

$$$ ⊞ **Plaza.** With its convenient location and plush homey atmosphere, this hotel attracts the likes of Tina Turner and Keith Richards. Close to Tivoli and the main station, the building opens with a stately lobby and the adjacent Russian restaurant, Alexander Nevski, with perhaps the best vodka selection in town. The older rooms are scattered with antiques; newer ones are furnished in a more modern style. ⊠ *Bernstorffsg. 4, DK–1577 KBH V,* ☎ *33/14–92–62,* 𝔽𝔸𝕏 *33/93–93–62. 93 rooms, 6 suites. Restaurant, bar, room service, concierge, meeting rooms, parking (fee). AE, DC, MC, V.*

$$ ⊞ **Triton.** Despite seedy surroundings, this streamlined hotel attracts a cosmopolitan clientele thanks to a central location in Vesterbro. The large rooms, in blond wood and warm tones, all include modern bathrooms and state-of-the-art fixtures. The buffet breakfast is exceptionally generous, the staff friendly. There are also family rooms, with a bedroom and a dining-sitting area with a foldout couch. ⊠ *Helgolandsg. 7–11, DK–1653 KBH V,* ☎ *31/31–32–66,* 𝔽𝔸𝕏 *31/31–69–70. 123 rooms, 2 suites, 4 family rooms. Bar, meeting room. AE, DC, MC, V.*

$ ⊞ **Cab-Inn Scandinavia.** This bright hotel is just west of the lakes and Vesterport Station. Its impeccably maintained rooms are distinctly small, but designed with superefficiency to include ample showers, stowaway and bunk beds, and even electric water kettles. The hotel is popular with business travelers in winter and kroner-pinching backpackers and families in summer. Its sister hotel, the Cab-Inn Copenhagen (☎ 31/21–04–00, 𝔽𝔸𝕏 31/21–74–09) is just around the corner, at Danasvej 32–34. ⊠ *Vodroffsvej 55–57, Frederiksberg C, DK–1900,* ☎ *35/36– 11–11,* 𝔽𝔸𝕏 *35/36–11–14. 201 rooms. Breakfast room, snack bar, exercise room, meeting rooms. AE, DC, MC, V.*

$ ⊞ **Missionhotellet Nebo.** Though it's between the main train station and Istedgade's seediest porn shops, this budget hotel is still prim, comfortable, and well maintained by a friendly staff. Its dormlike guest rooms are furnished with industrial carpeting, polished pine furniture, and gray-stripe duvet covers. Baths, showers, and toilets are at the center of each hallway, and downstairs there's a breakfast restaurant with a tiny courtyard. ⊠ *Istedg. 6, DK–1650 KBH V,* ☎ *31/21–12–17,* 𝔽𝔸𝕏 *31/23–47–74. 96 rooms, 40 with bath. AE, DC, MC, V.*

NIGHTLIFE AND THE ARTS

Nightlife

Most nightlife is concentrated in the area in and around Strøget, though there are student and "leftist" cafés and bars in Nørrebro and more upscale spots in Østerbro. Many restaurants, cafés, bars, and clubs stay open after midnight, a few until 5 AM. Copenhagen used to be famous for jazz, but unfortunately that has changed in recent years, with many of the best clubs closing down. However, you'll find nightspots catering to almost all musical tastes, from bop to ballroom music— and for the younger crowd, house, rap, and techno—in trendy clubs soundtracked by local DJs. The area around Nikolaj Kirken has the highest concentration of trendy discos and dance spots.

Bars and Lounges

Peder Oxe's basement (⊠ Gråbrødretorv 11, ☎ 33/11–11–93) is casual and young, though nearly impossible to squeeze into on weekends. The **Library,** in the Plaza (⊠ 4 Bernstorffsg., ☎ 33/14–92–62), is an elegant spot for a quiet drink. The more than 270-year-old **Hviids Vinstue** (⊠ Kongens Nytorv 19, ☎ 33/15–10–64) attracts all kinds, young and old, single and coupled, for a glass of wine or cognac. **Vin & Ølgod** (⊠ Skinderg. 45, ☎ 33/13–26–25) draws a diverse crowd for singing, beer drinking, and linking of arms for old-fashioned dancing to corny swing bands.

Cafés

Café life appeared in Copenhagen in the '70s and quickly became a compulsory part of its urban existence. The cheapest sit-down eateries in town, where a cappuccino and sandwich often cost less than DKr40, cafés are lively and relaxed at night, the crowd always interesting. **Café Sommersko** (⊠ Kronprinsensg. 6, ☎ 33/14–81–89) is the granddaddy, with a surprisingly varied menu (try the delicious french fries with pesto) and an eclectic crowd. **Krasnapolsky** (⊠ Vesterg. 10, ☎ 33/32–88–00) packs a young, hip, and painfully well-dressed audience at night, a more mixed group for its quiet afternoons. **Café Dan Turrell** (⊠ Skt. Regneg. 3, ☎ 33/14–10–47), another old café, as of late has become terribly chic with good food and candlelight. **Victors Café** (⊠ Ny Østerg. 8, ☎ 33/13–36–13) is all brass and dark wood, lovely for a light lunch. At the very chic **Europa** (⊠ Amagertorv 1, ☎ 33/14–28–09), people-watching and coffee far surpass the fare. The juncture of Købmagergade and Strøget marks the art nouveau–style **Café Norden** (⊠ Østerg. 61, ☎ 33/11–77–91), where substantial portions make up for minimal table space. On Nørrebro's main square, Skt. Hanstorv, the all-in-one rock club-restaurant-café **Rust** (⊠ Guldbergsg. 8, ☎ 35/ 37-72-83) is packed all the time. Hearty, fresh dishes are served inside, and there's grill food outside on the terrace. Come evening, **Sebastopol** (Guldbergsg. 2, ☎ 35/36–30–02) is packed with gussied-up locals; sample the ample weekend brunch.

Casino

The **Casino Copenhagen** at the SAS Scandinavia (⊠ Amager Boulevard 70, ☎ 33/11–51–15) has American and French roulette, blackjack, baccarat, and slot machines. Admission is DKr80 (you must be 18 yea old and show a photo ID), and a dress code (jackets required and no sportswear or jeans) is enforced. The casino is open 2 PM to 4 AM.

Discos and Dancing

Most discos open at 11 PM, have cover charges of about DKr40, and pile on steep drink prices. Among the most enduring clubs is **Woodstock** (⊠ Vesterg. 12, ☎ 33/11–20–71), where a mixed audience grooves to '60s music. The very popular English-style **Rosie McGees** (⊠ Vesterbrog. 2A, ☎ 33/32–19–23) pub serves up Mexican eats and dancing. At the fashionable **Park Café** (⊠ Østerbrog. 79, ☎ 35/26–63–42), there's an old-world café with live music downstairs, a disco upstairs, and a movie theater next door. The lively **Club Absalon** (⊠ Frederiksbergg. 38, ☎ 33/16–16–99), popular with folks in uniforms (policemen, soldiers, and nurses among them), has live music on the ground floor and a disco above. **Søpavillionen** (⊠ Gyldenløvesg. 24, ☎ 33/15–12–24), between St. Jørgen's and Peblinge lakes, glows white on the outside; within there's pop and disco on Friday and Saturday night for an older crowd. At the **Røde Pimpernel** (⊠ Hans Christian Andersen Blvd. 7, ☎ 33/12–20–32), an adult audience gathers for dancing to live orchestras, trios, and old-time music. **Sabor Latino** (⊠ Vester Voldg. 85, ☎ 33/11–97–66) is the United Nations of discos, with an international crowd dancing to salsa and other Latin rhythms.

Gay Bars

Women and men pack **Pan Café**'s (⊠ Knabrostr. 3, off Strøget, ☎ 33/11–37–84) five floors of coffee-and-cocktail bars; the disco's open Wednesday through Saturday night (DKr40 cover). The **Amigo Bar** (⊠ Schønbergsg. 4, ☎ 31/21–49–15) serves light meals and is popular with men of all ages. Much larger is the mammoth **Club Amigo** (⊠ Studiestr. 31A, ☎ 33/15–33–32), which includes a indoor pool and sauna, as well as a disco, GeO2. The dark, casual **Cosy Bar** (⊠ Studiestr. 24, ☎ 33/12–74–27) is the place to go in the wee hours (it usually stays open until 8 AM). **Sebastian Bar Café** (⊠ Hyskenstr. 10, ☎ 33/32–22–79) is relaxed for a drink or coffee, and is among the best cafés in town, with art exhibits upstairs and a bulletin board downstairs.

The small **Central Hjørnen** (⊠ Kattesundet 18, ☎ 33/11–85–49) has been around for about 70 years. **Masken** (⊠ Studiestr. 33, ☎ 33/91–67–80) is a relaxed bar welcoming both men and women. The cozy lesbian café **Babooshka** (⊠ Turesensg. 6, ☎ 33/15–05–36) also welcomes men. **Hotel Windsor** (⊠ Frederiksborgg. 40, ☎ 33/11–08–30, FAX 33/11–63–87) is a gay-friendly hotel that doubles as a great breakfast greasy spoon. The men-only **Men's Bar** (⊠ Teglgaardstraede 3, ☎ 33/12–73–03) is dark and casual, with a leather and rubber dress code. It's easy to meet mostly men at **Can Can** (⊠ Mikkel Bryggesg. 11, ☎ 33/11–50–10), a small place with a friendly bartender.

For more information, call or visit the **Lesbiske og Bøsser Landsforening** (Lesbian and Gay Association, ⊠ Teglgaardstr. 13, 1452 KBH K, ☎ 33/13–19–48), which has a library and more than 45 years of experience. Check out *Xpansion*, a supplement of the larger free paper *Pan Bladet*, for listings of nightlife events and clubs.

Jazz Clubs

Hard times have thinned Copenhagen's once-thriving jazz scene. Among the clubs still open, most headline local talents, but European and international artists also perform, especially in July, when the Copenhagen Jazz Festival spills over into the clubs. **La Fontaine** (⊠ Kompagnistr. 11, ☎ 33/11–60–98) is Copenhagen's quintessential jazz dive, with sagging curtains, impenetrable smoke, and lounge lizards. **Copenhagen Jazz House**

(✉ Niels Hemmingsensg. 10, ☎ 33/15–26–00) is infinitely more up-scale, attracting European and some international names to its chic, modern, bar-like ambience. **Jazzhus Slukefter** (✉ Vesterbrog. 3, ☎ 33/11–11–13) is Tivoli's jazz club, attracting big names.

Rock Clubs

Copenhagen has a good selection of rock clubs, most of which cost less than DKr40. Almost all are filled with young, fashionable crowds. They tend to open and go out of business with some frequency, but you can get free entertainment newspapers and flyers advertising gigs at almost any café. **Cafe'en Funk** (✉ Blegdamsvej 2, ☎ 31/35–17–41) plays jazz, rock, and folk. The **Pumpehuset** (✉ Studiestr. 52, ☎ 33/93–19–60) is the place for soul and rock. For good old-fashioned rock and roll, head to **Lades Kælder** (✉ Kattesundet 6, ☎ 33/14–00–67), a local hangout just off Strøget.

The Arts

The most complete English calendar of events is listed in the tourist magazine **Copenhagen This Week,** and includes musical and theatrical events as well as films and exhibitions. Copenhagen's main theater and concert season runs from September through May, and tickets can be obtained either directly from theaters and concert halls or from ticket agencies. **Billetnet** (✉ Main post office, Tietgensg. 37, ☎ 35/28–91–83), a box-office service available at all post offices, has tickets for most major events. The main phone line is impossible to get through to: for information go in person to the post office on Købmagergade, just off Strøget, or check in at any post office. Billetnet's owner, **ARTE** (✉ Hvidkildevej 64, ☎ 38/88–49–00), is another good source for tickets; same-day purchases at the ARTE box office (✉ Near the Nørreport train station, Fiolstr. side, no phone) are half off. Tivoli's **Billetcenter** (✉ Vesterbrog. 3, ☎ 33/15–10–12) issues tickets for its own events.

Film

Films open in Copenhagen a few months to a year after their U.S. premieres. Nonetheless, the Danes are avid viewers, willing to pay DKr60 per ticket, wait in lines for premieres, and read subtitles. Call the theater for reservations, and pick up tickets (which include a seat number) an hour before the movie. Most theaters have a café. Among the city's alternative venues for second-run films is **Vester Vov Vov** (✉ Absalonsg. 5, ☎ 31/24–42–00) in Vesterbro. The **Grand** (✉ Mikkel Bryggersg. 8, ☎ 33/15–16–11) shows new foreign and artsy films, and is just next door to its sister café.

Opera, Ballet, and Theater

Tickets at the **Kongelige Teater** (Danish Royal Theater, ✉ Tordenskjoldsg. 3, ☎ 33/14–10–02; ☞ Exploring Copenhagen, *above*) are reasonably priced at DKr70–DKr400; the season runs October to May. It is home to the Royal Danish Ballet, one of the premier companies in the world. Not as famous, but also accomplished, are the **Royal Danish Opera** and the **Royal Danish Orchestra**, the latter of which performs in all productions. Plays are exclusively in Danish. For information and reservations, call the theater. Beginning at the end of July, you can order tickets for the next season by writing to the theater (✉ Danish Royal Theater, Attn. Ticket Office, Box 2185, DK–1017 KBH). For English-language theater, call either the professional **London Toast Theater** (☎ 33/33–80–25) or the amateur **Copenhagen Theater Circle** (☎ 31/86–20); both troupes perform in various venues.

OUTDOOR ACTIVITIES AND SPORTS

Beaches

North of Copenhagen along the old beach road, **Strandvejen,** you'll find a string of lovely old seaside towns and beaches. **Bellevue Beach** (⊠ Across the street from Klampenborg Station) is packed with locals and has cafés, kiosks, and surfboard rentals. **Charlottelund Fort** (⊠ Bus 6 from Rådhuspl.) is a bit more private, but you'll have to pay (about DKr10) to swim off the pier. The beaches along the tony town of **Vedbæk,** 18 km (11 mi) north of Copenhagen, are not very crowded.

Biking

Bike rentals (DKr100–DKr200 deposit and DKr30–DKr60 per day) are available throughout the city, and most roads have bike lanes. Follow all traffic signs and signals; bicycle lights must be used at night. For more information, contact the **Dansk Cyclist Forbund** (Danish Cyclist Federation, ⊠ Rømersg. 7, ☎ 33/32–31–21).

Golf

Some clubs do not accept reservations; call for details. Virtually all clubs in Denmark require your being a member of another club for admittance. Handicap requirements vary widely.

One of Denmark's best courses, often the host of international tournaments, is the 18-hole **Rungsted Golf Klub** (⊠ Vestre Stationsvej 16, ☎ 42/86–34–44). A 30 handicap for all players is required on weekdays; on weekends and holidays there's a 24 handicap for men and a 29 handicap for women. The 18-hole **Københavns Golf Klub** (⊠ Dyrehaven 2, ☎ 39/63–04–83) is said to be Scandinavia's oldest. Greens fees range from DKr180 to DKr240.

Health and Fitness Clubs

A day pass for weights and aerobics at the **Fitness Club** (⊠ Vesterbrog. 2E at Scala, across the street from Tivoli, ☎ 33/32–10–02) is DKr65. **Form og Figur** (Form and Figure) offers one-hour aerobics classes for DKr75 at the SAS Globetrotter Hotel (⊠ Engvej 171, ☎ 31/55–00–70) in Amager, and weights, treadmill, and stationary bikes for DKr75 at the SAS Scandinavia Hotel (⊠ Amager Boulevarden 70, ☎ 31/54–28–88) and Øbro-Hallen (⊠ Ved Idrætsparken 1, ☎ 35/26–79–39).

Horseback Riding

You can ride at the Dyrehavebakken (Deer Forest Hills) in Lyngby at the **Fortunens Ponyudlejning** (⊠ Ved Fortunen 33, ☎ 45/87–60–58). A one-hour session, in which both experienced and inexperienced riders go out with a guide, costs about DKr85.

Running

The 6-km (4-mi) loop around the three lakes just west of city center— St. Jorgens, Peblinge, and Sortedams—is a runner's nirvana. There are also paths at the Rosenborg Have; the Frederiksberg Garden (near Frederiksberg Station, corner of Frederiksberg Allé and Pile Allé); and the Dyrehaven, north of the city near Klampenborg.

Soccer

Danish soccer fans call themselves *Rolegans*—which loosely translates as well-behaved fans—as opposed to hooligans, and idolize the national team's soccer players as superstars. When the rivalry is most intense (especially against Sweden and Norway), fans don face paint, wear head-to-toe red and white, incessantly wave the *Dannebrog* (Danish flag), and have a good time whether or not they win. The biggest stadium in town for national and international games is **Parken** (✉ Øster Allé 50, ☎ 35/43–31–31). Tickets (DKr120 for slightly obstructed views, DKr250–DKr300 for unobstructed; local matches are less expensive than international ones) can be bought at any post office.

Swimming

Swimming is very popular here, and pools are crowded but well maintained. Separate bath tickets can also be purchased. Admission to local pools (DKr20–DKr50) includes a locker key, but you'll have to bring your own towel. Most pools are 25 m long. The beautiful **Frederiksberg Svømmehal** (✉ Helgesvej 29, ☎ 38/14–04–04) still maintains its old Art Deco decor with sculptures and decorative tiles. **Øbro Hallen** (✉ Ved Idrætsparken 3, ☎ 31/42–30–65) is in the large sports compound north of the center. The pool is lined with sculptures, and there is a 10-m diving tower; massage is also available. In the modern concrete **Vesterbro Svømmehal** (✉ Angelg. 4, ☎ 31/22–05–00), many enjoy swimming next to the large glass windows. The 50-m **Lyngby Svømmehal** (✉ Lundoftevej 53, ☎ 45/87–44–56) is one of metropolitan Copenhagen's newest pools, with a separate diving pool.

Tennis

Courts fees for guests are very high, often including court rental (DKr75 per person) and a separate nonmembers' user fee (as high as DKr130). If you must volley, courts are available to guests at some sports centers before 1 PM only. **Københavns Boldklub** (✉ PeterBangs Vej 147, ☎ 38/71–41–50) is in Frederiksberg, a neighborhood just west of central Copenhagen. **Hellerup Idræts Klub** (✉ Hartmannsvej 37, ☎ 31/62–14–28) is about 5 km (3 mi) north of town. **Skovshoved Idræts Forening** (✉ Krørsvej 5A, ☎ 31/64–23–83) is along the old beach road about 10 km (6 mi) north of town.

SHOPPING

A showcase for world-famous Danish design and craftsmanship, Copenhagen seems to have been designed with shoppers in mind. The best buys are such luxury items as crystal, porcelain, silver, and furs. Look for sales (*tilbud* or *udsalg* in Danish) and check antiques and secondhand shops for classics at cut-rate prices.

Although prices are inflated by a hefty 25% Value-Added Tax (Danes call it MOMS), non–European Union citizens can receive about a 20% refund. For more details and a list of all tax-free shops, ask at the tourist board for a copy of the *Tax-Free Shopping Guide* (☞ Sales-Tax Refunds *in* Denmark A to Z, *below*).

Department Stores

Illum (✉ Østerg. 52, ☎ 33/14–40–02), not to be confused with Illums Bolighus (☞ Design, *below*), is well stocked, with a lovely rooftop café and excellent basement grocery. **Magasin** (✉ Kongens Nytorv 13, ☎ 33/11–44–33), Scandinavia's largest, also has a top-quality basement marketplace. **Daells** (⊠ Fiolstr., ☎ 33/12–78–25) is best for basic Danish goods, like wool underwear and frying pans, at relatively reasonable prices.

Shopping Districts, Streets, and Malls

The pedestrian-only **Strøget** and adjacent **Købmagergade** are *the* shopping streets, but wander down the smaller streets for lower-priced, off-beat stores. You'll find the most exclusive shops at the end of Strøget, around Kongens Nytorv, and on Ny Adelgade, Grønnegade, and Pistolstræde. **Scala,** the city's glittering café- and boutique-studded mall, is across the street from Tivoli and has a trendy selection of clothing stores. Farther south in the city, on **Vesterbrogade,** you'll find discount stores—especially leather and clothing shops.

Specialty Stores

Antiques
For silver, porcelain, and crystal, the well-stocked shops on **Bredgade** are upscale and expensive. On Strøget, **Royal Copenhagen Porcelain** (⊠ Amagertorv 6, ☎ 33/13–71–81) carries old and new china, porcelain patterns, and figurines, as well as seconds. **Kaabers Antikvariat** (⊠ Skinderg. 34, ☎ 33/15–41–77) is an emporium for old and rare books, prints, and maps. For silver, Christmas plates, or porcelain, head to **H. Danielsens** (⊠ Læderstr. 11, ☎ 33/13–02–74). **Danborg Gold and Silver** (⊠ Holbergsg. 17, ☎ 33/32–93–94) is one of the best places for estate jewelry and silver flatware. For furniture, the dozens of **Ravnsborggade** stores carry traditional pine, oak, and mahogany furniture, and smaller items as lamps and tableware. (Some of them sell tax-free items and can arrange shipping.)

Audio Equipment
For high-tech design and acoustics, **Bang & Olufsen** (⊠ Østerg. 3, ☎ 33/15–04–22) is so renowned that its products are in the permanent design collection of New York's Museum of Modern Art. (Check prices at home first to make sure you are getting a deal.) You'll find B&O and other international names at **Fredgaard** (⊠ Nørre Voldg. 17, ☎ 33/13–82–45), near Nørreport Station.

Clothing
At **Jens Sørensen** (⊠ Vester Voldg. 5, ☎ 33/12–26–02) you'll find fine men's and women's clothing and outerwear, and a Burberry collection. **Petitgas Chapeaux** (⊠ Købmagerg. 5, ☎ 33/13–62–70) is a venerable shop for old-fashioned men's hats. The **Company Store** (⊠ Frederiksbergg. 24, ☎ 33/11–35–55) is for trendy, youthful styles, typified by the Danish Matinique label. If you are interested in the newest Danish designs, keep your eyes open for cooperatives and designer-owned stores. Among the most inventive handmade women's clothing shops is **Met Mari** (⊠ Vesterg. 11, ☎ 33/15–87–25). Thick, traditional, patterned, and solid Scandinavian sweaters are available at the **Sweater Market** (⊠ Frederiksbergg. 15, ☎ 33/15–27–73). **Artium** (⊠ Vesterbrog. 1, ☎ 33/12–34–88) offers an array of colorful, Scandinavian-designed sweaters and clothes alongside useful and artful household gifts.

Crystal and Porcelain
Minus the V.A.T., such Danish classics as Holmegaard crystal and Royal Copenhagen porcelain are less expensive than they are back home. Signed art glass is always more expensive, but be on the lookout for seconds as well as secondhand and unsigned pieces. Tucked in a lovely courtyard is the elegant shop **Hinz/Kjær Glasdesign** (⊠ Østerg. 24, ☎ 33/32–83–82), where the work of this American-Danish couple includes

bright glasses, bowls, and other functional art. **Chicago** (⊠ Vimmel-skaftet 47 on Strøget, ☏ 33/12–30–31) shows off a wide variety of Scandinavian art and functional glass. **Skandinavisk Glas** (⊠ Ny Østerg. 4, ☏ 33/13–80–95) has a large selection of Danish and international glass and a helpful, informative staff.

Holmegaards Glass has a Strøget store (⊠ Østerg. 15, ☏ 33/12–44–77), as well as a factory (☏ 55/54–62–00), 97 km (60 mi) south of Copenhagen near the town of Næstved, that is smaller than the shop in Copenhagen but has a larger selection of seconds, discounted 20% to 50%. (The store on Østergade has a limited selection of seconds.) The **Royal Copenhagen** shop (⊠ Amagertorv 6, ☏ 33/13–71–81) has firsts and seconds. For a look at the goods at their source, try the **Royal Copenhagen Factory** (⊠ Smalleg. 45, ☏ 31/86–48–48).

Design
Part gallery, part department store, **Illums Bolighus** (⊠ Amagertorv 6, ☏ 33/14–19–41) shows off cutting-edge Danish and international design—art glass, porcelain, silverware, carpets, and loads of grown-up toys. **Lysberg, Hansen and Therp** (⊠ Bredg. 3, ☏ 33/14–47–87), one of the most prestigious interior-design firms in Denmark, has sumptuous showrooms done up in traditional and modern styles. **Interieur** (⊠ Gothersg. 91, ☏ 33/13–15–56) displays fresh Danish style and chic kitchenware. Wizard florist **Tage Andersen** (⊠ Ny Adelg. 12, ☏ 33/93–09–13) has a fantasy-infused gallery-shop filled with one-of-a-kind gifts and arrangements; browsers (who generally don't purchase the pricey items) are charged a DKr40 admission.

Fur
Denmark, the world's biggest producer of ranched minks, is the place to go for quality furs. Furs are ranked into four grades: Saga Royal, Saga, Quality 1, and Quality 2. Copenhagen's finest furrier, dealing only in Saga Royal quality, and purveyor to the royal family is **Birger Christensen** (⊠ Østerg. 38, ☏ 33/11–55–55), which presents a new collection yearly from its in-house design team. Expect to spend about 20% less than in the United States for same-quality furs ($5,000–$10,000 for mink, $3,000 for a fur-lined coat). Birger Christensen is also among the preeminent fashion houses in town, carrying Donna Karan, Chanel, Prada, Kenzo, Jil Sander, and Yves Saint Laurent. **A. C. Bang** (⊠ Østerg. 27, ☏ 33/15–17–26) carries less expensive furs, but has an old-world, old-money aura and very high quality. **Otto D. Madsen** (⊠ Vesterbrog. 1, ☏ 33/13–41–10) is not as chichi as some of Copenhagen's furriers, but has less expensive items.

Silver
Check the silver standard of a piece by its stamp. Three towers and "925S" (which means 925 parts out of 1,000) mark sterling. Two towers are used for silver plate. The "826S" stamp (also denoting sterling, but less pure) was used until the 1920s. Even with shipping charges, you can expect to save 50% versus American prices when buying Danish silver (especially used) at the source. For one of the most recognized names in international silver, visit **Georg Jensen** (⊠ Amagertorv 4, ☏ 33/11–40–80), an elegant, austere shop aglitter with velvet-cushioned sterling. **Peter Krog** (⊠ 4 Bredg., ☏ 33/12–45–55) stocks collectors' items in silver, primarily Georg Jensen place settings, compotes, and jewelry. **Ketti Hartogsohn** (⊠ Palæg. 8, ☏ 33/15–53–98) carries all sorts of silver knick-knacks and settings. The **English Silver House** (⊠ Pilestr. 4, ☏ 33/14–83–81) is an emporium of used estate silver. The city's largest (and brightest) silver store is **Sølvkælderen** (⊠ Kompagnistr. 1, ☏ 33/13–36–34), with an endless selection of tea services, place settings, and jewelry.

Street Markets

Check with the tourist board or the tourist magazine *Copenhagen This Week* for flea markets. Bargaining is expected. For a good overview of antiques and junk, visit the flea market at **Israels Plads** (⊠ Near Nørreport Station), open May–October, Saturday 8–2. It is run by more than 100 professional dealers, and prices are steep, but there are loads of classic Danish porcelain, silver, jewelry, and crystal, plus books, prints, postcards, and more. Slightly smaller than the Israels Plads market, and with lower prices and more junk, is the market behind **Frederiksberg Rådhus** (summer Saturday mornings). The junk and flea market that takes place Saturday in summer and stretches from Nørrebros Rundel down the road along the Assistens Kirkegårn (cemetery) claims to be one of the longest in the world.

SIDE TRIPS FROM COPENHAGEN

Eksperimentarium

8 km (6 mi) north of Copenhagen.

In the beachside town of Hellerup is the user-friendly **Experimentarium,** where more than 300 exhibitions are clustered in various Discovery Islands, each exploring a different facet of science, technology, and natural phenomena. A dozen body- and hands-on exhibits allow you to take skeleton-revealing bike rides, measure your lung capacity, stir up magnetic goop, play ball on a jet stream, and gyrate to gyroscopes. Once a bottling plant for the Tuborg Brewery, this center organizes one or two special exhibits a year; one past installation had interactive exhibits of the brain. Until mid-April, 1998, the special exhibition will focus on dinosaurs. Take Bus 6 or 650S from Rådhus Plads or the S-train to Hellerup; transfer to bus 21, 23, or 650S. ⊠ *Tuborg Havnevej 7,* ☎ *39/27–33–33.* ☜ *DKr69; combined admission for a child and parent, DKr98.* ◷ *Mid-June–mid-Aug., daily 10–5; mid-Aug.–mid-June, Mon. and Wed.–Fri. 9–5, Tues. 9–9, weekends 11–5.*

Dragør

22 km (14 mi) east of Copenhagen (take Bus 30 or 33 from Rådhus Pladsen).

On the island of Amager, less than a half hour from Copenhagen, the quaint fishing town of Dragør (pronounced *drah*-wer) feels far away in distance and time. The town's history is apart from the rest of Copenhagen's because it was settled by Dutch farmers in the 16th century. King Christian II ordered the community to provide fresh produce and flowers for the royal court. Today, neat rows of white, terra-cotta-roofed houses trimmed with wandering ivy, roses, and the occasional waddling goose characterize the still meticulously maintained community. According to local legend, the former town hall's chimney was built with a twist so that meetings couldn't be overheard.

The **Dragør Museum** (⊠ Strandlinien 4, ☎ 32/53–41–06), in one of the oldest houses in town, contains a collection of furniture, costumes, drawings, and model ships. Admission is DKr20; it's open weekends 2–5. A ticket to the Dragør Museum also affords entrance to the nearby **Mølsted Museum** (⊠ Dr. Dichs Pl. 4, ☎ 32/53–41–06), displaying paintings by the famous local artist Christian Mølsted; call ahead for hours. If you're still energetic, swing by the **Amager Museum** (⊠ Hovedg. 4 and 12, ☎ 32/53–93–07), which details the Dutch colony. It's open Tuesday through Sunday noon to 4; admission is DKr20.

Frilandsmuseet

16 km (10 mi) north of Copenhagen.

Just north of Copenhagen is Lyngby, its main draw the Frilandsmuseet, an open-air museum. About 50 farmhouses and cottages representing various periods of Danish history have been painstakingly dismantled, moved, reconstructed, and filled with period furniture and tools. The museum is surrounded by trees and gardens; bring lunch and plan to spend the day. To get here, take the S-train to the Sorgenfri Station, then walk right and follow the signs. ⊠ *Frilandsmuseet, 100 Kongevejen, Lyngby,* ☎ *45/85–02–92.* ☎ *DKr30.* ⊙ *Easter–Sept., Tues.–Sun. 10–5; Oct., daily 10–4; call to confirm Oct. hrs.*

Museet for Moderne Kunst

20 km (12 mi) south of Copenhagen (take the S-train in the direction of either Hundige, Solrød Strand, or Køge to Ishøj Station, then pick up bus 128 to the museum).

Architect Søren Robert Lund was just 25 when awarded the commission for this forward-looking museum, which he designed in metal and white concrete set against the flat coast south of Copenhagen. The museum, also known as the Arken, opened in March 1996 to great acclaim, both for its architecture and its collection. Unfortunately, it has been plagued with a string of stranger-than-fiction occurrences, including a director with a completely bogus resume and financial difficulties that often leave it depressingly bare of art. Nonetheless, when filled, its massive sculpture room exhibits both modern Danish and international art, as well as experimental works. Dance, theater, film, and multimedia exhibits are additional attractions. ⊠ *Skovvej 42,* ☎ *43/42–02–22.* ☎ *DKr45.* ⊙ *Tues.–Sun., 10–5.*

COPENHAGEN A TO Z

Arriving and Departing

By Car

The E–66 highway, via bridges and ferry routes, connects Fredericia (on Jylland) with Middelfart (on Fyn), a distance of 16 km (10 mi), and goes on to Copenhagen, another 180 km (120 mi) east. Farther north, from Århus (in Jylland), you can get direct ferry service to Kalundborg (on Sjælland). From there, Route 23 leads to Roskilde, about 72 km (45 mi) east. Take Route 21 east and follow the signs to Copenhagen, another 40 km (25 mi). Make reservations for the ferry in advance through the Danish State Railways (DSB, ⊠ Hovedbanegården, DK–1570 KBH K, ☎ 33/14–17–01).

By Ferry

Frequent ferries connect Copenhagen with Sweden, including several daily ships from Malmö, Limhamn, Landskrona, and Helsingborg. There is also a high-speed craft from Malmö.

By Plane

Copenhagen Airport, 10 km (6 mi) southeast of downtown in Kastrup, is the gateway to Scandinavia. International and domestic flights are served by **SAS** (☎ 32/33–68–48). Among the other airlines that serve Copenhagen Airport are **British Airways** (☎ 33/14–60–00), **Icelandair** (☎ 33/12–33–88), and **Delta** (☎ 33/11–56–56).

Between the Airport and Downtown: Although the 10-km (6-mi) drive from the airport to downtown is quick and easy, public transportation is also a good option. **SAS coach buses** leave the international arrivals terminal every 15 minutes, from 5:42 AM to 9:45 PM, cost DKr32, and take 25 minutes to reach Copenhagen's main train station on Vesterbrogade. Another SAS coach from Christianborg, on Slotsholmsgade, to the airport runs every 15 minutes between 8:30 AM and noon, and every half-hour from noon to 6 PM. **HT** city buses depart from the international arrivals terminal every 15 minutes, from 4:30 AM (Sunday 5:30) to 11:52 PM, but take a long, circuitous route. Take Bus 250S for the Rådhus Pladsen and transfer. Tickets (one way) cost DKr15.

The 20-minute **taxi** ride downtown costs from DKr75 to DKr120 and up. Lines form at the international arrivals terminal. In the unlikely event there is no taxi available, call ☎ 31/35–35–35.

By Train

Copenhagen's **Hovedbanegården** (Central Station, ✉ Vesterbrog.) is the hub of the DSB network and is connected to most major cities in Europe. Intercity trains leave every hour, usually on the hour, from 6 AM to 10 PM for principal towns in Fyn and Jylland. Find out more from **DSB** (☎ 33/14–17–01). You can make reservations at the central station, at most other stations, and through travel agents.

Getting Around

Copenhagen is small, with most sights within its one square-mi center. Wear comfortable shoes and explore it on foot. Or follow the example of the Danes and rent a bike. For those with aching feet, an efficient transit system is available.

By Bicycle

Bikes are delightfully well suited to Copenhagen's flat terrain and are popular among Danes as well as visitors. Bike rental costs DKr25–DKr60 a day, with a deposit of DKr100–DKr200. You may also be lucky enough to find a free city bike chained up at bike racks in various spots throughout the city, including Nørreport and Nyhavn. Insert a DKr20 coin, which will be returned to you when you return the bike.

RENTALS
Københavns Cycle (✉ Reventlowsg. 11, ☎ 33/33–86–13). **Danwheel-Rent-a-Bike** (✉ Colbjørnsensg. 3, ☎ 31/21–22–27). **Urania Cykler** (✉ Gammel Kongevej 1, ☎ 31/21–80–88).

By Bus and Train

The **Copenhagen Card** offers unlimited travel on buses and suburban trains (S-trains), admission to more than 60 museums and sites around Sjælland, and a reduction on the ferry crossing to Sweden. You can buy the card, which costs DKr140 (24 hours), DKr255 (48 hours), or DKr320 (72 hours) and is half-price for children, at tourist offices and hotels and from travel agents.

Trains and buses operate from 5 AM (Sunday 6 AM) to midnight. After that, night buses run every half hour from 1 AM to 4:30 AM from the main bus station at Rådhus Pladsen to most areas of the city and surroundings. Trains and buses operate on the same ticket system and divide Copenhagen and surrounding areas into three zones. Tickets are validated on a time basis: on the basic ticket, which costs DKr10 per hour, you can travel anywhere in the zone in which you started. A discount *klip kort* (clip card), good for 10 rides, costs DKr75 and must be stamped in the automatic ticket machines on buses or at stations. Get zone details for S-trains by their information line (☎ 33/14–17–01). The buses have an automatic answering menu that is barely helpful in Danish. You'll do better by asking a bus driver.

By Car

If you are planning on seeing the sites of central Copenhagen, a car is not convenient. Parking spaces are at a premium and, when available, are expensive. A maze of one-way streets, relatively aggressive drivers, and bicycle lanes make it even more complicated. If you are going to drive, choose a small car that's easy to parallel park, bring a lot of small change to feed the meters, and be very aware of the cyclists on your right-hand side: they always have the right-of-way.

By Taxi

The shiny computer-metered Mercedes and Volvo cabs are not cheap. The base charge is DKr15, plus DKr8–DKr10 per km. A cab is available when it displays the sign FRI (free); it can be hailed or picked up in front of the main train station or at taxi stands, or by calling ☎ 31/35–35–35. Outside of the central city, always call for a cab, as your attempts will be in vain.

Contacts and Resources

Car Rentals

All major international car rental agencies are represented in Copenhagen; most are located near the Vesterport Station. Try **Europcar** (✉ Copenhagen Airport, ☎ 32/50–30–90). Also try **Pitzner Auto** (✉ Copenhagen Airport, ☎ 32/50–90–65).

Currency Exchange

Almost all banks (including the Danske Bank at the airport) exchange money. Most hotels cash traveler's checks and exchange major foreign currencies, but they charge a substantial fee and give a lower rate. The exception to the rule—if you travel with cash—are the several locations of **Forex** (including the main train station and close to the Nørreport station). For up to $500, Forex charges only DKr20 for the entire transaction. Keep your receipt and they'll even change it back to dollars for free. For travelers checks, they charge DKr10 per check.

Den Danske Bank exchange is open during and after normal banking hours at the **main railway station,** daily June to August 7 AM–10 PM, and daily September to May, 7 AM–9 PM. **American Express** (✉ Amagertorv 18, ☎ 33/12–23–01) is open weekdays 9–5 and Saturday 9–noon. In Copenhagen center are the four locations of the **Danish Change** (✉ Vesterbrog. 9A; Østerg. 61; Vimmelskaftet 47; Frederiksbergg. 5; ☎ 33/93–04–18), open April to October, daily 10–8, November to March, daily 10–6. **Tivoli** (✉ Vesterbrog. 3, ☎ 33/15–10–01) also exchanges money; it is open May to September, daily noon–11 PM.

You can use **ATM**s to get cash with credit cards; you will find machines in all of Denmark's cities and many larger towns. ATMs typically accept Visa, MasterCard, and Cirrus cards, and Jyske Bank machines accept PLUS cards.

Doctors and Dentists

Emergency dentists (✉ 14 Oslo Pl.), near Østerport Station, are available weekdays 8 PM–9:30 PM and weekends and holidays 10 AM–noon. Cash only is the accepted payment.

Look in the phone book under *læge*. After normal business hours, **emergency doctors** (☎ 38/88–60–41) make house calls in the central city. Fees are payable in cash only; night fees are approximately DKr300–DKr400.

Embassies

U.S. (✉ Dag Hammarskjölds Allé 24, DK-2100 Copenhagen O, ☎ 35/55–31–44). **Canada** (✉ Kristen Bernikows G. 1, DK-1105 Copenhagen K, ☎ 33/12–22–99). **U.K.** (✉ Kastesvej 36–40, DK-2100 Copenhagen O, ☎ 35/26–46–00).

Emergencies

Police, fire, and **ambulance** (☎ 112). **Auto Rescue/Falck** (☎ 31/14–22–22). **Rigshospitalet** (✉ Blegdamsvej 9, ☎ 35/45–35–45). **Frederiksberg Hospital** (✉ Nordre Fasanvej 57, ☎ 38/34–77–11).

English-Language Bookstores

Steve's Books and Records (✉ Ved Stranden 10, ☎ 33/11–94–60) stocks new and used English books. **Boghallen** (✉ Rådhus Pl. 37, ☎ 33/11–85–11, ext. 309), the bookstore of the Politiken publishing house, offers a good selection of English-language books. **Arnold Busck** (✉ Kobmagerg. 49, ☎ 33/12–24–53), has an excellent selection, and also textbooks, CDs, and comic books.

Guided Tours

The Copenhagen Tourist Board monitors all tours and has brochures and information. Most tours run through the summer until September. Only the Grand Tour of Copenhagen is year-round. In any case, it's always a good idea to call first to confirm availability. For tour information call **Copenhagen Excursions** (☎ 31/54–06–06).

BIKING TOURS (SELF-GUIDED)

BikeDenmark (✉ Åboulevarden 1, ☎ 35/36–41–00) offers two different self-guided city cycling tours. Choose between the 3- to 4-hour **Copenhagen Tour,** which includes the exteriors of the "musts" of the city, including *The Little Mermaid* and Amalienborg. The second is the 8- to 9-hour **Dragør Tour,** during which you leave the city and bike to the old-fashioned fishing hamlet near Copenhagen. There, you can swim at the beach and explore the ancient heart of the former Dutch colony. The tour package includes maps and a detailed route description. The rental price of the bike, which is available from **Københavns Cycle** (✉ Reventlowsg. 11, ☎ 33/33–86–13) is an additional DKr50 per bike.

BOAT TOURS

The **Harbor and Canal Tour** (1 hour) leaves from Gammel Strand and the east side of Kongens Nytorv from May to mid-September. Contact Canal Tours (☎ 33/13–31–05) or the tourist board (☞ Visitor Information, *below*). The **City and Harbor Tour** (2½ hours) includes a short bus trip through town and sails from the Fish Market on Holmens Canal through several more waterways, ending near Strøget. Just south of the embarkation point for the City and Harbor Tour, you'll find the equally charming **Netto Boats,** which also offer an hourlong tour for about half the price of their competitors.

COMMERCIAL TOURS

Tours of the **Carlsberg Bryggeri** (✉ Ny Carlsbergvej 140, ☎ 33/27–13–14; ☞ Exploring Copenhagen, *above*), which include a look into the draft horse stalls, meet at the Elephant Gate weekdays at 11 and 2. **The Royal Porcelain Factory** (✉ Smalleg. 45, ☎ 31/86–48–48) conducts tours that end at its shop on weekdays at 9, 10, and 11 from mid-September through April, and weekdays at 9, 10, 11, 1, and 2 from May through mid–September.

WALKING TOURS

All tours begin at Lurblæserne, in front of the Palace Hotel at the Rådhus Pladsen, and reservations are not necessary. Walking tours begin in front of the Tourist Information Office (✉ Bernstorffsg. 1, ☎ 33/11-13-25) at 10:30 and 2 daily (call to confirm); the 2-hour tour takes in the exteriors of most of the city's major sights. **The Royal Tour of Copenhagen** (2¾ hours) covers the exhibitions at Christiansborg and

Rosenborg, and visits Amalienborg Square. **The Grand Tour of Copenhagen** (2½ hours) includes Tivoli, the New Carlsberg Museum, Christiansborg Castle, Stock Exchange, Danish Royal Theater, Nyhavn, Amalienborg Castle, Gefion Fountain, Grundtvig Church, and Rosenborg Castle. The **City Tour** (1½ hours) is more general, passing the New Carlsberg Museum, Christiansborg Castle, Thorvaldsen's Museum, National Museum, Stock Exchange, Danish Royal Theater, Rosenborg Castle, National Art Gallery, Botanical Gardens, Amalienborg Castle, Gefion Fountain, and *The Little Mermaid*.

Late-Night Pharmacies

Steno Apotek (✉ Vesterbrog. 6C, ☎ 33/14–82–66) is open 24 hours a day. **Sønderbro Apotek** (✉ Amangerbrog. 158, ☎ 31/58–01–40) is also open around the clock.

Travel Agencies

American Express (✉ Amagertorv 18, ☎ 33/12–23–01). **Carlsen Wagons-Lits** (✉ Ved Vesterport 6, ☎ 33/14–27–47). **Skibby Rejser** (✉ Vandkunsten 10, ☎ 33/32–85–00).

For student and budget travel, try **Kilroy Travels Denmark** (✉ Skinderg. 28, ☎ 33/11–00–44). For charter packages, stick with **Spies** (✉ Nyropsg. 41, ☎ 33/32–15–00). **Star Tours** (✉ H. C. Andersens Boulevard 12, ☎ 33/11–50–70 also handles packages.

Visitor Information

Danmarks Turistråd (Danish Tourist Board, ✉ Bernstorffsg. 1, DK–1577 Copenhagen V, ☎ 33/11–13–25) is open May through the first two weeks of September, weekdays 9–8, weekends 9–5; and the rest of September through April, Monday to Saturday 9–5. Youth information in Copenhagen is available at **Use-It** (✉ Huset, Rådhusstr. 13, ☎ 33/15–65–18).

3 Sjælland and Its Islands

THE GODDESS GEFION is said to have carved Sjælland (Zealand) from Sweden. If she did, she must have sliced the north deep with a fjord, while she chopped the south to pieces and left the sides bowing west. Though the coasts are deeply serrated, Gefion's myth is more dramatic than the flat, fertile land of rich meadows and beech stands.

Slightly larger than the state of Delaware, Sjælland is the largest of the Danish islands. From Copenhagen, almost any point on it can be reached in an hour and a half, making it the most traveled portion of the country—and it is especially easy to explore thanks to the road network. To the north of the capital, ritzy beach towns line up between Hellerup and Humlebæk. Helsingør's Kronborg, which Shakespeare immortalized in *Hamlet,* and Hillerød's stronghold of Frederiksborg, considered one of the most magnificent Renaissance castles in Europe, also lie to the north. To the west of Copenhagen is Roskilde, medieval Denmark's most important town, with an eclectic cathedral that served as northern Europe's spiritual center 1,000 years ago.

West and south, rural towns and farms edge up to seaside communities and fine white beaches, often encompassed by forests. Beaches with summer cottages, white dunes, and calm waters surround Gilleleje and the neighboring town of Hornbæk. The beach in Tisvildeleje, farther west, is quieter and close to woods. Even more unspoiled are the lilliputian islands around southern Sjælland, virtually unchanged over the past century. Most of Sjælland can be explored in day trips from Copenhagen. The exceptions are the northwestern beaches around the Sejerø Bugt (Sejerø Bay) and those south of Møn, all of which require at least a night's stay and a day's loll.

Biking
Sjælland's flat landscape allows easy biking. Most roads have cycle lanes, and tourist boards stock with maps detailing local routes.

Canoeing
About 15 km (10 mi) north of Copenhagen, especially in the Lynby area, several calm lakes and rivers are perfect for canoeing: the Mølleå (Mølle River) and the Bagsværd, Lyngby, and Furesø (Bagsværd, Lyngby, and Fur lakes). **Frederiksdal Kanoudlejning** (⌧ Nybrovej, Lyngby, ☎ 45/85–67–70) offers hourly and daily rentals and package canoe tours throughout the region.

Fishing
Sjælland's takes, rivers, and coastline teem with plaice, flounder, cod, and catfish. Buy the DKr100 license, required to fish along Sjælland's coast, at any post office. Elsewhere, check with the local tourist office for license requirements. It is illegal to fish within 1,650 ft of the mouth of a stream.

Shopping
Shopping here can be considerably cheaper than in Copenhagen. Pedestrian streets run through the center of most towns, and flea markets are usually held Saturday morning.

Rungsted

㊷ *21 km (13 mi) north of Copenhagen.*

Between Copenhagen and Helsingør is **Rungstedlund,** the elegant, airy former manor of Baroness Karen Blixen. The author of *Out of Africa* and several accounts of aristocratic Danish life wrote under the pen name Isak Dinesen. The manor house, where she lived as a child and to which she returned in 1931, is open as a museum and displays manuscripts, photographs, and memorabilia documenting her years in Africa and Denmark. Leave time to wander around the gardens. ⊠ *Rungstedlund,* ☎ *42/57–10–57.* 🎫 *DKr30 (for combined train and admission tickets, call DSB (☞ Arriving and Departing in Sjælland and Its Islands A to Z, below).* ☉ *May–Sept., daily 10–5; Oct.–Apr., Wed.–Fri. 1–4, weekends 11–4.*

Dining

$$ ✕ **Strandmollekroen.** Stop for a meal at this 200-year-old beachfront
★ inn in Klampenborg as you drive north from Copenhagen to Rungsted. It's burnished with deep-green walls and filled with antiques and hunting trophies, but the best views are of the Øresund from the back dining room. Elegantly served seafood and steaks are the mainstays, and for a bit of everything, try the seafood platter, with lobster, crab claws, and Greenland shrimp. ⊠ *Strandvejen 808,* ☎ *31/63–01–04. AE, DC, MC, V.*

Humlebæk

㊽ *10 km (6 mi) north of Rungsted, 30 km (19 mi) north of Copenhagen.*

★ ℭ This elegant seaside town is home of the must-see **Louisiana,** a modern art museum famed for its stunning location and architecture as much as for its collection. Even if you can't tell a Monet from a Duchamp, you should make the 30-minute trip to see its elegant rambling structure, surrounded by a large park. Housed in a pearly 19th-century villa surrounded by dramatic views of the Øresund waters, the permanent collection includes modern American paintings and Danish paintings from the COBRA (a trend in northern European painting that took its name from its active locations, Copenhagen, Brussels, Amsterdam) and Deconstructionism movements. Be sure to see the haunting collection of Giacomettis backdropped by picture windows overlooking the sound. The children's wing has pyramid-shape chalkboards, kid-proof computers, and weekend activities under the guidance of an artist or museum coordinator. This makes for a good side trip from Copenhagen; walk north from the station about 10 minutes. ⊠ *Gammel Strandvej 13,* ☎ *49/19–07–19.* 🎫 *DKr48 (for combined train and admission tickets, call DSB ☞ Arriving and Departing in Sjælland and Its Islands A to Z, below).* ☉ *Daily 10–5, Wed. until 10.*

Helsingør

㊹ *19 km (12 mi) north of Humlebæk, 47 km (29 mi) north of Copenhagen.*

At the northeastern tip of the island is Helsingør, the departure point
★ for ferries to the Swedish town of Helsingborg, and the site of **Kronborg Slot** (Kronborg Castle). William Shakespeare based *Hamlet* on Danish mythology's Amleth, and used this castle as the setting even though he had never seen it. Built in the late 16th century, it's 600 years younger than the Elsinore we imagine from the tragedy. It was built as a Renaissance tollbooth: From its cannon-studded bastions, forces collected Erik of Pomerania's much-hated Sound Dues, a tariff charged to all ships crossing the sliver of water between Denmark and Sweden. Well worth seeing are the 200-ft-long dining hall and the dungeons, where there is a brooding statue of Holger Danske. According to legend, the Viking chief sleeps, but will awaken to defend Denmark when it is in danger. (The largest Danish resistance group during World War II called itself Holger Danske after its fearless forefather.) ⊠ *Helsingør,*

SCANDINAVIA BY TRAIN

The best way to experience the sights Scandinavia has to offer is by train.

With a *Scanrail Pass* choose unlimited rail travel throughout Denmark, Finland, Norway and Sweden for as many days as you need. Individual country rail passes are also available.

And with a *Scanrail 'n Drive,* you can take advantage of the benefits of both rail *and* car to get even more out of your Scandinavian vacation.

For information or reservations call your travel agent or Rail Europe:

1-800-4-EURAIL(US)

1-800-361-RAIL(CAN)

Your one source for European travel!

www.raileurope.com

Pick up the phone.

Pick up the miles.

MCI Calling Card

415 555 1234 2244
J.D. SMITH

WorldPhone

Use your MCI Card® to make an international call from virtually anywhere in the world and earn frequent flyer miles on one of seven major airlines.

Enroll in an MCI Airline Partner Program today. In the U.S., call **1-800-FLY-FREE.** Overseas, call MCI collect at **1-916-567-5151.**

1. To use your MCI Card, just dial the WorldPhone access number of the country you're calling from. (For a complete listing of codes, visit www.mci.com.)
2. Dial or give the operator your MCI Card number.
3. Dial or give the number you're calling.

# Austria (CC) ♦	022-903-012		# Netherlands (CC) ♦	0800-022-91-22
# Belarus (CC)			# Norway (CC) ♦	800-19912
From Brest, Vitebsk, Grodno, Minsk	8-800-103		# Poland (CC) ÷	00-800-111-21-22
From Gomel and Mogilev regions	8-10-800-103		# Portugal (CC) ÷	05-017-1234
# Belgium (CC) ♦	0800-10012		Romania (CC) ÷	01-800-1800
# Bulgaria	00800-0001		# Russia (CC) ÷ ♦	
# Croatia (CC) ★	99-385-0112		To call using ROSTELCOM ■	747-3322
# Czech Republic (CC) ♦	00-42-000112		For a Russian-speaking operator	747-3320
# Denmark (CC) ♦	8001-0022		To call using SOVINTEL ■	960-2222
# Finland (CC) ♦	08001-102-80		# San Marino (CC) ♦	172-1022
# France (CC) ♦	0-800-99-0019		# Slovak Republic (CC)	00-421-00112
# Germany (CC)	0130-0012		# Slovenia	080-8808
# Greece (CC) ♦	00-800-1211		# Spain (CC)	900-99-0014
# Hungary (CC) ♦	00▼800-01411		# Sweden (CC) ♦	020-795-922
# Iceland (CC) ♦	800-9002		# Switzerland (CC) ♦	0800-89-0222
# Ireland (CC)	1-800-55-1001		# Turkey (CC) ♦	00-8001-1177
# Italy (CC) ♦	172-1022		# Ukraine (CC) ÷	8▼10-013
# Kazakhstan (CC)	8-800-131-4321		# United Kingdom (CC)	
# Liechtenstein (CC) ♦	0800-89-0222		To call using BT ■	0800-89-0222
# Luxembourg	0800-0112		To call using MERCURY ■	0500-89-0222
# Monaco (CC) ♦	800-90-019		# Vatican City (CC)	172-1022

Is this a great time, or what? :-)

MCI

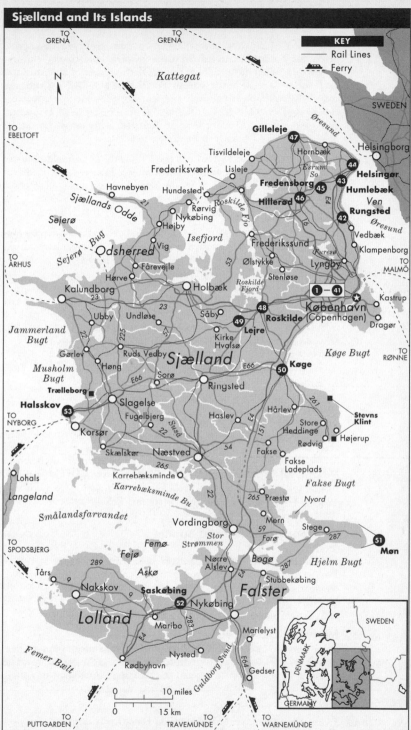

Sjælland and Its Islands

TO GRENÅ
TO GRENÅ

N

KEY
— Rail Lines
🚢 Ferry

Kattegat

SWEDEN

TO EBELTOFT

Øresund

Gilleleje ⑰

Tisvildeleje
Hornbæk
Helsingborg

Frederiksværk
Lisleje
Esrum So
㊹ Helsingør

Havnebyen
Hundested
Rørvig
Fredensborg
㊸
Humlebæk

Sjællands Odde
Nykøbing
Højby
Roskilde Fjo
Hillerød ㊻
㊺
Ven
Rungsted

Sejerø
Vig
Isefjord
E4
㊷
Øresund
Vedbæk

TO ÅRHUS
Sejerø Bug
Odsherred
Fåreveile
Frederikssund
Furesø
Klampenborg

Hørve
Holbæk
Ølstykke
Stenløse
Lyngby
TO MALMÖ

Kalundborg
Roskilde Fjord
① — ㊶
København
(Copenhagen)
Kastrup

Jammerland Bugt
Ubby
Undløse
Sáby
㊽
Roskilde
Dragør

㊾
Lejre
Kirke Hvalsø
Køge Bugt
TO RØNNE

Gørlev
Høng
Ruds Vedby
Sjælland
E66
㊿ **Køge**

Musholm Bugt
Sorø

Trælleborg
E66

Halsskov ㊼
Slagelse
Ringsted
Hårlev
261
Stevns Klint

TO NYBORG
Fugelbjerg
Haslev
E4
Store Heddinge
Højerup

Korsør
22
151
Rødvig

Skælskør
Næstved
54
Fakse

Lohals
265
Karrebæksminde
Fakse Ladeplads
Fakse Bugt

Langeland
Karrebæksminde Bu
22
265
Præstø
Nyord

Smålandsfarvandet
Vordingborg
Mern
Stege
287

TO SPODSBJERG
Femø
Stor Strømmen
59
Farø
(51)
Møn

Tårs
Askø
Nørre Alslev
Bogø
287
Hjelm Bugt

Nakskov
Saskøbing
Stubbekøbing
SWEDEN

Lolland
(52)
Nykøbing
Falster

Maribo
283
Marielyst
DENMARK

Femer Bælt
Nysted
GERMANY

Rødbyhavn
Gedser

0 — 10 miles
0 — 15 km
Guldborg Sund
E64

TO PUTTGARDEN
TO TRAVEMÜNDE
TO WARNEMÜNDE

☜ 49/21–30–78. ▨ DKr30. ☉ May–Sept., daily 10:30–5; Oct. and Apr., Tues.–Sun. 11–4; Nov.–Mar., Tues.–Sun. 11–3.

Thanks to the hefty tolls collected by Erik of Pomerania, Helsingør prospered. Stroll past the carefully restored medieval merchants' and ferrymen's houses in the middle of town. On the corner of Stengade and Skt. Annæ Gade near the harbor you'll find **Skt. Olai's Kirke,** the country's largest parish church and worth a peek for its elaborately carved wooden altar. ▨ St. Olai G. 51, ☜ 49/21–00–98 between 9 and noon only. ▨ Free. ☉ May 15–Sept. 14, daily noon–3, tours at 2; Sept. 15–May 14, daily noon–2.

Next door to Skt. Olai's Kirke is the 15th-century **Carmelite Kloster** (Carmelite Convent), one of the best-preserved examples of medieval architecture in Scandinavia. After the Reformation it was used as a hospital, and by 1630 it had become a poorhouse. ▨ Skt. Annæ G. 38, ☜ 49/21–17–74. ▨ DKr10. ☉ Tour daily at 2; call ahead.

If you want to know more about Helsingør, head to the modest **By Museum** (Town Museum), which has exhibits of 19th-century handicrafts, dolls, and a model of the town. ▨ Skt. Annæ G. 36, ☜ 49/21–00–98. ▨ DKr10. ☉ Daily noon–4.

OFF THE
BEATEN PATH

MARIENLYST SLOT – One kilometer (½ mile) north of Helsingør is the Louis XVI–style Marienlyst Castle. Built in 1587, it provided King Frederik II with a garden, as well as a delicate change of scenery from the militant Kronborg. Today the gardens have been replanted, and inside are paintings by north Sjælland artists and a gallery with changing arts and crafts exhibitions. ▨ Marienlyst Allé, ☜ 49/28–37–91. ▨ DKr20. ☉ Daily noon–5.

Dining and Lodging

$$$ ✕▥ **Hotel Hamlet.** A few minutes from the harbor, this overly renovated hotel has lost some of its charm but makes an attempt at character with raw timbers and deep-green walls. The rooms are furnished in rose schemes and dark wood, and all are comfortable, if nondescript. Downstairs, the Ophelia Restaurant serves traditional Danish seafood, steaks, and open-face sandwiches. ▨ Bramstrstrædet 5, DK–3000, ☜ 49/21–28–02, ℻ 49/26–01–30. 36 rooms. Restaurant, bar, meeting room. AE, DC, MC, V.

Outdoor Activities and Sports

GOLF

The **Helsingør Golf Klub** (▨ Gamle Hellebækvej, Helsingør, ☜ 49/21–29–70) has 18 holes on a beautiful, parklike course, with trees and, on clear days, views across the sound to Sweden. A weekday handicap of 36 for men and women, and a weekend handicap of 24 for men and 36 for women, is expected.

Nightlife and the Arts

Some summers, **Kronborg Castle** (☞ above) is the site of outdoor performances of Hamlet by internationally renowned theater groups. The schedule varies from year to year, so check with the tourist board.

Fredensborg

㊻   15 km (9 mi) southwest of Helsingør, 33 km (20 mi) northwest of Copenhagen.

Commanding this town is the **Fredensborg Slot** (Castle of Peace), built by Frederik IV to commemorate the 1720 peace treaty with Sweden. The castle, with a towering domed hall in the center, was originally inspired by French and Italian castles, but 18th-century reconstructions, concealing the original design, instead serve as a review of domestic architecture. The castle became a favorite of Frederik V, who lined the gardens with marble sculptures of ordinary people. It is now the summer residence of the royal family, and interiors are closed except in July. The lovely Baroque Gardens include a series of wide, horizontal waterfalls, called Cascades. The neatly trimmed park around the palace, connecting with Lake Esrum, is lovely for a stroll. ☎ 42/28–00–25. ☉ *Palace July, daily 1–5; Baroque Gardens, May–Aug., daily 10–9; Sept., daily 10–7; Mar., Apr., and Oct., daily 10–5; Nov.–Feb., daily 10–4.*

Dining and Lodging

$$$$ ✕🏨 **Hotel Store Kro.** Built by King Frederik IV, this magnificent Re-
★ naissance annex to Fredensborg Castle is the archetypal stately inn. Inside it's appointed with European antiques and paintings; outside, glass gazebos and classical statues overlook a lovely garden. The rooms are equally sumptuous, with delicately patterned wallpapers and antiques. The romantic restaurant, specializing in French fare, has a fireplace and a grand piano. ✉ *Slotsg. 6, DK–3480,* ☎ *42/28–00–47,* FAX *42/28–45–61. 49 rooms. Restaurant, bar, room service, sauna, meeting rooms. AE, DC, MC, V.*

$$$$ 🏨 **Marienlyst.** This hotel is full of flashy neon, bolts of drapery, and
★ glass. A large casino and endless lounges provide weekend entertainment, but when guests tire of gambling, there's a huge second-floor "Swinging Pool," with a water slide, swim-up bar, and sauna. The rooms are all plush and pastel, with every convenience. ✉ *Nordre Strandvej 2, DK–3000,* ☎ *49/21–40–00,* FAX *49/21–49–00. 220 rooms, 11 suites. 2 restaurants, 2 bars, room service, indoor pool, sauna, casino, nightclub, meeting rooms. AE, DC, MC, V.*

Hillerød

㊻ *10 km (6 mi) southwest of Fredensborg, 41 km (26 mi) northwest of Copenhagen.*

Hillerød's **Frederiksborg Slot** was acquired and rebuilt by Frederik II, but the fortress was demolished by his son, king-cum-architect Christian IV, who rebuilt it as one of Scandinavia's most magnificent castles. With three wings and a low entrance portal, the moated Dutch-Renaissance structure covers three islets and is peaked with dozens of gables, spires, and turrets. The two-story marble gallery known as the **Great Hall,** audaciously festooned with drapery, paintings, and reliefs, sits on top of the vaulted chapel, where monarchs were crowned for 200 years. Devastated by a fire in 1859, the castle was reconstructed with the support of the Carlsberg Foundation, and it now includes the National Portrait Gallery. ☎ *42/26–04–39.* 🎫 *DKr30.* ☉ *May–Sept., daily 10–5; Apr. and Oct., daily 10–4; Nov.–Mar., daily 11–3.*

Dining

$ ✕ **Slotsherrenskro.** Under the shadow of the Frederiksborg Castle, this family restaurant bustles in what used to be the castle stables. Antique on the outside, it's bright orange inside, with prints and paintings of royalty and the castle. Popular with visitors to the castle, the Danish menu ranges from quick open-face sandwiches to savory stews, soups, and steaks. ✉ *Slotherrens Kro,* ☎ *42/26–75–16. DC, MC, V. Nov.– Mar., no dinner Thurs.*

Gilleleje

㊼ *25 km (16 mi) north of Hillerød, 55 km (35 mi) northwest of Copen-hagen.*

Gilleleje is at the very top of Sjælland. Once a small fishing commu-nity, it experiences a population explosion every summer, when north-ern Europeans take to its woods and fine, sandy beaches. It was a favorite getaway of philosopher Søren Kierkegaard, who wrote: "I often stood there and reflected over my past life. The force of the sea and the strug-gle of the elements made me realize how unimportant I was." The less existential will go for a swim and visit the philosopher's monument on a nearby hill. The old part of town, with its thatched and color-fully painted houses, is good for a walk.

Odsherred

34 km (21 mi) southwest of Gilleleje, 80 km (50 mi) northwest of Copen-hagen (via Roskilde).

This hammer-shape peninsula is curved by the Sejerø Bugt (Sejerø Bay) and dotted with hundreds of **burial mounds.** Getting here involves driving to Hundested, then taking the 25-minute ferry ride to Rørvig.

If you are a devotee of ecclesiastical art, make a pilgrimage to explore the frescoes of the Romanesque-Gothic-Renaissance **Højby Kirke** (Højby Church) in the town of Højby, near Nykøbing Sjælland. In the town of Fårevejle is the Gothic **Fårevejle kirke,** with the earl of Both-well's chapel. **Sjællands Odde** (Zealand's Tongue), the tiny strip of land north of the Sejerø Bay, offers slightly marshy but private beach strands. Inside the bay, the beaches are once again smooth and blond.

Roskilde

㊽ *101 km (63 mi) southeast of Odsherred, 32 km (20 mi) west of Copen-hagen (on Rte. 156).*

Roskilde is Sjælland's second-largest town and one of its oldest, cele-brating its 1,000-year anniversary in 1998 (☞ Nightlife and the Arts, *below*). For a weekend in the end of June, it's filled with the rock music of the **Roskilde Festival,** said to be the largest outdoor concert in north-ern Europe, attracting some 75,000 people.

Roskilde was the royal residence in the 10th century and became the spiritual capital of Denmark and northern Europe in 1170, when Bishop Absalon built the **Roskilde Domkirke** (Roskilde Cathedral) on the site of a church erected 200 years earlier by Harald Bluetooth. Over-whelming the center of town, the current structure took more than 300 years to complete and thus provides a one-stop crash course in Dan-ish architecture. Inside are an ornate Dutch altarpiece and the sar-cophagi—ranging from opulent to modest—of 38 Danish monarchs. Predictably, Christian IV is interred in a magnificent chapel with a mas-sive painting of himself in combat and a bronze sculpture by Thorvaldsen. In modest contrast is the newest addition, the simple brick chapel of King Frederik IX, who died in 1972, outside the church. On the inte-rior south wall above the entrance is a 16th-century clock showing St. George charging a dragon, which hisses and howls, echoing through-out the church and causing Peter Døver, "the Deafener," to sound the hour. A squeamish Kirsten Kiemer, "the Chimer," shakes her head in fright but manages to strike the quarters. ✉ *Domkirkestr. 10,* ☎ *46/35–27–00.* ⚏ *DKr10.* ☉ *Hours vary; call ahead.*

Less than a kilometer (½ mi) north of the cathedral, on the fjord, is the modern **Vikingeskibshallen** (Viking Ship Museum), containing five Viking ships sunk in the fjord 1,000 years ago. Submerged to block the passage of enemy ships, they were discovered in 1957. The painstaking recovery involved building a watertight dam and then draining the water from that section of the fjord. The splinters of wreckage were then preserved and reassembled. A deep-sea trader, warship, ferry, merchant ship, and fierce 92½-ft man-of-war attest to the Vikings' sophisticated and aesthetic boat-making skills. ⊠ *Strandengen,* ☎ *46/35–65–55.* ✇ *DKr40.* ☉ *Apr.–Oct., daily 9–5; Nov.–Mar., daily 10–4.*

Dining and Lodging

$$ ✕ **Club 42.** This popular Danish restaurant spills out into the walking
★ street with a few tables in the summertime, while inside the roof opens over the dining room. The fare is typically Danish, including smørrebrød and spare ribs, simply prepared and served with potato salad. The rest of the menu includes lots of meat and potatoes, as well as fish. ⊠ *Skomagerg. 42,* ☎ *46/35–17–64. DC, MC, V.*

$$ ⊞ **Hotel Prindsen.** Central in downtown Roskilde, this convenient hotel, built 100 years ago, is popular with business guests. The elegant dark-wood lobby leads to nondescript rooms that are, nonetheless, homey and comfortable. Downstairs, the restaurant La Bøf serves up grill and fish fare, and next door there's a cozy bar. ⊠ *Alg. 13, DK–4000,* ☎ *46/35–80–10,* ⅟ᴀ̃ˣ *42/35–81–10. 38 rooms. Restaurant, bar, meeting room. AE, DC, MC, V.*

$ ⊞ **Roskilde Vandrehjem Hørgården.** In front of a grassy yard, this youth hostel is perfect for families and budget travelers. In a former schoolhouse 2 km (1 mi) east of the Roskilde Domkirke, it looks straight out of third grade, and the rooms, with bunks, look like camp. You can have use of the kitchen. ⊠ *Hørhusene 61, DK–4000,* ☎ *42/35–21–84,* ⅟ᴀ̃ˣ *46/32–66–90. 21 rooms with 4 beds each, 8 showers. No credit cards. Closed Oct.–Apr.*

Nightlife and the Arts

To celebrate the town's 1,000th birthday in 1998, concerts, performances, and exhibits will run all year, and on September 5th, a cultural blowout will keep shops, cinemas, museums, and libraries open late into the night. Call the Roskilde Tourist Board (☞ Visitor Information *in* Sjælland and Its Islands A to Z, *below*) for a schedule of events.

The young head to **Gimle** (⊠ Ringstedg. 30, ☎ 46/35–12–13) for live rock on the weekends. At **Bryggerhesten** (⊠ Alg. 15, ☎ 46/35–01–03), or "The Draft Horse," adults have a late supper and beer in cozy surroundings. During the summer, **Mullerudi** (⊠ Djalma Lunds Gord 7, ☎ 46/37–03–25) is an arty spot with indoor and outdoor seating and live jazz.

Outdoor Activities and Sports

GOLF

Roskilde has an 18-hole **golf course** (⊠ Kongemarken 34, ☎ 46/37–01–80) with views of the twin-peaked Roskilde Cathedral and an encircling forest.

Shopping

CRAFTS

Between Roskilde and Holbæk is **Kirke Sonnerup Kunst-håndværk** (Art Handicrafts, ⊠ Englerupvej 62, Såby, ☎ 46/49–25–77), with a good selection of pottery, glass, clothing, and woodwork produced by more than 50 Danish artists.

Lejre

🔵 *10 km (6 mi) west of Roskilde, 40 km (25 mi) west of Copenhagen.*

Ⓒ The 50-acre **Lejre Forsøgscenter** (Lejre Archaeological Research Center) compound contains a reconstructed village dating from the Iron Age and two 19th-century farmhouses. In summer a handful of hardy Danish families live here and are under the observation of researchers; they go about their daily routine—grinding grain, herding goats—providing a clearer picture of ancient ways of life. In Bodalen (Fire Valley), visitors (especially children) can grind corn, file an ax, and sail in a dugout canoe. ⊠ *Slangæleen,* ☎ *46/48–08–78.* 🎫 *DKr50.* ⊙ *May–Sept., daily 10–5.*

Køge

🔵 *20 km (13 mi) southeast of Lejre, 40 km (25 mi) southwest of Copenhagen.*

The well-preserved medieval town of Køge is known for its historic witch hunts. In the centrally located **Køge Museum,** a 17th-century merchant's house, you will see souvenirs from Hans Christian Andersen, costumes, local artifacts, an executioner's sword, and a 13th-century stone font. The story goes that the font had to be removed from the town church after a crippled woman committed an unsavory act into it, hoping her bizarre behavior would cure her. Also on exhibit are 16th-century silver coins from a buried treasure of more than 2,000 coins found in the courtyard of Langkildes Gård. ⊠ *Nørreg. 4,* ☎ *56/63–42–42.* 🎫 *DKr20.* ⊙ *June–Aug., daily 10–5; Sept.–May, weekdays 2–5, weekends 1–5.*

The old part of Køge is filled with 300 half-timber houses, all protected by the National Trust; it's a lovely area for a stroll. At the end of Kirkestræde, the 15th-century **Skt. Nikolai Kirke** (St. Nicholas Church) was once a lighthouse; its floor is covered with more than 100 tombs of Køge VIPs. Carved angels line the church's walls, but most have had their noses struck off—a favorite pastime of drunken Swedish soldiers in the 1700s. ⊠ *Kirkestr.,* ☎ *53/65–13–59.* 🎫 *Free.* ⊙ *June–Aug., weekdays 10–4; Sept.–May, weekdays 10–noon. Tower tours late July–mid-Aug., weekdays at 11, noon, and 1.*

If you have time, visit the **Køge Kunst Museet** (Køge Art Museum) for its changing exhibitions and an extensive permanent collection of sketches, sculpture, and other modern Danish art. ⊠ *Nørreg. 29,* ☎ *53/66–24–14.* 🎫 *DKr15. Free with admission ticket from the Køge Museum (☞ above).* ⊙ *Tues.–Sun. 11–5.*

En Route Twenty-four kilometers (15 miles) south of Køge near Rødvig, you should stop at the chalk cliffs called Stevns Klint to see the 13th-century **Højerup Kirke** built above them. As the cliffs eroded, first the cemetery, then the choir toppled into the sea. In recent years the church has been restored and the cliffs below bolstered by masonry to prevent further damage. ⊠ *Højerup Church, Stevns Klint.* 🎫 *DKr5.* ⊙ *Apr.–Sept., daily 11–5.*

Møn

🔵 *85 km (52 mi) south of Stevns Klint, 130 km (81 mi) south of Copenhagen.*

The whole island of Møn is pocked with nearly 100 Neolithic burial mounds, but it is most famous for its dramatic chalk cliffs, the northern **Møns Klint,** three times as large as Stevns Klint (☞ En Route, *above*). Rimmed by a beech forest, the milky-white 75-million-year-old bluffs plunge 400 ft to a small, craggy beach—accessible by a path and more than 500 steps. Wear good walking shoes, and take care; though a park ranger checks the area for loose rocks, the cliffs crumble suddenly. Once there, Danish families usually hunt for blanched fossils of cuttlefish, sea urchins, and other sea life. The cliffs are an important navigational marker for ships, defining south Sjælland's otherwise flat topography.

You can walk to a delightful folly of the 18th century, **Liselund Slot** (not to be confused with a hotel of the same name), 4 km (2½ mi) north of the cliffs. Antoine de la Calmette, the island's sheriff and a royal chamberlain, took his inspiration from Marie Antoinette's *Hameau* (*Hamlet*) at Versailles and built the structure in 1792 for his beloved wife. The thatched palace, complete with English gardens, combines a Norwegian country facade with elegant Pompeian interiors. In this lovely setting, Hans Christian Andersen wrote his fairy tale *The Tinder Box*. The palace has been open to the public since 1938. ☎ 55/81–21–78. 🎫 DKr20. ☼ *Tours (Danish and German only) May–Oct., Tues.–Fri. 10:30, 11, 1:30, and 2; weekends also 2, 4, and 4:30.*

Møn's capital, **Stege**, received its town charter in 1268. Take time to explore its medieval churches, including Elmelunde, Keldby, and Fanefjord, all famous for their naive frescoes. Thought to have been completed by a collaborative group of artisans, the whimsical paintings include pedagogic and biblical doodlings.

Lodging

$$ ★ 🏨 **Liselund Ny Slot.** Set in a grand old manor on an isolated estate, this modern hotel offers refined accommodations minus stodginess. The square staircase and painted ceilings have been preserved. The rooms are fresh and simple, with wicker and pastel schemes, half of them overlooking a swan-filled pond and the forest. The downstairs restaurant serves Danish cuisine. ✉ *Liselund Ny Slot, DK–4791 Børre*, ☎ 55/81–20–81, 🏠 55/81–21–91. *25 rooms, 1 suite. Restaurant, meeting rooms. AE, DC, MC, V.*

Falster

3 km (2 mi) south of Bogø, 24 km (15 mi) south of Møn, 99 km (62 mi) south of Copenhagen.

Accessible by way of the striking Farø Bridge or the parallel Storstrømsbroen (Big Current Bridge) from Vordingborg, Falster is shaped like a tiny South America and has excellent blond beaches to rival those of its tropical twin. Among the best are the southeastern Marielyst and southernmost Gedser. Almost everywhere on the island you'll find cafés, facilities, and water-sports rentals. Falster is also one of the country's major producers of sugar beets.

☾ The **Middelaldercentret** (Center for the Middle Ages), a reconstructed medieval village, invites school classes to dress up in period costumes and experience life a millennium ago. Day guests can participate in activities that change weekly—from cooking to medieval knife-making to animal herding and, on weekends, folk dances and other cultural happenings. ✉ *Nykøbing Falster*, ☎ 54/86–19–34. 🎫 DKr45. ☼ *May–mid-Sept., Tues.–Sat., 10–4, Sun. 10–5.*

Dining and Lodging

$$$ ✕ **Czarens Hus.** This stylish old inn dates back more than 200 years, when it was a guest house and supply store for area farmers and merchants. Deep-green walls, gold trim, and chandeliers provide a background for antique furnishings. The specialty of the house is Continental Danish cuisine, which translates as creative beef and fish dishes, often served with cream sauces. Try the *Zar Beuf* (calf tenderloin in a mushroom-and-onion cream sauce). ⊠ *Langg. 2, Nykøbing Falster,* ☎ *54/85–28–29. AE, DC, MC, V.*

$$ ✕ **Brasserie Kæller and Køkken.** Done up in bright colors with a modern decor, this central and very popular café-restaurant is touted as one of the best in the area. The menu varies, with basics like steaks, sandwiches, and nachos, as well as the slightly more experimental, including ham with pineapple sauce, grilled ostrich steaks, and beef slices with Gorgonzola. ⊠ *Torvet 19, Nykøbing Falster,* ☎ *54/85–82–82. DC, MC, V. Closed Dec. 24–Jan. 2.*

$$ ⊡ **Hotel Falster.** This sleek and efficient hotel accommodates conference guests as well as vacationers with a comfortable and businesslike ambience. Rustic brick walls and Danish antiques mix with sleek Danish-design lamps and sculpture. Rooms are comfortably done with dark wood and modular furniture. ⊠ *Skovalleen, Nykøbing Falster, DK–4800,* ☎ *54/85–93–93,* 🖷 *54/82–21–99. 70 rooms. Restaurant, bar, meeting room. AE, DC, MC, V.*

Outdoor Activities and Sports
GOLF

The 18-hole **Sydsjælland Golf Klub** (⊠ Præstolandevej 39, Mogenstrup, ☎ 53/76–15–55) is more than 25 years old, and the park course is lined with a number of small lakes.

Lolland

19 km (12 mi) west of Nykøbing Falster.

The history of Lolland dates back more than 1,000 years, to a man named Saxe, who sat at the mouth of the fjord and collected a toll. He later cleared the surrounding land and leased it. It became known as Saxtorp and eventually **Sakskøbing,** the island's capital. Though most people head straight for the beaches, the area has a few sights, including a water tower with a smiling face and an excellent car museum near the central 13th-century **Ålholm Slot** (closed to the public). The **Ålholm Automobile Museum** is northern Europe's largest, with more than 200 vehicles. The town is accessible by bridge from Nykøbing Falster. ⊠ *Ålholm Parkvej, Nysted,* ☎ *53/87–15–09.* 🖾 *DKr60.* ☉ *Sept. and Oct., Thurs. and Sun. 11–4.*

☾ The **Knuthenborg Safari Park,** just 8 km (5 mi) west of Sakskøbing and also on Lolland, has a drive-through range where you can rubberneck at tigers, zebras, rhinoceroses, and giraffes, and pet camels, goats, and ponies. Besides seeing 20 species of animals, children can also play in Miniworld's jungle gym, minitrain, and other rides. ⊠ *Knuthenborg Safaripark, DK–4930 Maribo,* ☎ *53/88–80–89.* 🖾 *DKr74.* ☉ *May–Sept. 15, daily 9–6.*

Lodging

$$ ⊡ **Lalandia.** This massive water-park hotel has an indoor pool, beachside view, and lots of happy families. On the southern coast of Lolland, about 27 km (16 mi) southwest of Sakskøbing, the modern white apartments, with full kitchen and bath, accommodate up to eight people. There are three family-style restaurants—a steak house, Italian buffet, and pizzeria. ⊠ *Rødbyhavn, DK–4970 Rødby,* ☎ *54/60–42–00,* 🖷 *54/60–41–44. 636 apartments. 3 restaurants, bar, indoor pool, sauna, 9-hole golf course, 5 tennis courts, health club, playground, meeting rooms. AE, DC, MC, V.*

$ ⊡ **Hotel Saxkjøbing.** Behind its yellow half-timber facade, this comfortable hotel is short on character and frills, but the rooms are bright, sunny, and modern, if very simply furnished. In town center, the hotel is convenient to everything. Its family-style restaurant serves pizzas, steaks, and salads. ⊠ *Torvet 9, Sakskøbing, DK–4990,* ☎ *54/70–40–39,* FAX *54/89–53–50. 30 rooms, 20 with bath. Restaurant, bar, meeting room. AE, DC, MC, V.*

En Route Kids adore and flock to **BonBon Land,** in the tiny southern Sjælland town of Holme Olstrup between Rønnede and Næstved. Filled with rides and friendly costumed grown-ups, the park is an old-fashioned playland, with a few eating and drinking establishments thrown in for adults. ☎ *53/76–26–00.* 🎫 *DKr95, DKr89 off-season.* ☉ *Early May–mid-June and early Aug.–mid-Sept., daily 10–7; mid-June–early Aug., daily 10–9.*

Halsskov

53 *95 km (60 mi) northwest of Falster, 110 km (69 mi) southwest of Copenhagen.*

Europe's second-longest tunnel-bridge, Storebæltsbro—the entire fixed-link length of which will be 18 km (11 mi)—will soon link Halsskov, on west Sjælland, to Nyborg, on east Fyn. Rail traffic traverses the west bridge and tunnel; at press time, auto traffic was scheduled to commence in summer 1998 on the east and west bridge. The **Storebæltsbro Udstillings Center** (Great Belt Exhibition Center), detailing the work, includes videos and models and makes for an informative stop. ⊠ *Halsskov Odde,* ☎ *58/35–01–00.* 🎫 *DKr35.* ☉ *May–Sept., daily 10–8; Oct.–Apr., Tues.–Sun. 10–5.*

Outdoor Activities and Sports
CANOEING
Just 15 km (10 mi) east of Slagelse and 30 km (19 mi) east of Halsskov is the Suså (Sus River), where you can arrange hour-, day-, and week-long trips. Call **Susåen Kanoudlejning** regarding canoe rentals (☎ 53/64–61–44).

GOLF
The 18-hole **Korsør Course** (⊠ Ørnumvej 8, Korsør, ☎ 53/57–18–36) is in Korsør, less than 3 km (2 mi) south of Halsskov.

Shopping
In Næstved, 49 km (31 mi) southeast of Halsskov, the **Holmegaards Glasværker** (Glass Workshop, ⊠ Glasværksvej 52, Fensmark, ☎ 55/54–62–00) sells seconds of glasses, lamps, and occasionally art glass, with savings of up to 50% off wholesale costs.

OFF THE BEATEN PATH **TRÆLLEBORG** – Viking enthusiasts will want to head 18 km (11 mi) northeast from Halsskov to Slagelse to see its excavated Viking encampment with a reconstructed army shelter. No longer content to rely on farmer warriors, the Viking hierarchy designed the geometrically exact camp within a circular, moated rampart, thought to be of Asian inspiration. The 16 barracks, of which there is one model, could accommodate 1,300 men. ⊠ Trælleborg Allé, ☎ 53/54–95–06. 🎫 DKr35. ☉ Mid-Mar.–Oct., daily 10–5; Nov.–mid-Mar., daily noon–4.

Sjælland and Its Islands A to Z

Arriving and Departing
BY CAR
There are several **DSB** car ferries from Germany. They connect Kiel to Bagenkop, on the island of Langeland (from there, drive north to Spodsbjerg and take another ferry to Lolland, which is connected to

Falster and Sjælland by bridges); Puttgarden to Rødbyhavn on Lolland; and Travemünde and Warnemünde to Gedser on Falster. Sjælland is connected to Fyn, which is connected to Jylland, by bridges and frequent ferries. If you are driving from Sweden, take a car ferry from either Helsingborg to Helsingør or Limhamn to Dragør. Or sail directly to Copenhagen (☞ Arriving and Departing *in* Copenhagen A to Z *in* Chapter 2). In Denmark, call DSB (☎ 33/14–17–01); in Sweden, call DSB Sweden (☎ 46/31–80–57–00).

BY PLANE

Copenhagen Airport is Sjælland's only airport (☞ Arriving and Departing *in* Copenhagen A to Z *in* Chapter 2).

BY TRAIN

Most train routes to Sjælland, whether international or domestic, are directed to Copenhagen. Routes to north and south Sjælland almost always require a transfer at Copenhagen's main station. For timetables, call **DSB** (☎ 33/14–17–01).

Getting Around

BY CAR

Highways and country roads throughout Sjælland are excellent, and traffic—even around Copenhagen—is manageable most of the time. As elsewhere in Denmark, take care to give right-of-way to the bikes driving to the right of the traffic.

BY PUBLIC TRANSPORTATION

The **Copenhagen Card,** which affords free train and bus transport, as well as admission to museums and sites, is valid within the HT-bus and rail system, which extends north to Helsingør, west to Roskilde, and south to Køge (☞ Getting Around *in* Copenhagen A to Z *in* Chapter 2). Every town in Sjælland has a central train station, usually within walking distance of hotels and sights. (For long distances, buses are not convenient.) The only part of the island not connected to the DSB network is the sliver of northwestern peninsula known as Sjællands Odde. Trains leave from Holbæk to Højby, where you can bus to the tip of the point. For information, call the private railway company **Odsherrede** (☎ 53/41–00–03). Two vintage trains dating from the 1880s run from Helsingør and Hillerød to Gilleleje; call for info (☎ 48/30–00–30 or 42/12–00–98).

Contacts and Resources

EMERGENCIES

Police, Fire, or **Ambulance:** (☎ 112).

Hospitals: Helsingør (✉ Esrumvej 145, ☎ 48/29–29–29). **Roskilde** (✉ Roskilde Amtssygehus, Køgevej 7, ☎ 46/32–32–00).

Pharmacies: Helsingør (✉ Axeltorvs, Groskenstr. 2A, ☎ 49/21–12–23). **Stengades** (✉ Steng. 46, ☎ 49/21–86–00). **Roskilde** (✉ Dom Apoteket, Alg. 8, ☎ 42/35–40–16). **Svane** (✉ Skomagerg. 12, ☎ 42/35–83–00).

GUIDED TOURS

Check with the local tourism boards for general sightseeing tours in the larger towns or for self-guided walking tours. Most tours of Sjælland begin in Copenhagen. For information, call Vikingbus (☎ 31/57–26–00) or Copenhagen Excursion (☎ 31/54–06–06).

Boat Tour: The turn-of-the-century *Saga Fjord* (☎ 46/35–35–75) gives tours of the waters of the Roskildefjord from April through September; meals are served on board. Schedules vary; call ahead.

Castle Tours: The **Afternoon Hamlet Tour** (4½ hours) includes Frederiksborg Castle and the exterior of Fredensborg Palace. The 7-hour **Castle Tour of North Zealand** visits Frederiksborg Castle and the outside of Fredensborg Palace, and stops at Kronborg Castle.

Walking Tours: The 6-hour Roskilde **Vikingland Tour** includes the market and cathedral, Christian IV's Chapel, and the Viking Ship Museum.

VISITOR INFORMATION
Helsingør (⊠ Havnepl. 3, ☎ 49/21–13–33). **Hillerød** (⊠ Slotsg. 52, ☎ 42/26–28–52). **Køge** (⊠ Vesterg. 1, ☎ 53/65–58–00). **Lolland** (⊠ Østergårdg. 7, Nykøbing Falster, ☎ 54/85–13–03). **Roskilde** (⊠ Fondens Bro 3, ☎ 42/35–27–00). **Sakskøbing** (⊠ Torveg. 4, ☎ 53/89–56–30 summer; ☎ 53/89–45–72 winter). **Stege** and **Møn** (⊠ Storeg. 2, Stege, ☎ 55/81–44–11).

4 Fyn and the Central Islands

CHRISTENED THE GARDEN of Denmark by its most famous son, Hans Christian Andersen, Fyn (Funen) is the smaller of the country's two major islands. A patchwork of vegetable fields and flower gardens, the flat-as-a-board countryside is relieved by beech glades and swan ponds. Manor houses and castles pop up from the countryside like magnificent mirages. Some of northern Europe's best-preserved castles are here: the 12th-century Nyborg Slot, travel pinup Egeskov Slot, and the lavish Valdemars Slot. The fairy-tale cliché often attached to Denmark really does spring from this provincial isle, where the only faint pulse emanates from Odense, its capital. Trimmed with thatched houses and green parks, the city makes the most of the Andersen legacy but surprises with a rich arts community at the Brandts Klædefabrik, a former textile factory turned museum compound.

Towns in Fyn are best explored by car. It's even quick and easy to reach the smaller islands of Langeland and Tåsinge—both are connected to Fyn by bridges. Slightly more isolated is Ærø, where the town of Ærøskøbing, with its painted half-timber houses and winding streets, seems caught in a delightful time warp.

Biking
Flat and smooth, Fyn is perfect for biking. Packages with bike rental, hotel accommodations, and half-board (breakfast and one meal) for the entire region are available from **Hotel Svendborg** (⊠ Centrumpl., 5700 Svendborg, ☎ 62/21–17–00).

Markets
Wednesday and Saturday are market days in towns across Fyn throughout the summer. Often held in the central square, these morning markets offer fresh produce, flowers, and cheeses.

Nightlife and the Arts
Castle concerts are held throughout the summer at Egeskov, Nyborg, and Valdemar castles and the rarely opened Krengenrup manor house near Assens.

Nyborg

⑤⓸ *75 km (47 mi) southwest of Copenhagen, including ferry passage across the Great Belt, 30 km (19 mi) southeast of Odense.*

Like most visitors, you should begin your tour of Fyn in Nyborg, a 13th-century town that was Denmark's capital during the Middle Ages. The city's major landmark, the moated 12th-century **Nyborg Slot** (Nyborg Castle), was the seat of the Danehof, the Danish parliament from 1200 to 1413. It was here that King Erik Klipping signed the country's first constitution, the Great Charter, in 1282. In addition to geometric wall murals and an armory collection, the castle houses changing art exhibits. ⊠ *Slotspl.,* ☎ *65/31–02–07.* ⌑ *DKr10.* ☉ *June–Aug., daily 10–5; Mar.–May and Sept.–Oct., Tues.–Sun. 10–3.*

Cross Gammel Torv and walk down the street to the **Nyborg Museum,** housed in a half-timber merchant's house from 1601, for a picture of 17th-century life. Aside from furnished rooms, there's a small brewery. ⊠ *Slotspl. 11,* ☎ *65/31–02–07.* ⌑ *DKr10.* ☉ *June–Aug., daily 10–5; Mar.–May and Sept.–Oct., Tues.–Sun. 10–3.*

Dining and Lodging
$$ ✕ **Danehofkroen.** Outside Nyborg Slot, this family-run restaurant does a brisk lunch business, serving traditional Danish meals to tourists

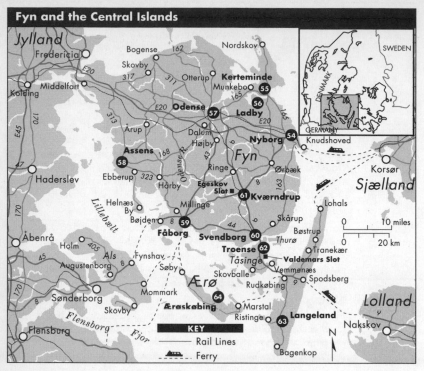

Fyn and the Central Islands

who enjoy a view of the castle and its tree-lined moat. The menu is basic meat and potatoes, with such dishes as *flæskesteg* (sliced pork served with the crisp rind). ⊠ *Slotspl.,* ☎ *65/31–02–02. Reservations essential. No credit cards. Closed Mon.*

$$$$ 🏨 **Hesselet.** A modern brick slab outside, this hotel is a refined Anglo-Asian sanctuary on the inside. Guest rooms have cushy, modern furniture, most with a splendid view of the Storebæltsbro. ⊠ *Christianslundsvej 119, DK–5800 Nyborg,* ☎ *65/31–30–29,* FAX *65/31–29–58. 43 rooms, 3 suites. Restaurant, bar, room service, indoor pool, sauna, tennis courts, meeting rooms. AE, DC, MC, V.*

Shopping
ANTIQUES

Many of Fyn's manor houses and castles now double as antiques emporiums. The largest is at **Hindemae** (⊠ Near Rte. 315, 12 km/7 mi west of Nyborg, exit 46 or 47 in Ullerslee, ☎ 65/35–22–05). A modest selection of antiques is for sale at **Hønnerup Hougård** (⊠ Hougårdsvej 6, Hønnerup, 40 km/25 mi northwest of Nyborg, ☎ 64/49–13–00); take exit 55 to Route 161 toward Middelfart; follow the signs to Hønnerup.

Kerteminde

⑤⑤ *21 km (13 mi) north of Nyborg, 20 km (13 mi) northeast of Odense.*

Kerteminde is an important fishing village and picturesque summer resort. On Langegade, walk past the neat half-timber houses to Møllebakken and the museum of the Danish painter **Johannes Larsen** (1867–1961). Across from a crimson strawberry patch and a 100-year-old windmill, the artist built a large country villa that has been perfectly preserved, right down to the teacups. In front, you'll see a sculpture of a woman by Kai Nielsen. Local legend has it that one night, after a particularly wild party in Copenhagen, its legs were broken off. An ambulance was called, and once it arrived, the enraged driver demanded that the artists pay a fine. A chagrined Larsen paid, and in return kept the wounded sculpture. ⊠ *Møllebakken,* ☎ *65/32–37–27.* 🗩 *DKr30.* ☉ *June–Aug., daily 10–5; Mar.–May and Sept.–Oct., Tues.–Sun. 10–4; Nov.–Feb., Tues.–Sun. 11–4.*

Dining

$$ ✕ **Rudolf Mathis.** This busy harborside restaurant is topped by two chimneys venting open grills that broil popular fish dishes. Favorites are catfish with butter, fennel, and Pernod sauce, and grilled turbot in green-pepper-and-lime sauce. ⊠ *Dosserengen 13,* ☎ *65/32–32–33. AE, DC, MC, V. Closed Mon. Jan.–Mar. and Sun. Oct. and Dec.*

Shopping

CERAMICS
Just a few miles north of Kerteminde is **Bjørnholt Keramik** (⊠ Risingevej 12, Munkebo, ☎ 65/97–40–90), where you can watch ceramics in the making.

Ladby

56 *4 km (2½ mi) south of Kerteminde, 16 km (10 mi) east of Odense.*

The village of Ladby is best known as the home of the 1,100-year-old remains of the **Ladbyskibet.** This Viking chieftain's ship burial is complete with hunting dogs and horses for his trip to Valhalla—the afterlife. ⊠ *Vikingevej 12,* ☎ *65/32–16–67.* 🗩 *DKr20.* ☉ *Mid-May–mid-Sept., daily 10–6; Mar.–mid-May and mid-Sept.–Oct., daily 10–4; Nov.–Feb., weekends 11–3.*

Odense

57 *20 km (12 mi) southwest of Ladby on Route 165, 144 km (90 mi) west of Copenhagen.*

It's no coincidence that Odense, the capital of Fyn and third largest city in Denmark, is reminiscent of a storybook village—much of its charm is built upon the legend of its most famous son, author Hans Christian Andersen. First see the flourishing **Kongens Have** (King's Garden) and 18th-century **Odense Castle,** now a government building. Walking east on Stationsvej to Thomas B. Thriges Gade and Hans Jensensstræde, you'll come to the **Hans Christian Andersen Hus** (Hans Christian Andersen House) amid half-timber houses and cobbled streets. Inside, the storyteller's life is chronicled through his photographs, drawings, letters, and personal belongings. The library has Andersen's works in more than 100 languages, and you can listen to fairy tales on tape. ⊠ *Hans Jensensstr. 37–45,* ☎ *66/13–13–72 ext. 4611.* 🗩 *DKr25.* ☉ *June–Aug., daily 9–6; Sept.–May, daily 10–4.*

The sleek **Carl Nielsen Museum** creates multimedia exhibits of the life and work of Denmark's most famous composer (1865–1931) and of his wife, the sculptor Anne Marie Carl-Nielsen (yes, that's the way she took his name). ⊠ *Claus-Bergs G. 11,* ☎ *66/13–13–72, ext. 4671.* 🗩 *DKr15.* ☉ *Daily 10–4.*

Møntergården, Odense's museum of urban history, occupies four 17th-century row houses in a shady, cobbled courtyard. Exhibits range from interiors of the Middle Ages to Denmark's Nazi occupation to an impressive coin collection. ⊠ *Overg. 48–50,* ☎ *66/13–13–72 ext. 4611.* 🗩 *DKr15.* ☉ *July and Aug., daily 10–5; Sept.–June, Tues.–Sun. 10–5.*

The stately **St. Knuds Kirke,** built from the 13th to the 15th century, is the only purely Gothic cathedral in Denmark. The intricate wooden altar covered with gold leaf was carved by German sculptor Claus Berg. Beneath the sepulchre are the bones of St. (King) Knud, killed during a farmers' uprising in 1086, and his brother. ⊠ *Toward the pedestrian zone of St. Knuds Kirkestræde, in front of Andersen Park.*

In the diminutive **H. C. Andersens Barndomshjem** (H. C. Andersen's Childhood Home), the young boy and his parents lived in a room barely 5 ft by 6 ft. ⊠ *Munkemøllestr. 3–5,* ☎ *66/13–13–72, ext. 4611.* ☺ *Jun.–Aug., daily 10–4; Sept.–May, daily 11–3.*

Filosofgangen is the embarkation point for the **Odense River Cruises** (☎ *65/95–79–96*). Here you can catch a boat (May–mid-Aug., daily 10, 11, 1, 2, 3, and 5, returning 35 minutes later) downriver to the Fruens Bøge (Lady's Beech Forest) and then walk down Erik Bøghs Sti (Erik Bøgh's Footpath) to **Den Fynske Landsby** (the Fyn Village). Among the country's largest open-air museums, it includes 25 farm buildings and workshops, a vicarage, a water mill, and a theater, which in summer stages adaptations of Andersen's tales. Afterward, cruise back to town center or catch Bus 21 or 22, and walk down the boutique- and café-lined pedestrian street Vestergade (Kongsgade running perpendicular to the town hall), which in summer is abuzz with street performers, musicians, and brass bands. ⊠ *Sejerskovvej 20,* ☎ *66/13–13–72 ext. 4642.* ⊠ *DKr20.* ☺ *June–Aug., daily 10–7; Apr.–May and Sept.–Oct., daily 10–5; Nov.–Mar., Sun. and holidays 10–4.*

★ Occupying a former textile factory, the four-story artist compound **Brandts Klædefabrik** now houses the **Museet for Fotokunst** (Museum of Photographic Art), **Danmarks Grafiske Museum** (Danish Graphics Museum), **Dansk Presse Museum** (Danish Press Museum), and **Kunsthallen** (Art Gallery). National and international exhibits vary widely, but the photography museum and the art gallery show especially experimental work. ⊠ *North of the river and parallel to Kongensgade, Brandts Passage 37,* ☎ *66/13–78–97.* ⊠ *Combined ticket DKr40; photography museum DKr20; graphics museum DKr20; press museum DKr20; art gallery DKr25.* ☺ *July and Aug., daily 10–5; Sept.–June, Tues.–Sun. 10–5.*

OFF THE
BEATEN PATH

HOLLUFGÅRD – This 16th-century manor now houses the city's archaeological department. Although the house itself remains closed, its grounds contain a completely renovated old barn and adjacent buildings showing special exhibits, including the archaeological find of the month and an ecology display. Nearby are a sculpture center, where you can see an artist at work, and a sculpture garden. Take Bus 91 from the railway center on Jernbanegade 10 km (6 mi) south of Odense. ⊠ *Hestehaven 201,* ☎ *66/14–88–14, ext. 4638* ⊠ *DKr25.* ☺ *Apr.–Oct., Tues.–Sun. 10–5.; Nov.–Apr., Sun. 11–4.*

Dining and Lodging

$$$ ✕ **La Petite Cuisine Française.** This romantic little restaurant, tucked in the Brandts Passage, can accommodate about 40 guests, all of whom must make reservations a least a few days in advance. The southern French specialties change every day according to what can be purchased fresh at the market. Typical dishes include Asian-inspired marinated duck breast, grilled skewered salmon or catfish with vegetables, and white mocha parfait for dessert. Dishes can be combined in three- to five-course menus. ⊠ *Brandts Passage 13,* ☎ *66/14–11–00. Reservations essential. DC, MC, V.*

$$$ ✕ **Marie Louise.** Near the pedestrian street, this elegant whitewashed dining room glitters with crystal and silver. The daily French-Danish menu typically offers such specialties as salmon scallop with bordelaise sauce and grilled veal with lobster-cream sauce. Business and holiday diners are sometimes treated to gratis extras—such as quail's egg appetizers or after-dinner drinks. ⊠ *Lottrups Gaard, Vesterg. 70–72,* ☎ *66/17–92–95. AE, DC, MC, V. Closed Sun. and July.*

$$ ✕ **Den Gamle Kro.** Built within the courtyards of several 17th-century homes, this popular restaurant has walls of ancient stone sliced by a sliding glass roof. The French-Danish menu includes fillet of sole stuffed with salmon mousse and chateaubriand with garlic potatoes, but there's also inexpensive smørrebrød. ⊠ *Overg. 23,* ☎ *66/12–14–33. DC, MC, V.*

$$ ✕ **La Provence.** A few minutes from the pedestrian street, this intimate restaurant with a bright yellow and orange dining room puts a modern twist on Provençal cuisine. Dishes might be venison in blackberry sauce and tender duck breast cooked in sherry. ⊠ *Dogstr. 31,* ☎ *66/12–12–96. DC, MC, V.*

$ ✕ **Den Grimme Ælling.** The name of this chain restaurant means the
★ Ugly Duckling, but inside it's simply homey, with pine furnishings and family-style interiors. It's also extremely popular with tourists and locals alike, thanks to an all-you-can-eat buffet heaped with cold and warm dishes. ⊠ *Hans Jensensstr. 1,* ☎ *65/91–70–30. DC, MC.*

$ ✕ **Målet.** A lively crowd calls this sports club its neighborhood bar. After the steaming plates of schnitzel served in a dozen ways, soccer is the chief delight of the house. ⊠ *Jernbaneg. 17,* ☎ *66/17–82–41. Reservations not accepted. No credit cards.*

$$$ 🛏 **Grand Hotel.** A century old, with renovated fin-de-siècle charm, this imposing four-story, brick-front hotel greets guests with old-fashioned luxury. The original stone floors and chandeliers lead to a wide staircase and upstairs guest rooms that are modern, with plush furnishings and sleek marble bathrooms. ⊠ *Jernabaneg. 18, DK–5000 Odense C,* ☎ *66/11–71–71,* FAX *66/14–11–71. 134 rooms, 13 suites. Room service, sauna. AE, DC, MC, V.*

$ 🛏 **Hotel Ydes.** Constantly under undisturbing renovation, this well-kept, bright, and colorful hotel is a good bet for students and budget-conscious travelers tired of barracks-type accommodations. The plain hospital-style rooms are spotless and comfortable. ⊠ *Hans Tausensg. 11, DK–5000 Odense C,* ☎ *66/12–11–31. 30 rooms, 24 with bath. Café. MC, V.*

Nightlife and the Arts
CAFÉS AND BARS
Odense's central Arcade is an entertainment mall, with bars, restaurants, and live music ranging from corny sing-alongs to hard rock. For a quiet evening, stop by **Café Biografen** (⊠ Brandts Passage, ☎ 66/13–16–16) for an espresso or beer, light snack, and the atmosphere of an old movie house. Or settle in to see one of the wide variety of films screened here.

The **Air Pub** (⊠ Kongsg. 41, ☎ 66/14–66–08) is a Danish café that caters to a slightly older crowd—30- and 40-something—with light meals and a small dance floor. **Klos Ands** (⊠ Vineg. 76, ☎ 66/13–56–00) used to be just for grown-ups, but its specialty, malt whiskey, is now drawing a younger crowd, too. At the **All Night Boogie Dance Café** (⊠ Nørreg. 21, ☎ 66/14–00–39), a laid-back crowd grooves to pop, disco, and '60s music.

CASINO

Fyn's sole casino is in the slick glass atrium of the **SAS Hans Christian Andersen Hotel** (⊠ Claus Bergs G. 7, Odense, ☎ 66/14–78–00), where you can gamble at blackjack, roulette, and baccarat.

JAZZ CLUBS

The Cotton Club (⊠ Pantheonsg. 5C, ☎ 66/12–55–25), with its crowd of old-timers and earnest youths, is a venue for traditional jazz. **Dexter's** (⊠ Vinderg. 65, ☎ 66/13–68–88) has all kinds of jazz—from Dixieland to fusion—Thursday to Saturday nights.

THEATER

In summer the thespians of the **Odense Street Theater** parade through the streets, dramatizing the tales of the town's most famous son, Hans Christian Andersen. **Den Fynske Landsby** (☞ *above*) stages regular Andersen plays from mid-July to mid-August.

Outdoor Activities and Sports

GOLF

The **Odense Eventyr Golfklub** (☎ 66/17–11–44) is 4 km (2½ mi) southwest of Odense, and was built in 1993. The 27-hole **Odense Golf Klub** (☎ 65/95–90–00), 6 km (4 mi) southeast of Odense, was built in 1980 and is relatively flat, with some trees and woods. The nine-hole driving range and putting greens in **Blommenlyst** (☎ 65/96–80–08) are 12 km (7 mi) from Odense, west toward Middlefart.

Shopping

Flensted Uromageren Hus (⊠ Ravnsherred 4, ☎ 66/12–70–44), famous for its paper mobiles, is just across from the Hans Christian Andersen Hus. Inside, handmade mobiles range from simple paper hangings to intricate ceramic balloons.

Assens

58 *38 km (24 mi) southwest of Odense; take Rte. 168, then drive south on the Strandvej (Beach Rd.) off Rte. 323 in the town of Å.*

★ Near the quiet town of Assens is one of the most extraordinary private gardens in Denmark: Tove Sylvest's sprawling **Seven Gardens.** A privately owned botanical United Nations, the gardens represent the flora of seven European countries, including many plants rare to Denmark. ⊠ *Å Strandvej 62, Ebberup,* ☎ *64/74–12–85.* ▨ *DKr40.* ☉ *May–Oct., daily 10–5.*

Children will appreciate a detour 18 km (11 mi) northeast to Fyn's **Terrarium,** where they can examine all kinds of slippery and slithery creatures, including snakes, iguanas, alligators, and the nearly extinct blue frog. ⊠ *Kirkehelle 5, Vissenbjerg,* ☎ *64/47–18–50.* ▨ *DKr40.* ☉ *May–Aug., daily 10–6; Sept.–Apr., daily 10–4.*

Fåborg

59 *30 km (18 mi) south of Odense (via Rte. 43).*

The surrounding beaches of this lovely 12th-century town are invaded by sun-seeking Germans and Danes in summer. Four times a day you can hear the dulcet chiming of a carillon, the island's largest. In town center is the controversial *Ymerbrønden* sculpture by Kai Nielsen, depicting a naked man drinking from an emaciated cow while it licks a baby. The 18th-century **Den Gamle Gård** (Old Merchant's House), of 1725, chronicles the local history of Fåborg through furnished interiors and exhibits of glass and textiles. ⊠ *Holkeg. 1,* ☎ *62/61–33–38.* ▨ *DKr20.* ☉ *Mid-May–Sept., daily 10:30–4:30.*

The **Fåborg Museum for Fynsk Malerkunst** (Fyn Painting Museum) has a good collection of turn-of-the-century paintings and sculpture by the Fyn Painters, a school of artists whose work captures the dusky light of the Scandinavian sun. ⊠ *Grønneg. 75,* ☎ *62/61–06–45.* ⊡ *DKr25.* ☉ *June–Aug., daily 10–5; Apr.–May and Sept.–Oct., daily 10–4; Nov.–Mar., daily 11–3.*

Dining and Lodging

$ ✕ **Vester Skerninge Kro.** Midway between Fåborg and Svendborg, this traditional inn is cluttered and comfortable. Pine tables are polished from years of serving hot stews and homemade *mediste pølse* (mild grilled sausage) and *æggkage* (fluffy omelet made with cream, smoked bacon, chives, and tomatoes). ⊠ *Krovej 9, Vester Skerninge,* ☎ *62/ 24–10–04. No credit cards. Closed Tues.*

$$$$ ✕▥ **Falsled Kro.** Once a smuggler's hideaway, the 500-year-old Fal-
★ sled Kro is now one of Denmark's most elegant inns. A favorite among well-heeled Europeans, it has appointed its cottages sumptuously with European antiques and stone fireplaces. The restaurant combines French and Danish cuisines, using ingredients from its garden and markets in Lyon. ⊠ *Assensvej 513, DK–5642 Millinge,* ☎ *62/68–11–11,* ⸬ *62/68–11–62. 14 rooms, 3 apartments. Restaurant, room service, 3-hole golf course, horseback riding, boating. AE, DC, MC, V. Closed Jan. and Feb.*

$$$$ ✕▥ **Steensgaard Herregårdspension.** A long avenue of beeches leads to this 700-year-old moated manor house, 7 km (4½ mi) northwest of Fåborg. The rooms are elegant, with antiques, four-poster beds, and yards of silk damask. The fine restaurant serves wild game from the manor's own reserve. ⊠ *Steensgaard 4, DK–5642 Millinge,* ☎ *62/61–94–90,* ⸬ *62/61–78–61. 15 rooms, 13 with bath. Restaurant, tennis court, horseback riding. AE, DC, MC, V. Closed Jan.*

Svendborg

⑥⓪ *25 km (15½ mi) east of Fåborg (via Rte. 44 east), 44 km (28 mi) south of Odense.*

Svendborg is Fyn's second-largest town, and one of the country's most important—not to mention happy—cruise harbors. It celebrates its eight-century-old maritime traditions every July, when old Danish wooden ships congregate in the harbor for the circular Fyn *rundt,* or regatta. Play your cards right, and you might hitch aboard and shuttle between towns. Contact the tourist board or any agreeable captain. With many charter-boat options and good marinas, Svendborg is an excellent base from which to explore the hundreds of islands of the South Fyn archipelago.

In Svendborg center is Torvet—the town's market square. To the left on Fruestræde is the black-and-yellow **Anne Hvides Gård,** the oldest secular structure in Svendborg and one of the four branches of **Svendborgs Omegns Museum** (Svendborg County Museum). This evocative exhibit includes 18th- and 19th-century interiors and glass and silver collections. ⊠ *Fruestr. 3,* ☎ *62/21–02–61.* ⊡ *DKr15.* ☉ *Late May–mid-June, daily 10–4; mid-June–late Oct., daily 10–5.*

Bagergade (Baker's Street) is lined with some of Svendborg's oldest half-timber houses. At the corner of Grubbemøllevej and Svinget is the **Viebæltegård,** the headquarters of the Svendborg County Museum, a former poorhouse. You can wander through dining halls, washrooms, and the "tipsy clink," where, as recently as 1974, inebriated citizens were left to sober up. ⊠ *Grubbemøllevej 13,* ☎ *62/21–02–61.* ⊡ *DKr20. Com-*

bined admission to Anne Hvides and Svendborgs Omegns museums
DKr30. ☺ May–mid-June, daily 10–4; mid-June–Oct., daily 10–5;
Nov., Dec., Mar., and Apr., daily 1–4; Jan. and Feb., weekdays 1–4.

Dining and Lodging

$ ✕ **Ærø.** A dim hodgepodge of ship parts and nautical doodads, this
restaurant looks like it's always been there, just as is. It's peopled by
brusque waitresses and serious local trenchermen who exchange orders from a menu that is staunchly old-fashioned, featuring *frikadeller*
(fried meatballs), fried *rødspætte* (plaice) with hollandaise sauce, and
dozens of smørrebrød options. ⊠ Brøg. 1 ved, Ærøfærgen, ☎ 62/21–
07–60. DC, MC, V. Closed Sun.

$$ ▦ **Margrethesminde.** The Fyn equivalent of a bed-and-breakfast, this
manor house is 16 km (10 mi) west of Svendborg. Owners Marlene
Philip and Henrik Nielsen furnished the sunny house with bright col-
ors and modern furnishings, and serve their guests a generous break-
fast, ranging from Danish pastries or dark bread and cheese to bacon
and eggs. Two of the six rooms are singles. ⊠ Fåborgvej 154, DK–
5762 Vester Skerninge, ☎ 62/24–10–44, FAX 62/24–10–62. 6 rooms,
1 with bath. Bicycles. MC.

Nightlife and the Arts

A diverse crowd congregates at **Bortløbne Banje** (⊠ Klosterpl. 7, ☎
62/22–31–21) to hear live rock and blues. **Chess** (⊠ Vesterg. 7, ☎ 62/
22–17–16) is popular with a young crowd that comes for the live
bands. **Crazy Daizy** (⊠ Frederiksg. 6, ☎ 62/21–67–60) attracts a ca-
sual, over-21 crowd to dance to oldies and rock on Saturday nights,
and a younger crowd on Fridays. The restaurant **Orangi** (⊠ Jessens
Mole, ☎ 62/22–82–92), an old sailing ship moored in the harbor, hires
live jazz in summer.

Kværndrup

⑥¹ *15 km (9 mi) north of Svendborg, 28 km (18 mi) south of Odense.*

★ Over this town presides the moated Renaissance **Egeskov Slot,** one of
the best-preserved island-castles in Europe. Peaked with copper spires
and surrounded by Renaissance, Baroque, English, and peasant gar-
dens, the castle has an antique-vehicle museum and the world's largest
maze, designed by the Danish scientist-turned-poet Piet Hein. The cas-
tle is still a private home, though visitors can see a few of the rooms,
including the great hall, the hunting room, and the Riborg Room, where
the daughter of the house was locked up from 1599 to 1604 after giv-
ing birth to a son out of wedlock. ⊠ Kværndrup, ☎ 62/27–10–16. 💷
Castle and museum DKr100. ☺ Castle May–June and Aug.–Sept., daily
10–5; July, daily 10–8. Museum June and Aug., daily 9–6; July, daily
9–8; May and Sept., daily 10–5.

Troense

⑥² *3 km (2 mi) south of Svendborg (via the Svendborg Sound Bridge), 43
km (27 mi) south of Odense.*

Tåsinge island is known for its local 19th-century drama involving Elvira
Madigan (recall the movie?) and her married Swedish lover, Sixten Sparre.
Preferring heavenly union to earthly separation, they shot themselves
and are now buried in the island's central Landet churchyard. Brides
throw their bouquets on the lovers' grave.

Troense is Tåsinge's main town, and one of the country's best-preserved
maritime villages, with half-timber buildings opening through hand-

★ carved doors. South of town is **Valdemars Slot** (Valdemars Castle), dating from 1610, one of Denmark's oldest privately owned castles. You can wander through almost all the sumptuously furnished rooms, libraries, and the candle-lit church. There's also an X-rated 19th-century cigar box not to be missed. ⊠ *Slotsalleen 100, Troense,* ☎ *62/22–61–06 or 62/22–50–04.* ☜ *DKr45.* ۞ *June–Aug., daily 10–6; May and Sept.–Oct., daily 10–5.*

Dining

$$$$ ✕ **Restaurant Valdemars Slot.** Beneath the castle, this domed restaurant is ankle-deep in pink carpet and aglow with candlelight. Fresh French and German ingredients and wild game from the castle's preserve are the menu staples. Venison with cream sauce and duck breast *à l'orange* are typical of the French-inspired cuisine. A less expensive annex, Den Grå Dame, serves traditional Danish food. The third eatery, Æblehaven, serves inexpensive sausages and upscale fast-food. ⊠ *Slotsalleen 100, Troense,* ☎ *62/22–59–00. AE, DC. Closed Mon.*

Shopping

For delicate hand-blown glass, visit **Glasmagerne** (⊠ Vemmenæsvej 10, Tåsinge, ☎ 62/54–14–94).

Langeland

63 *16 km (10 mi) southeast of Troense, 64 km (40 mi) southwest of Odense.*

Reached by a causeway bridge from Tåsinge and also by a one-hour ferry ride from Fåborg, Langeland is the largest island of the southern archipelago, rich in relics, with smooth, tawny beaches. Bird-watching is excellent on the southern half of the island, where migratory flocks roost before setting off on their cross-Baltic journey. To the south are Ristinge and Bagenkop, two towns with good beaches; at Bagenkop you can catch the ferry to Kiel, Germany.

Outdoor Activities and Sports

FISHING

Langeland has particularly rich waters for fishing, with cod, salmon, flounder, and gar. For package tours, contact **Ole Dehn** (⊠ Sønderg. 22, Lohals, DK–5953 Tranekær, ☎ 62/55–17–00).

Ærøskøbing

★ **64** *30 km (19 mi) south of Svendborg, 74 km (46 mi) south of Odense, plus a one-hour ferry ride, either from Svendborg or Langeland.*

The island of Ærø, where country roads wend through fertile fields, is aptly called the Jewel of the Archipelago. About 27 km (16 mi) southeast of Søby on the island's north coast, the storybook town of Ærøskøbing is the port for ferries from Fåborg. Established as a market town in the 13th century, it did not flourish until it became a sailing center during the 1700s. At night when the street lights illuminate the cobbled streets, it is as though time has stood still.

Ferries provide the only access to Ærø. The ferry from Svendborg to Ærøskøbing takes 1 hour, 15 minutes. In addition, there's a one-hour ferry from Fåborg to Søby, a town on the northwest end of the island; and a shorter one from Rudkøbing—on the island of Langeland—to Marstal, on the eastern end of Ærø.

Down the main central road in Ærøskøbing, take a left onto Smegade to visit one of Denmark's most arresting shrines to obsession. History is recorded in miniature at the **Flaskeskibssamlingen** (Bottle Ship Collection), thanks to a former ship's cook known as Peter Bottle, who painstakingly built nearly 2,000 bottle ships in his day. The combination of his life's work and the enthusiastic letters he received from fans and disciples around the world make for a surprisingly moving collection. ⊠ *Smeg. 22, Ærøskøbing,* ☎ *62/52–29–51.* ☒ *DKr20.* ⊙ *May–Oct., daily 10–5; Nov.–Apr., Tues.–Thurs. 1–3, Sat., 10–2, Sun. 10–1.*

Lodging

$$ 🏨 **Ærøhus.** A half-timber building with a steep red roof, the Ærøhus looks like a rustic cottage on the outside, an old, but overly renovated, aunt's house on the inside. Hanging pots and slanted walls characterize the public areas, and pine furniture and cheerful duvets keep the guest rooms simple and bright. The garden's five cottages have small terraces. ⊠ *Vesterg. 38, DK–5970,* ☎ *62/52–10–03,* 𝔽𝔸𝕏 *62/52–21–23. 30 rooms, 17 with bath; 5 cottages. Restaurant. AE, V.*

Fyn and the Central Islands A to Z

Arriving and Departing

BY CAR AND FERRY

From Copenhagen, take the E20 west to Halsskov, near Korsør, and drive aboard the Great Belt ferry, which costs about DKr300 per car, with up to five passengers and a reservation. For ferry reservations, call **DSB** (☎ 33/14–17–01). The ferry departs daily every 40 minutes. You'll arrive in Knudshoved, near Nyborg, which is a half hour from either Odense or Svendborg. Passage on the Great Belt Bridge costs DKr200.

BY PLANE

Odense Airport (☎ 65/95–50–72), 11 km (7 mi) north of Odense, is served by Mærsk Air (☎ 65/95–53–55) and Muk Air (☎ 65/95–50–20 or 98/19–03–88), which make eight daily flights between Copenhagen and Odense. The 25-minute hop costs about DKr1,300. You can make reservations with the airlines themselves or through SAS (☎ 32/32–00–00).

Between the Airport and Downtown: Metered **airport taxis** charge about DKr140 for the 15-minute drive downtown. A **Mærsk Airbus** meets each flight and stops at the Grand Hotel, Hans Christian Andersen Hotel, and the main railway station. The fare is about DKr60.

BY TRAIN

Trains from Copenhagen's main station depart for the three-hour trip to Odense's train station hourly, every day. Stations in both towns are central, close to hotels and sites. The one-way fare is about DKr150. A reservation costs an additional DKr30 (☎ 33/14–17–01).

Getting Around

BY BICYCLE

With their level terrain and short distances, Fyn and the Central Islands are perfect for cycling. You can rent bikes at **Cykel Biksen** (⊠ Nederg. 14–16, Odense, ☎ 66/12–40–98). **Fåborg Sportshandel** (⊠ Havneg. 40, Fåborg, ☎ 62/61–28–22) also lets bikes.

BY BUS AND TRAIN

Large towns are served by intercity trains. The Nyborg–Odense–Middelfart and the Odense–Svendborg routes are among the two most important. The other public transportation option is by bus. Timetables are posted at all bus stops and central stations. Passengers buy tickets on board and pay according to the distance traveled (☎ 66/11–71–11). For central Odense, the **Odense Eventyrpas** (Adventure Pass), available at the tourism office, affords admission to sites and museums and free city bus and train transport. The cost for a two-day pass is DKr90; for a one-day pass, DKr50.

BY CAR

The highways of Fyn are excellent, and small roads meander beautifully on two lanes through the countryside. Traffic is light, except during the height of summer in highly populated beach areas.

Contacts and Resources

EMERGENCIES

Police, fire, or **ambulance** (☎ 112). **Odense Hospital,** (✉ J. B. Winsløws Vej, ☎ 66/11–33–33). **Doctor** (☎ 65/90–60–10 between 4 PM and 7 AM). **Other Emergencies** (Falck, ☎ 66/11–22–22). **Ørnen Apoteket** (✉ Vesterg. 80, Odense, ☎ 66/12–29–70).

GUIDED TOURS

Few towns offer organized tours, but check the local tourist offices for step-by-step walking brochures.

Hans Christian Andersen Tours: Full-day tours to Odense depart from Copenhagen's Rådhus Pladsen mid-May–mid-September, Sunday at 8:30 AM, and cost DKr480. (Six of 11 hours are spent in transit.) Call ☎ 31/54–06–06 for reservations.

Walking Tours: The two-hour Odense tour departs from the tourist office during July and early August at 11 AM every Tuesday, Wednesday, and Thursday. It includes the exteriors of the Hans Christian Andersen sites and the cathedral.

VISITOR INFORMATION

Odense (✉ City Hall, ☎ 66/12–75–20). **Kerteminde** (✉ Strandg. 1, ☎ 65/32–11–21). **South Fyn Tourist Board** (✉ Centrumpl., Svendborg, ☎ 62/21–09–80). **Nyborg** (✉ Torvet 9, ☎ 65/31–02–80). **Ærøskøbing** (✉ Torvet, ☎ 62/52–13–00).

5 Jylland

J YLLAND (JUTLAND), Denmark's western peninsula, is the only part of the country naturally connected to mainland Europe; its southern boundary is the frontier with Germany. In contrast to the smooth, postcard-perfect land of Fyn and Sjælland, this Ice Age–chiseled peninsula is bisected at the north by the craggy Limfjord and spiked below by the Danish "mountains." Himmelbjerget, the zenith of this modest range, peaks at 438 ft. Farther south, the Yding Skovhøj plateau rises 568 ft—modest hills just about anywhere else.

Hunters first inhabited Denmark, in southern Jylland, some 250,000 years ago. You can see flint tools and artifacts from this period locked away in museums, but the land holds more stirring relics from a later epoch: after 1,000 years, Viking burial mounds and stones still swell the land, some in protected areas, others lying in farmers' fields, tended by grazing sheep.

The windswept landscapes filmed in *Babette's Feast,* the movie version of the Karen Blixen (Isak Dinesen) novel, trace the west coast northward to Skagen, a luminous, dune-covered point (geographically similar to the Outer Banks of North Carolina). To the west, facing Fyn, Jylland is cut by deep fjords rimmed with forests. The center is dotted with castles, parklands, and the famed Legoland. Ribe, Denmark's oldest town, lies to the south and west; Århus and Aalborg, respectively Denmark's second- and fourth-largest cities, face east and have nightlife and sights to rival Copenhagen's.

Nearly three times the size of the rest of Denmark, with long distances between towns, the peninsula of Jylland can easily take at least several days, even weeks, to explore. If you are pressed for time, concentrate on a single tour or a couple of cities. Delightful as they are, the islands are suitable only for those with plenty of time, as many require an overnight stay. The following tour focuses on chunks of the peninsula and is organized as you would explore them with a car.

Canoeing

Canoe rentals (about DKr200 per day) are available in the lake district, Limfjord, and almost all lakes and rivers. One- to three-day package tours are available throughout the region, with either camping or hostel accommodations. For more information, contact the local tourist boards.

Fishing

The lake district is a great place for fishing and angling. License requirements vary and package tours are also available; contact any local tourist office for details.

Kolding

65 *71 km (44 mi) northwest of Odense (via the Little Belt Bridge), 190 km (119 mi) west of Copenhagen.*

The well-preserved **Koldinghus,** a massive stonework structure that was once fortress, then a royal residence in the Middle Ages, is today a historical museum. In the winter of 1808, during the Napoleonic Wars, Spanish soldiers set fire to most of it while trying to stay warm. ⊠ *Rådhusstr.,* ☎ *75/50–15–00, ext. 5400.* ☜ *DKr40.* ☉ *Daily 10–5.*

Dining and Lodging

$$$ ✕⊠ **Hotel Koldingfjord.** This impressive neoclassical hotel has mahogany
★ floors and pyramid skylights. It's five minutes from town and faces the

Jylland

N

KEY

Ferry

SWEDEN

DENMARK

GERMANY

Skagen 76

TO SWEDEN

Hirtshals   Tuen

Hjørring   Frederikshavn

Skagerrak

Brønderslev   Sæby

Hanstholm   11   Nørresundby

Thisted   Lim-fjord   Limfjord

Mors   Nibe   75 **Aalborg**

Løgstør

Nykøbing Mors

Kattegat

Lemvig   Venø Bugt   Skive   Hadsund

Struer   Hobro

Holstebro   **Viborg** 74   Mariager

Nissum Fjord   Råsted

Randers

Gudenå   Gammel Estrup Slot   Grenå

Ringkøbing   Herning   71 **Silkeborg**   **Århus** 72   **Ebeltoft** 73

Ringkøbing Fjord   Skjern   Brande   Skanderborg

Skjernå

Grindsted   Givskud   **Jelling** 70   Horsens

Varde   68   **Vejle** 69   Juelsminde

Billund   Vejle Fjord

Varde Å   **Samsø**   TO KALUNDBORG

Esbjerg   Holsted   **Kolding**   Fredericia   **Fyn**   **Storebælt**

Fanø   **Sønderho**   65   Middelfart   311

TO HARWICH, NEWCASTLE   67   Kongeå   Lillebæltsbro   Odense

Ribe 66   Christiansfeld

Ribe Å   Vojens   Nyborg

Rømø   Skærbæk   Haderslev   TO HALSSKOV

Åbenrå   Fåborg   Svendborg

Kolding Fjord and 50 acres of countryside. The rooms vary in size (with 39 in a separate annex), but all have mahogany beds and bright prints. There's also an excellent French-Danish restaurant. ⊠ *Fjordvej 154, DK–6000 Strandhuse,* ☎ *75/51–00–00,* ℻ *75/51–00–51. 115 rooms, 8 suites. Restaurant, bar, indoor pool, sauna, 2 tennis courts, health club. AE, DC, MC, V.*

Ribe

★ ⑥ *60 km (36 mi) southwest of Kolding, 150 km (103 mi) southwest of Århus.*

In the southeastern corner of Jylland, the country's oldest town is well worth the detour for its medieval center preserved by the Danish National Trust. From May to mid-September, a night watchman circles the town, recalling its history and singing traditional songs. If you who want to accompany him, gather at the main square at 10 PM.

The **Ribe Domkirke** (Cathedral) stands on the site of one of Denmark's earliest churches, built around AD 860. The present structure dates from the 12th century, with a 14th-century bell tower. Note the Cat Head Door, said to be for the exclusive use of the devil. ⊠ *Torvet,* ☎ *75/ 42–06–19.* ▣ *DKr5.* ⊙ *May and Sept., Mon.–Sat. 10–5, Sun. noon–5; June–Aug., Mon.–Sat. 10–6, Sun. noon–6; Oct.–Apr., Mon.–Sat. 11–3, Sun. noon–3. Call first to confirm hours.*

The **Ribes Vikinger** (Museum for the Viking Period and the Middle Ages) chronicles Viking history with conventional exhibits of household goods, tools, and clothing. There's a multimedia room, with an interactive computer screen where you can search for more Viking information in the form of text, pictures, and videos. ⊠ *Odinspl.,* ☎ *75/ 42–22–22.* ▣ *DKr40.* ⊙ *June–Aug., daily 10–5; Apr.–May and Sept.–Oct., daily 10–4; Nov.–Mar., Tues.–Sun. 10–4.*

Take Bus 52 from the railway station across the street from the Ribes Vikinger 2 km south, and you'll arrive at the **Viking Center,** an outdoor exhibit detailing how the Vikings lived day-to-day, with demonstrations about homes, food, and crafts by real people. ⊠ *Lustrupsholm, Lustrupvej 4,* ☎ *75/41–16–11.* ▣ *DKr30.* ⊙ *Mid-May–mid-Sept., Tues.–Sun. 11–4.*

Dining and Lodging

$ ✕ **Sælhunden.** This 300-year-old canal-side "Male Seal" tavern barely fits a dozen tables, but its cozy atmosphere draws wayfarers and locals. The only seal mementos left are a few skins and pictures, but you can still order a "seal's special" of cold shrimp, sautéed potatoes, and scrambled eggs or—an old Danish favorite—fat strips of bacon served with cream gravy and boiled potatoes, only served Wednesday in the winter. Console yourself in summer with *rød grød med fløde* (red porridge with cream); the pronunciation of the dessert—which defies phonetic spelling—is so difficult Danes get a kick out of making foreigners pronounce it. ⊠ *Skibbroen 13,* ☎ *75/42–09–46. Reservations not accepted. DC, MC, V. Sept.–June, closed for dinner after 8:45.*

$$$ ✕▦ **Hotel Dagmar.** In Ribe's quaint center, this cozy half-timber hotel
★ encapsulates the charm of the 16th century—with stained-glass windows, sloping wooden floors, and carved chairs. The lavish rooms are all appointed with antique canopy beds, fat armchairs, and chaise longues. The fine French restaurant serves such specialties as fillet of salmon in sorrel cream sauce. ⊠ *Torvet 1, DK–6760,* ☎ *75/42–00–33,* ℻ *75/42–36–52. 48 rooms. Restaurant, bar, meeting rooms. AE, DC, MC, V.*

$ 🏠 **Ribe Family and Youth Hostel.** In town center, this plain, redbrick hostelry is run by helpful wardens Jens Philipsen and Gudrun Rishede. Six- and four-bed family rooms are arranged in clusters of two, each with its own private bath and toilet in a small hallway. There are also eight newish four-bed rooms with completely private facilities. They are functional and childproof, with pine bunks and industrial carpeting. A kitchen is available for use. ⊠ *Ribehallen, Skt. Pedersg. 16, DK–6760,* ☎ *75/42–06–20,* 𝔽𝔸𝕏 *75/42–42–88. 152 beds in 34 family rooms. Cafeteria. No credit cards. Closed Dec. and Jan.*

Sønderho

67 *30 km (19 mi) northwest of Ribe, plus 12-min ferry from Esbjerg, 153 km (96 mi) southwest of Århus, plus 12-min ferry from Esbjerg.*

During the 19th century, the tiny island of **Fanø** had an enormous ship-building industry and a fleet second only to Copenhagen's. The shipping industry deteriorated, but the proud maritime heritage remains.

From Fanø's ferry port in Nordby, take a bus south to Sønderho. Along the tiny winding lanes are thatched cottages decorated with ships' relics, figureheads, painted doors, and brass lanterns. You may even see people wearing the traditional costumes, especially on *Sønderhodag,* a town festival held on the third Sunday in July.

Dining and Lodging

$$ ✕🏠 **Sønderho Kro.** Just 13 km (8 mi) from Fanø's main town of
★ Nordby, this 270-year-old thatched inn is one of Jylland's finest, its charm preserved with a beamed foyer, painted doors, and timbered ceilings. Rooms are jazzed up with four-poster beds, elegant tapestries, and gauzy curtains. The French-Danish restaurant serves excellent seafood on its old tables. ⊠ *Kropl. 11, DK–6720, Sønderho,* ☎ *75/16–40–09. 6 rooms, 2 suites. Restaurant. AE, DC, MC, V. Closed Feb. and weekdays Nov.–Jan.*

Billund

68 *101 km (63 mi) southwest of Århus.*

★ ☺ Billund's only claim to fame is **Legoland,** an amusement park in which everything is constructed from 35 million plastic Lego bricks. Among its incredible structures are scaled-down versions of cities and villages, working harbors and airports, a Statue of Liberty, statue of Sitting Bull, Mount Rushmore, safari park, and Pirate Land. Grown-ups might marvel at toys from pre-Lego days, the most exquisite of which is Titania's Palace, a sumptuous dollhouse built in 1907 by Sir Neville Wilkinson for his daughter. The Lego empire is expanding: the company's goal is to open one park globally every three years, but Danes maintain that theirs, the original, will always be the best. ⊠ *Billund,* ☎ *75/33–13–33.* 💳 *DKr110.* ☉ *Apr.–Sept., daily 10–8.*

Vejle

69 *40 km (25 mi) east of Billund, 73 km (46 mi) southwest of Århus.*

On the east coast, Vejle is beautifully positioned on a fjord, amid forest-clad hills. You can hear the time of day chiming on the old **Dominican monastery clock**; the clock remains, but the monastery long ago gave way to the town's imposing 19th-century city hall.

In town center, at Kirke Torvet, is **Skt. Nikolai Kirke** (St. Nicholas Church). In the left arm of the cross-shape church, lying in a glass Empire-style coffin, is the body of a bog woman found preserved in a peat marsh in 1835; she dates to 500 BC. The church walls contain the skulls of 23 thieves executed in the 17th century. ⊠ *Kirke Torvet,* ☎ *75/82–41–39.* ⊙ *May–Sept., weekdays 9–5, Sat. 9–noon, Sun. 9–11:30.*

Lodging

$$$$ 🏨 **Munkebjerg Hotel.** Seven kilometers (4½ miles) southeast of town, surrounded by a thick beech forest and majestic views of the Vejle Fjord, this elegant hotel attracts guests who prefer privacy. Beyond the rustic lobby, rooms furnished in blond pine and soft green overlook the forest. There are also two top-notch French-Danish restaurants and a swank casino. ⊠ *Munkebjergvej 125, DK–7100,* ☎ *75/72–35–00,* FAX *75/72–08–86. 145 rooms, 2 suites. 2 restaurants, room service, indoor pool, sauna, tennis court, health club, casino, meeting rooms, helipad. AE, DC, MC, V.*

Nightlife

The casino at the **Munkebjerg Hotel** (☞ *above*) has blackjack, roulette, baccarat, and slot machines.

Jelling

⑳ *10 km (6 mi) northwest of Vejle (via Rte. 18), 83 km (52 mi) southwest of Århus.*

In Jelling, two 10th-century burial mounds mark the seat of King Gorm and his wife, Thyra. Between the mounds are two **Runestener** (runic stones), one of which is Denmark's certificate of baptism, showing the oldest known figure of Christ in Scandinavia. The inscription explains that the stone was erected by Gorm's son, King Harald Bluetooth, who brought Christianity to the Danes in AD 960.

The most scenic way to get to Jelling is via the **vintage steam train** that runs from Vejle every Sunday in July and the first Sunday in August. Call the Jelling tourist office for schedules.

Silkeborg

㉑ *60 km (38 mi) north of Jelling, 43 km (27 mi) west of Århus.*

At the banks of the River Gudenå begins Jylland's lake district. Stretching from Silkeborg in the west to Skanderborg in the east, this area contains some of Denmark's loveliest scenery and most of its meager mountains, including the 438-ft **Himmelbjerget,** at Julsø (Lake Jul). You can climb the narrow paths through the heather and trees to the top, where an 80-ft tower stands sentinel, placed there on Constitution Day in 1875 in memory of King Frederik VII.

The best way to explore the lake district is by water, as the Gudenå winds its way some 160 km (100 mi) through lakes and wooded hillsides down to the sea. Take one of the excursion boats or the world's last coal-fired paddle steamer, **Hjejlen,** which departs in summer from Silkeborg Harbor. Since 1861 it has paddled its way through narrow stretches of fjord, where the treetops meet overhead, to the foot of the Himmelbjerget. ⊠ *Havnen, Silkeborg,* ☎ *86/82–07–66 (reservations).* 🎫 *DKr76 round-trip.* ⊙ *Mid-June–early Aug., Sun. 10 and 1:45.*

★ Silkeborg's main attractions are housed in the **Kulturhistoriske Museum** (Museum of Cultural History): the 2,200-year-old Tollund Man and Elling Girl, two bog people preserved by natural ingredients in the soil and water. Discovered in 1950, the Tollund Man remains the best-preserved human face from the Iron Age. He was killed by strangulation—the noose remains around his neck—with a day's worth of stubble that can still be seen on his hauntingly serene face. ⊠ *Hovedgådsvej,* ☎

86/82–15–78. ⊡ *DKr20.* ◉ *Apr. 15–Oct. 23, daily 10–5; Oct. 24–
Apr. 14, Wed. and weekends noon–4.*

Dining

$$ ✕ **Spisehuset Christian VIII.** Cut off from Silkeborg's center by a high-
way, this tiny crooked building seems transported from another time.
Inside it's elegant and busy, with an international group of diners oc-
cupying the dozen cramped tables. The inventive menu includes tourne-
dos of guinea fowl with mushrooms, and fish specialties such as
poached turbot with scallops and spring onions. ⊠ *Christian VIII Vej
54,* ☎ *86/82–25–62. AE, DC, MC, V. Closed Sun.*

Århus

72 *40 km (24 mi) east of Silkeborg.*

Århus is Denmark's second-largest city, and, with its funky arts and
college community, one of its most pleasant. The town is liveliest dur-
ing the 10-day **Århus Festival** in September, which combines everything
from concerts, theater, and exhibitions to beer tents and sports. In ad-
dition, the **Århus International Jazz Festival** in early or mid-July bills
international and local greats. In July, the **Viking Moot** draws afi-
cionados to the beach below the Museum of Prehistory at Moesgård.
Activities and exhibits include market booths, ancient defense techniques,
and rides on Viking ships.

A good starting point is the **Rådhus,** probably the most unusual city
hall in Denmark. Built in 1941 by noted architects Arne Jacobsen and
Erik Møller, the pale Norwegian-marble block building is controver-
sial but cuts a startling figure when illuminated in the evening. ⊠ *Park
Allé,* ☎ *86/12–16–00.* ⊡ *City hall DKr10, tower DKr5.* ◉ *Guided
tours in Danish only mid-June–early Sept., weekdays at 11; tower
tours weekdays at noon and 4.*

★ Don't miss the town's open-air museum, known as **Gamle By** (Old
Town). Its 70 half-timber houses, mill, and millstream were carefully
moved from locations throughout Jylland and meticulously re-cre-
ated, inside and out. ⊠ *Viborgvej,* ☎ *86/12–31–88.* ⊡ *DKr50.* ◉ *June–
Aug., daily 9–6; May and Sept., daily 9–5; Jan.–Mar. and Nov., daily
11–3; Apr., Oct., and Dec., daily 10–4. Grounds always open.*

In a 250-acre forest south of Århus is the **Moesgård Forhistorisk Mu-
seum** (Prehistoric Museum), with exhibits on ethnography and ar-
chaeology, including the famed Grauballe Man, a 2,000-year-old corpse
so well bog-preserved that scientists could determine his last meal. Also,
take the Forhistoriskvej (Prehistoric Trail) through the forest, which
leads past Stone- and Bronze-Age displays to reconstructed houses from
Viking times. ⊠ *Moesgård Allé,* ☎ *86/27–24–33.* ⊡ *DKr30.* ◉ *Apr.–
Sept., daily 10–5; Oct.–Mar., Tues.–Sun. 10–4.*

ⓒ If you are visiting Århus with children, visit its provincial **Tivoli,** with
rides, music, and lovely gardens. ⊠ *Skovbrynet,* ☎ *86/14–73–00.* ⊡
DKr30. ◉ *Mid-Apr.–May, daily 1–9; May–mid-June, daily 1–10; mid-
June–mid-Aug., daily 1–11.*

Be sure to ask at the tourist office about the **Århus Pass,** which affords
free passage on buses, free or discounted admission to museums and
sites, and tours. A two-day pass is DKr110, and a seven-day is DKr155.

Dining and Lodging

$ ✕ **Rio Grande.** Full of the standard-issue blankets, straw hats, and bright
colors ubiquitous in Mexican restaurants the world over, Rio Grande
is a favorite with youngsters, families, and even businesspeople. Heap-

ing plates of tacos, enchiladas, and chili are a good value—and tasty, too. ✉ *Vesterg. 39,* ☎ *86/19–06–96. AE, MC, V.*

$$$ 🏨 **Royal Hotel.** In operation since 1838, Århus's grand hotel has welcomed such greats as Arthur Rubinstein and Marian Anderson. Wellheeled guests are welcomed into a stately lobby appointed with Chesterfield sofas, modern paintings, and a winding staircase. Plush rooms vary in style and decor, but all have rich drapery, velour and brocade furniture, and marble bathrooms. ✉ *Store Torv 4, DK–8100 Århus C,* ☎ *86/12–00–11,* ℻ *86/76–04–04. 105 rooms, 7 suites. Restaurant, bar, sauna, casino, business services. AE, DC, MC, V.*

$ 🏨 **Youth Hostel Pavilionen.** As in all Danish youth and family hostels, the rooms here are clean, bright, and functional. The secluded setting in the woods near the fjord is downright beautiful. Unfortunately, the hostel can get a bit noisy. You can have use of the kitchen. ✉ *Marienlunsdvej 10, DK–8100,* ☎ *86/16–72–98,* ℻ *86/10–55–60. 32 rooms, 11 with private shower, 4 shared showers and toilets. Cafeteria (breakfast only). AE, MC, V. Closed mid-Dec.–mid-Jan.*

Nightlife and the Arts

There's no better time to visit Århus than during the 10-day **Århus Festival Week** in September, when jazz, classical, and rock concerts are nonstop, in addition to drama, theater, and dance.

BARS, LOUNGES, AND DISCOS

The **Café Mozart** (✉ Vesterport 10, ☎ 86/18–55–63) plays classical music and serves homemade organic Middle Eastern and other ethnic specialties, including what it claims as the world's biggest pita bread. The **Hotel Marselis** (✉ Strandvejen 25, ☎ 86/14–44–11) attracts a varied crowd to its two venues: the **Beach Club** with danceable rock and disco and the more elegant **Nautilas** piano bar for an older crowd. **Blitz** (✉ Klosterg. 34, ☎ 86/19–10–99) is one of the more trendy and alternative spots in Århus, cranking out techno-pop tunes.

CASINO

The **Royal Hotel** (✉ Store Torv 4, ☎ 86/12–00–11) is the city's casino with blackjack, roulette, baccarat, and slot machines.

JAZZ CLUBS

For jazz, head to **Bent J's** (✉ Nørre Allé 66, ☎ 86/12–04–92), a small club with free-admission jam sessions three times a week and occasional big-name concerts. **Glazz Huset** (✉ Åboulevarden 35, ☎ 86/12–13–12) is Århus's big jazz club, attracting some international stars.

Ebeltoft

❼ *45 km (28 mi) east of Århus.*

Drive northeast to the tip of what Danes call Jylland's nose, Ebeltoft, a town of crooked streets, sloping row houses, and local crafts shops. Danish efficiency is showcased beside the ferry, at the **Vindmølleparken,** one of the largest windmill parks in the world, where 16 wind-powered mills on a curved spit of land generate electricity for 600 families. ✉ *Færgehaven,* ☎ *86/34–12–44.* 🎟 *Free.* ☉ *Daily.*

You can't miss the **Frigate Jylland,** dry-docked on the town's main harbor. The renovation of the three-masted tall ship was financed by Danish shipping magnate Mærsk McKinney Møller, and it's a testament to Denmark's seafaring days of yore: Wander through to examine the bridge, gun deck, galley, captain's room, and perhaps most impressive of all, the 10½-ton pure copper and pewter screw, and view the voluptuous Pomeranian pine figurehead. ⊠ *Strandvejen 4,* ☎ *86/34–10–99.* 🖾 *DKr40.* 𝄫 *Daily 10–5.*

Also on the Ebeltoft harbor is the small, light, and airy **Glasmuseum.** The setting is perfect for the collection, ranging from mysterious symbol-imbedded monoliths of Swedish glass sage Bertil Vallien to the luminous gold pavilions of Japanese artist Kyohei Fujita. Once a customs and excise house, the museum has a glass workshop where international students come to study. Functional pieces, art, and books are sold at the shop. ⊠ *Strandvejen 8,* ☎ *86/34–17–99.* 🖾 *DKr40.* 𝄫 *Mid-May–mid-Sept., daily 10–5; mid-Sept.–mid-May, daily 1–4.*

Viborg

⑦ *60 km (36 mi) west of Randers, 66 km (41 mi) northwest of Århus.*

Viborg dates to at least the 8th century, when it was a trading post and a place of pagan sacrifice. Later it became a center of Christianity, with monasteries and an episcopal residence. The 1,000-year-old **Hærvejen,** the old military road that starts near here, was once Denmark's most important connection with the outside world—though today it lives on as a bicycle path. Legend has it that in the 11th century, King Canute set out from Viborg to conquer England; he succeeded, of course, and ruled from 1016 to 1035. Today you can buy reproductions of a silver coin minted by the king, embossed with the inscription "Knud, Englands Kong" (Canute, King of England).

Built in 1130, Viborg's **Domkirke** (Cathedral) was once the largest granite church in the world. Today only the crypt remains of the original building, restored and reopened in 1876. The dazzling early 20th-century biblical frescoes are by Danish painter Joakim Skovgard. ⊠ *Mogensg.,* ☎ *86/62–10–60.* 🖾 *Free.* 𝄫 *June–Aug., Mon.–Sat. 10–4, Sun. noon–5; Sept. and Apr.–May, Mon.–Sat. 11–4, Sun. noon–4; Oct.–Mar., Mon.–Sat. 11–3, Sun. noon–3.*

Aalborg

⑦ *80 km (50 mi) northeast of Viborg, 112 km (70 mi) north of Århus.*

The gentle waters of the Limfjord sever Jylland completely. Clamped to its narrowest point is Aalborg, Denmark's fourth-largest community. The town celebrated its 1,300th birthday with a year of festivities in 1992—once and for all cementing the town's party reputation. The gateway between north and south Jylland, the city is a charming combination of new and old: twisting lanes filled with medieval houses and, nearby, broad modern boulevards.

★ The local favorite site is the magnificent 17th-century **Jens Bang Stenhus** (Jens Bang's Stone House), built by a wealthy merchant. Chagrined he was never made a town council member, the cantankerous Bang avenged himself by caricaturing his political enemies in gargoyles all over the building and then adding his own face, its tongue sticking out at town hall. The five-story building dating from 1624 has a vaulted stone beer-and-wine cellar, **Duus Vinkælder,** one of the most atmospheric in the country (☞ Dining and Lodging, *below*). ⊠ *Østerå 9.*

The Baroque **Budolfi Kirke** (Budolfi Cathedral) is dedicated to the English saint Botolph. The church, originally made of wood, has been rebuilt several times in its 800-year history and is now made of stone. It includes a copy of the original tower of the Rådhus in Copenhagen, which was taken down about a century ago. The money for the construction was donated to the church by a generous local merchant and

In case you want to be welcomed there.

We're here to see that you're always welcomed at establishments everywhere. That's why millions of people carry the American Express® Card – for peace of mind, confidence, and security, around the world or just around the corner.

do more

In case you're running low.

We're here to help with more than 118,000 Express Cash locations around the world. In order to enroll, just call American Express before you start your vacation.

do more

AMERICAN EXPRESS

Express Cash

And just in case.

We're here with American Express® Travelers Cheques and Cheques *for Two*.® They're the safest way to carry money on your vacation and the surest way to get a refund, practically anywhere, anytime.

Another way we help you...

do more ®

AMERICAN
EXPRESS

Travelers
Cheques

his sister, both of whom, locals say, had no other family on which to lavish their wealth. ✉ *Gammel Torv.*

Next to Budolfi Kirke is the 15th-century **Helligandsklosteret** (Monastery of the Holy Ghost). One of Denmark's best-preserved monasteries—and perhaps the only one that admitted both nuns and monks—it is now a home for the elderly; unfortunately, it is generally not open to the public. During World War II the monastery was the meeting place for the Churchill Club, a group of Aalborg schoolboys who became world-famous for their sabotage of the Nazis, even after the enemy thought they were locked up. ✉ *C.W. Obels Plads, Gammel Torv,* ☎ *98/12–02–05.*

In the center of the old town is **Jomfru Ane Gade,** named, as the story goes, for an aristocratic maiden accused of being a witch, then beheaded. Now the street's fame is second only to that of Copenhagen's Strøget. Despite the flashing neon and booming music of about 30 discos, bars, clubs, and eateries, the street attracts a thick stream of mixed pedestrian traffic and appeals to all ages.

The only Fourth of July celebrations outside the United States annually blast off in nearby **Rebild Park,** a salute to the United States for welcoming some 300,000 Danish immigrants. The tradition dates back to 1912.

Just north of Aalborg at Nørresundby (still considered a part of greater Aalborg) is **Lindholm Høje,** a Viking and Iron Age burial ground where stones placed in the shape of a ship enclose many of the site's 682 graves and sheep often outnumber tourists. At its entrance there's a museum that chronicles Viking civilization and recent excavations. ✉ *Hvorupvej,* ☎ *98/17–55–22.* ⊠ *Museum DKr20; burial-ground free.* ☉ *Easter–mid-Oct., daily 10–5; mid-Oct–Easter, daily 10–4.*

Dining and Lodging

$$ ✕ **Dufy.** Light and bright on an old cobbled street, this is one of the most popular eateries in town. Downstairs, it has a French-style bistro ambience, with marble-topped tables, engraved mirrors, and windows overlooking Jomfru Ane Gade. The upstairs is more elegant and quieter. The French menu includes lobster-and-cognac soup for two, sliced roast duck with Waldorf salad, and beef fillet. ✉ *Jomfru Ane G. 8,* ☎ *98/16–34–44. AE, DC, MC, V.*

$$ ✕ **Spisehuset Knive og Gaffel.** In a 400-year-old building parallel to
★ Jumfru Ane Gade, this busy restaurant is crammed with oak tables, crazy slanting floors, and candlelight; the year-round courtyard is a veritable greenhouse. Young waitresses negotiate the mayhem to deliver inch-thick steaks, the house specialty. ✉ *Maren Turisg. 10,* ☎ *98/16–69–72. DC, MC, V. Closed Sun.*

$ ✕ **Duus Vinkælder.** Most people come to this cellar—part alchemist's
★ dungeon, part neighborhood bar—for a drink, but you can also get a light bite. In summer enjoy smørrebrød, in winter sup on grilled specialties like frikadeller and *biksemad* (a meat-and-potato hash), and the restaurant's special liver pâté. ✉ *Østerä 9,* ☎ *98/12–50–56. DC, V. Closed Sun.*

$$$$ ⌂ **Helnan Phønix.** In a central and sumptuous old mansion, this hotel is popular with international and business guests. The rooms are luxuriously furnished with plump chairs and polished, dark-wood furniture; in some the original raw beams are still intact. The Brigadier serves excellent French and Danish food. ✉ *Vesterbro 77, DK–9000,* ☎ *98/12–00–11,* ℻ *98/16–31–66. 185 rooms, 3 suites. Restaurant, bar, café, room service, sauna, meeting room. AE, DC, MC, V.*

Nightlife and the Arts

BEER-WINE CELLAR

Duus Vinkælder (☞ Dining and Lodging, *above*) is extremely popular, one of the most classic beer and wine cellars in all of Denmark.

CASINO

The city's sole casino is at the **Limsfjordshotellet** (⊠ Ved Stranden 14–16, ☎ 98/16–43–33) with blackjack and more.

MUSIC AND DISCOS

Aalborg doesn't have a regular jazz club, but local musicians get together at least once a week for **jam sessions.** Ask the tourist board for details. If you're there in the fall or winter, head to the harborside **Kompasset** (⊠ Vesterbådehavn, ☎ 98/13–75–00), where live jazz is paired with a Saturday-afternoon lunch buffet. **Gaslight** (⊠ Jomfrue Ane G. 23, ☎ 98/10–17–50) plays rock and grinding dance music to a young crowd. **Rendez-Vous** (⊠ Jomfrue Ane G. 5, ☎ 98/16–88–80) has an upstairs dance floor packed with 18- to 25-year-olds dancing to standard disco. **Ambassadeur** (⊠ Vesterbro 76, ☎ 98/12–62–22), with four dance restaurants and live music, is popular with a mature audience.

Skagen

⓰ *88 km (55 mi) northeast of Aalborg, 212 km (132 mi) north of Århus.*

At the windswept northern tip of Jylland is Skagen (pronounced *skane*), a very popular summer beach area for well-heeled Danes, where, historically, the long beaches and luminous light have inspired painters and writers alike. The 19th-century Danish artist Holger Drachmann (1846–1908) and his friends, including the well-known P. S. Kroyer, founded the Skagen School of painting, which captured the special quality of northern light; you can see their efforts on display in the **Skagen Museum.** ⊠ *Brøndumsvej 4,* ☎ *98/44–64–44.* ⊡ *DKr40.* ☉ *June–Aug., daily 10–6; May and Sept., daily 10–5; Apr. and Oct., Tues.–Sun. 11–4; Nov.–Mar., Wed.–Fri. 1–4, Sat. 11–4, Sun. 11–3.*

Danes say that in Skagen you can stand with one foot on the Kattegat, the strait between Sweden and eastern Jylland, the other in the Skagerrak, the strait between western Denmark and Norway. The point is so thrashed by storms and clashing waters that the 18th-century **Tilsandede Kirke** (Sand-Buried Church), 2 km (1 mi) south of town, is completely covered by dunes.

Even more famed than the Buried Church is the west coast's dramatic
★ **Råbjerg Mile,** a protected migrating dune that moves about 33 ft a year and is accessible on foot from the Kandestederne.

Dining and Lodging

$$$ ✕⊡ **Brøndums Hotel.** A few minutes from the beach, this 150-year-
★   old gabled inn is furnished with antiques and Skagen School paintings. The very basic 21 guest rooms in the main building are beginning to show their age; their old-fashioned decor includes wicker chairs, Oriental rugs, and pine four-poster beds. The 25 annex rooms are more modern. The fine French-Danish restaurant, where the Skagen School often gathered, has a lavish cold table. ⊠ *Anchersvej 3, DK–9990,* ☎ *98/44–15–55,* ℻ *98/45–15–20. 46 rooms, 12 with bath. Restaurant, meeting rooms. AE, DC, MC, V.*

Jylland A to Z

Arriving and Departing

BY CAR AND FERRY

More than 25 ferry routes connect the peninsula to the rest of Denmark (including the Faroe Islands), as well as England, Norway, and Sweden, with additional connections to Kiel and Puttgarden, Germany, the Baltics, Poland, and Russia. Most travelers however, drive north from Germany, or arrive from the islands of Sjælland or Fyn. Ferry prices can get steep, and vary according to how many are traveling and the size of the vehicle. For most ferries, you can get information and make reservations by calling **FDM,** the Danish automobile association (☎ 35/43–02–00).

From Copenhagen or elsewhere on Sjælland, you can drive the 110 km (69 mi) across the island, then cross the Storebæltsbro aboard either the Halsskov–Knudshoved (1 hour) or the Korsør–Nyborg (1 hour, 15 minutes) ferry. You then drive the 85 km (53 mi) across Fyn and cross from Middelfart to Fredericia, Jylland over the Lillebæltsbro (Little Belt Bridge). More choices abound here, since two bridges link Middelfart to Fredericia. The older, lower bridge (2 km/1¼ mi) follows Route 161, whereas the newer suspension bridge (1 km/½ mi) on E20 is faster. For direct Sjælland to Jylland passage, you can take the ferry between Sjællands Odde and Ebeltoft (1 hour, 40 minutes), or a car-ferry hydrofoil (1 hour, 25 minutes) between Århus and Kalundborg. The conventional DSB ferry (3¼ hours) is larger and slower, but more akin to a cruise ship. Also from Kalundborg, you can sail to Juelsminde (3 hours), 74 km (46 mi) south of Århus. Keep in mind that once the Great Belt train and auto links between Sjælland and Fyn are completed, many of the connections between Jylland and the rest of Denmark will be shortened by an hour. For ferry schedules, call **DSB** (☎ 33/14–17–01).

Ferries from Hundested, Sjælland, to Grena in east Jylland take 2½ hours; those from Kalundborg to Århus take three hours. For information, call **DSB** (☎ 33/14–17–01). Other major routes include those of **Scandinavian Seaways** (Esbjerg, ☎ 79/17–79–17; Copenhagen, ☎ 33/42–33–42), which links England's Harwich and Newcastle to Esbjerg in the southwest. There are ferries from Göteborg (3¼ hours), on Sweden's west coast and Oslo, Norway (10 hours), to Frederikshavn in the northeast. Call **Stena Line** (☎ 96/20–02–00) for both.

BY PLANE

Billund Airport, 2 km (1¼ mi) southwest of downtown, receives flights from London, Stockholm, Brussels, Amsterdam, and Frankfurt on **Mærsk Air** (☎ 75/33–28–44) and on the Norwegian carrier **Braathens** (☎ 75/35–44–00 Billund Airport, ☎ 47/67–58–60–00 Oslo Fornebu Airport) from Oslo. **Sunair** (☎ 75/33–16–11) serves Billund, Århus, Oslo, Stockholm, and Göteborg. Several domestic airports, including Aalborg, Århus, and Esbjerg, are served by Mærsk and **SAS** (75/16–03–33), both of which have good connections to Copenhagen. **Cimber Air** (☎ 74/42–22–77) links Sønderborg, just north of the German border with Copenhagen.

BY TRAIN

DSB (☎ 33/14–17–01) makes hourly runs between Copenhagen and Fredericia. The 3½-hour trip includes train passage aboard the ferry, which crosses the Store Bælt between Korsør, on west Sjælland, and Nyborg, on east Fyn.

Getting Around

At the Århus tourist office check out the **Århus Pass,** which affords free bus travel, free or discounted admission to museums and sites, and tours.

BY BICYCLE

Jylland has scores of bike paths, and many auto routes also have cycle lanes. Keep in mind that distances are much longer here than elsewhere in the country, and that even these humble hills are a challenge for children and novice cyclists. Consider prearranged package holidays, which range from island day trips to eight-day excursions. Among the offices that can help with bike tips are the tourist boards in Viborg, Silkeborg, and Vejen (☞ Visitor Information, *below*), or the **County of North Jylland** tourist office (⊠ Niels Bohrsvej, Box 8300, DK–9220 Aalborg, ☎ 96/35–10–00).

Bike rentals are available in most towns from the tourism board, which can also supply maps and brochures. In the west, the **Vestkyst-stien** (west-coast path) goes from Skagen in the north to Bulbjerg in the south. In the east, the **Vendsyssel-stien** (winding path) goes from Frederikshavn to the mouth of the Limfjord. The **Stkyst-stien** (east-coast path) follows and leads to the south of the Limfjord. In the south, much of the 1,000-year-old **Hærvejen** (Old Military Road) has been converted into a network of picturesque cycling lanes. It's signposted for all 240 km (145 mi) through the center of Jylland, from Padborg in the south to Viborg in the north.

BY BUS

Intercity buses are punctual but slower than trains. Passengers can buy tickets on the bus and pay according to destination. For schedules and fares, call **DSB** (☎ 86/12–67–03) weekdays. For intercity travel, schedules are posted at all bus stops and fares are usually under DKr10.

BY CAR

Although train and bus connections are excellent, sites and towns in Jylland are widely dispersed, and the peninsula is best explored by car. Whether you decide to take speedy, modern highways or winding old roads, traffic is virtually nonexistent.

BY TRAIN

For long trips, the **DSB** (☎ 86/13–17–00) trains are fast and efficient, with superb views of the countryside. Smaller towns do not have innercity trains, so you'll have to switch to buses once you arrive.

Contacts and Resources

EMERGENCIES

Ambulance, fire, or **police** (☎ 112).

Doctor: Aalborg (☎ 98/13–62–11). **Århus** (☎ 86/20–10–22).

Pharmacies: Aalborg (⊠ Budolfi Apotek, corner of Vesterbro and Algade, ☎ 98/12–06–77). **Århus** (⊠ Løve Apoteket, Store Torv 5, ☎ 86/12–00–22).

GUIDED TOURS

Guided tours are few and far between, but check with the local tourism offices for tips and reservations. Some carry brochures that describe walking tours.

Legoland Tours: Between mid-June and mid-August, the tour departs from Copenhagen at 7:30 AM on Thursday (call ☎ 31/57–26–00 to reserve) and Saturday (call ☎ 31/54–06–06 to reserve), and costs DKr350. The trip takes about 13 hours, with four hours spent at the park; you'll also have to pay admission into the park.

Walking Tours: The **Århus Round the City** tour (2½ hours) begins at the tourist office and includes Den Gamle By, the Domkirke, concert hall, university, and harbor. **Aalborg's City Tour** (two hours) departs from Adelgade and includes most of the town museums, the Budolfi Cathedral, Monastery of the Holy Ghost, Town Hall, the Jens Bang Stone House, and Jomfru Ane Gade.

VISITOR INFORMATION

County of North Jylland tourist office (✉ Niels Bohrsvej, Box 8300, DK–9220 Aalborg, ☎ 96/35–10–00).

Aalborg (✉ Østerå 8, ☎ 98/12–60–22). **Århus** (✉ Rådhuset, ☎ 86/12–16–00). **Billund** (✉ c/o Legoland A/S, Åstvej, ☎ 75/33–19–26). **Jelling** (✉ Gormsg. 4, ☎ 75/87–13–01). **Randers** (✉ Erik Menveds Pl. 1, ☎ 86/42–44–77). **Ribe** (✉ Torvet 3–5, ☎ 75/42–15–00). **Silkeborg** (✉ Godthåbsvej 4, ☎ 86/82–19–11). **Vejen** (✉ Sønderg., ☎ 75/36–26–96). **Vejle** (✉ Den Smiatske Gård, Sønderg. 14, ☎ 75/82–19–55). **Viborg** (✉ Nytorv 5, ☎ 86/61–16–66).

6 Bornholm

ALLED THE PEARL OF THE BALTIC for its natural beauty and winsomely rustic towns, Bornholm, 177 km (110 mi) southeast of Sjælland, is geographically unlike the rest of Denmark. A temperate climate has made this 588-square-km (436-square-mi) jumble of granite bluffs, clay soil, and rift valleys an extravagance of nature. Rich plantations of fir bristle beside wide dunes and vast heather fields; lush gardens teem with fig, cherry, chestnut, mulberry, and blue-blooming Chinese Emperor trees; and meadows sprout 12 varieties of orchids. Denmark's third-largest forest, the Almindingen, crowns the center; the southern tip is ringed with some of Europe's whitest beaches.

During the Iron and Bronze ages, Bornholm was inhabited by seafaring and farming cultures that peppered the land with burial dolmens and engravings. From the Middle Ages to the 18th century, the Danes battled the Swedes for ownership of the island, protecting it with strongholds and fortified churches, many of which still loom over the landscape.

Today Bornholmers continue to draw their livelihood from the land and sea—and increasingly from tourism. Chalk-white chimneys rise above the rooftops, harbors are abob with painted fishing boats, and in spring and summer fields blaze with amber mustard and grain.

Certainly, few people come to Bornholm to stay indoors. Long, silky beaches, rolling hills, and troll-inspiring forests make this a summer haven for walking, hiking, and swimming—particularly for families, many of whom take their summer vacations by packing provisions and children onto a pair of bikes, and winding throughout the island.

Bornholm is famous throughout Scandinavia for its craftspeople, especially glassblowers and ceramicists, whose work is often pricier in Copenhagen and Stockholm. In the center of each town (especially Gudhjem and Svaneke), you'll find crafts shops and *værksteder* (workshops). When you're on the road, watch for *keramik* (ceramics) signs, which direct you to artists selling from home.

Fishing

Cod, salmon, and herring fishing are excellent in season, though better from a boat than from shore. Licenses cost DKr25 per day, DKr75 per week, and DKr100 per year. Contact the tourist board for details and information on charter trips. Among the handful of charter companies is **Peter Prüssing** (✉ Gudhjem, ☎ 56/48–54–63), who arranges three-day trips from either Gudhjem and Snogebæk between July and September.

Hiking

In contrast to the rest of Denmark, Bornholm is hilly and rugged. Marked trails crisscross the island, including three 4-km (2½-mi) hikes through the Almindingen Forest and several more through its Ekkodalon (Echo Valley). The northern coastline is beautiful but a rocky and more strenuous walk. Ask for a map, routes, and tips from any tourism office. The *Bornholm Green Guide,* available in shops and tourism offices, offers suggestions for walking and hiking tours.

Swimming

Beach worshipers thrive in Bornholm. The swimming and sunning are best south, between Pedersker and Snogebæk, where the dunes are tall and the beaches wide. As elsewhere in Denmark, topless bathing is common and nude bathing is tolerated.

Rønne

☞ *190 km (120 mi) southeast of Copenhagen (7 hrs by ferry).*

Borhholm's capital, port, and largest town is Rønne, a good starting point for exploring northward or eastward. East of Nørrekås Harbor on Laksegade, you'll find an enchanting area of rose-clad 17th- and 18th-century houses, among them the tile-roof **Erichsens Gård** (farm). The home of the wealthy Erichsen family, whose daughter married the Danish poet Holger Drachmann, it is preserved with paintings by Danish artist Kristian Zahrtmann, period furnishings, and a lovely garden. ✉ *Lakseg. 7,* ☎ *56/95–87–35.* ✉ *DKr25.* ☉ *June–Aug., Tues.–Sat. 10–5.*

Near Store Torv, the main square, is the **Bornholm Museum,** which features local geologic and archaeological exhibits in addition to more than 4,500 pieces of ceramics and glass. The museum also displays 25 18th-century *Bornholmure* (Bornholm Clocks), as characteristic of the island as smoked herring. In 1744, a Dutch ship was wrecked on Bornholm, and the English grandfather clocks it carried became the models for the island's clocks. ✉ *Skt. Mortensg. 29,* ☎ *56/95–07–35.* ✉ *DKr25.* ☉ *May–Oct., Tues.–Sat. 10–5; Nov.–Apr., Tues., Thurs., and Sat. 1–4.*

Dining and Lodging

$$ ✕ **Rådhuskroen.** With exposed timbers, comfortable armchairs, and close-set tables, this restaurant provides a softly lit change from Rønne's busy streets. The menu has changed in recent years to highlight substantial beef dishes like pepper steak with wine and cream sauce, but you can still get a couple of local fish specialities—like poached Baltic salmon or grilled filet of sole, both served with lobster sauce. ✉ *Nørreg. 2,* ☎ *56/95–00–69. AE, DC, MC, V.*

$$$ 🏨 **Fredensborg.** The island's standard for luxury is set at this hotel, situated on a curve of forest near a small beach. The glass-and-tile lobby is spare and sunny, the staff pleasant and eager. The dozen ample apartments have full kitchens, and guest rooms are done in pastel schemes, with modern furniture and balconies overlooking the sea. The rustic restaurant, De Fem Ståuerne, serves traditional French-Danish food. ✉ *Strandvejen 116, DK–3700,* ☎ *56/95–44–44,* FAX *56/95–03–14. 60 rooms, 12 apartments. Restaurant, bar, room service, hot tub, sauna, tennis court, meeting rooms. AE, DC, MC, V.*

$$$ 🏨 **Hotel Griffen.** Just off a busy street and the Rønne harbor, this is one of Bornholm's largest and most modern hotels. It's three stories tall, with plenty of windows and views of the sea on one side and Rønne on the other. The rooms, done in deep-brown tones, have every modern convenience. ✉ *Kredsen 1, DK–3700,* ☎ *56/95–51–11,* FAX *56/95–52–97. 140 rooms, 2 suites. Restaurant, bar, room service, indoor pool, sauna, dance club, meeting rooms. AE, DC, MC, V.*

$ ⛺ **Galløkken Camping.** This site is just a short walk from the Rønne center, near an old military museum. The grounds are open, but trees surround the perimeter. There are good shower and cooking facilities. ✉ *Strandvejen 4, DK–3700 Rønne,* ☎ *56/95–23–20.*

Nightlife and the Arts

Bornholm's nightlife is limited to a handful of discos and clubs in Rønne, which open and close frequently as tastes change. An old stand-by however, is **Vise Vesth Huset** (✉ *Brøddeg. 24,* ☎ *56/48–50–80*), popular for light meals and live folk music.

Outdoor Activities and Sports

GOLF

The **Bornholm Golf Club** near Rønne (☎ *56/95–68–54*) is an 18-hole park course in a natural setting with plenty of wildlife and fauna—the

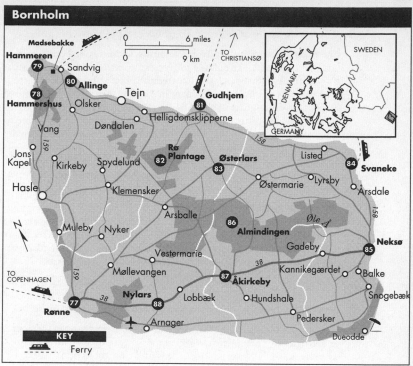

Bornholm

brochure even boasts that you can enjoy nightingales and wild orchids along the course. There's also a restaurant and pro shop.

Shopping

CLOCKS

A Bornholmure is a type of grandfather clock handmade on the island. Antique versions cost from DKr10,000 to DKr80,000 and more. The clocks often have round faces but can be rectangular as well and are completely hand-painted. On the hour, the modern clocks sound the hour with music—which ranges from Mozart and Verdi to Sondheim and Andrew Lloyd Webber. New reproductions modeled from museum originals are custom-made by **Bornholmerure** (⊠ Torneværksvej 26, Rønne, ☎ 56/95–31–08). A handmade custom clock costs, on the average, DKr37,000.

CLOTHING

You can pick up unusual gifts and one-of-a-kind clothing made of hand-printed textiles at **Bente Hammer** (⊠ Nyker Hovedg. 32, Rønne, ☎ 56/96–33–35).

MARKET

There is a large **vegetable and fruit market** on Wednesday and Saturday mornings in Store Torv, the main square in Rønne.

En Route   Fourteen kilometers (8½ miles) north of Rønne is the bluff known as **Jons Kapel.** A medieval legend has it that a monk, Brother Jon, lived in a cave and used these treacherous sea cliffs as a pulpit for his impassioned sermons. Wear rubber-sole hiking boots to climb the stairs that lead to the pulpit, where the agile friar stood atop the dramatic 72-ft-high cliffs that loom over the crashing waves.

Hammershus

★ ⑱ *8 km (5 mi) north of Jons Kapel, 30 km (19 mi) north of Rønne.*

The ruins of the fortress of Hammershus constitute northern Europe's largest stronghold. The hulking fortress was begun in 1255 by the archbishop of Lund (Sweden), and became the object of centuries of struggle between Denmark and Sweden. In 1658 Danes under Jens Kofoed killed its Swedish governor, and the castle was given back to Denmark. Used until 1743, it became a ruin when it was quarried for stone to fortify Christiansø and that island's buildings. The government finally intervened in 1822, and the site is now a mass of snaggletoothed walls and towers atop a grassy knoll. During restoration work in 1967, 22 gold German guilders were found. Occasionally, concerts and other performances are held at the ruins. ▨ *Free.*

Nightlife and the Arts

They don't happen nearly enough, but check with the local tourism office (☞ Visitor Information *in* Bornholm A to Z, *below*) to see if any special events are planned at or near Hammershus: the ruins add a spectacular dimension to classical music and the performing arts.

Hammeren

⑲ *5 km (3 mi) north of Hammershus, 36 km (23 mi) north of Rønne.*

Despite constant Baltic winds, rare plants and trees grow on the warm, granite-scattered Hammeren (the Hammer), including radiant anemones. The knuckle of land jutting from the island's northern tip is nearly separated from the island by a deep rift valley and the Hammer Sø (Hammer Lake). Look across the water south of the tip to the stone formation known as the Camel Heads.

En Route A little more than 3 km (2 mi) southeast of Hammeren, **Madsebakke** is the largest collection of Bronze Age rock carvings in Denmark. They are presumed to be ceremonial carvings, which ancient fishermen and farmers hoped would bring good weather and bountiful crops. The most interesting of them depicts 11 ships, including one with what's called a sun wheel.

Allinge

⑳ *3 km (2 mi) east of Madsebakke, 21 km (13 mi) north of Rønne.*

In Allinge and its twin town Sandvig, you'll find centuries-old neighborhoods and, particularly in Allinge, half-timber houses and herring smokehouses sprouting tall chimneys. Just south is a wood that the islanders call the **Trolleskoven** (Troll Forest). Legend says trolls live in the woods, and when they "brew" fog, they escape the heat in the kitchen and go out looking for trouble. The most mischievous is the littlest troll, Krølle Bølle.

Lodging

$$ ★ ▥ **Strandhotellet.** Romantic old-world charm is the draw at this venerable hotel. On a corner across from the harbor, it has a white arched entry into a stone-and-whitewashed lobby. The rooms are furnished in plain beech furniture with woolen covers and pastel colors. ⊠ *Strandpromenaden 7, Sandvig, DK–3770,* ☎ *56/48–03–14,* ℻ *56/48–02–09. 50 rooms, 1 suite. Restaurant, bar, sauna, steam room, health club. AE, DC, MC, V. Closed mid-Oct.–mid-Apr.*

$ ⌂ **Sandvig Familie Camping.** This site is pleasantly close to the beach, so that most of its sites enjoy a view of the water. The large kitchen and bathing facilities were renovated a few years ago. ⊠ *Sandlinien 5, DK–3770 Allinge,* ☎ *56/48–04–47 or 56/48–00–01.*

Shopping

Kampeløkken (⊠ Havneg. 45, Allinge, ☎ 56/48–17–66) gallery shop stocks the work of 24 potters and four glassblowers.

En Route Eight kilometers (5 miles) southeast of Allinge along the coastal path, you'll come upon the grottoes and granite cliffs of the **Helligdoms-klipperne** (Cliffs of Sanctuary), which contain a well-known rock formation best seen from the boats that ply the nearby waters in summer. In the Middle Ages, people used to visit these waters, believing that they had holy, healing powers—hence the name.

Just southeast of the Helligdomsklipperne, a pastoral coastal path leads to the tiny, preserved **Døndalen Forest.** Its fertile soil bears a surprising array of Mediterranean vegetation, including fig and cherry trees. During rainy periods look for a waterfall at the bottom of the dale.

Gudhjem

★ ⑧ *18 km (11 mi) east of Allinge, 33 km (21 mi) northeast of Rønne.*

Especially at the height of summer, Gudhjem (God's Home) is perhaps the most tourist-packed town on Bornholm—and the reason is obvious. Tiny half-timber houses and gift shops with lace curtains and clay roofs line steep stone streets that loop around the harbor. The island's first smokehouses still produce alder-smoked golden herring.

★ ◐ Walk down Brøddegade, which turns into Melstedvej; here you'll find the **Landsbrugs Museum** (Agricultural Museum) and Mestedgaard, a working farm with cows, horses, sheep, pigs, geese, and wandering kittens. The farm includes the well-kept house and garden of a 19th-century farm family. Notice the surprisingly bright colors used on the interior of the house, and leave time to visit the old shops, where you can buy locally produced woolen sweaters, wooden spoons, and even homemade mustard. ⊠ *Melstedvej 25,* ☎ *56/48–55–98.* ☞ *DKr25.* ◷ *Mid-May–mid-Oct., Tues.–Sun. 10–5.*

OFF THE
BEATEN PATH

BORNHOLM KUNST MUSEUM – Follow the main road, Hellidomsvej, out of town in the direction of Allinge/Sandvig, and you'll come to Bornholm's art museum, an excellent example of the Danes' ability to integrate art, architecture, and natural surroundings. Built by the architectural firm of Fogh and Følner, the white-painted brick, granite, and sandstone building is centered by a thin stream of "holy" trickling water that exits the building and leads the visitor to a walkway and overlook above the Hellig-domsklipperne (☞ *above*). Throughout, the walls of the museum are punched out by picture windows overlooking nearby grazing cows and the crashing Baltic: a natural accompaniment to the art. Most of the works are by Bornholmers, including a body of Modernist work by Olaf Høst, Karl Esaksen, and Olaf Rude, who recognized a particular ability in Bornholm's sea-surrounded light to bring out the poignancy in abstract scenes of local life. The museum also displays some sculpture and glass, as well as a survey of more historical paintings. Check out the restaurant and shop. ⊠ *Hellidomsvej 95,* ☎ *56/48–43–86.* ☞ *DKr30.* ◷ *May–mid-Oct., Tues.–Sun. 10–5; mid-Oct.–Apr., Tues., Thurs., Sun. 1–5.*

Lodging

$ ☒ **Skt. Jørgens Gård Vandrehjem.** In a half-timber 100-year-old former manor house, this hostel in the middle of Gudhjem offers single-to eight-bed rooms with standard Danish hostel style: pine bunks and industrial carpeting. There are six kitchens available for use. ⊠ *Gud-*

hjem Vandrehjem, DK–3760, ☎ 56/48–50–35, FAX 56/48–56–35. 52 rooms, 26 with bath. Restaurant. No credit cards.

Shopping

Baltic Sea Glass (✉ Melstedvej 47, Gudhjem, ☎ 56/48–56–41), on the main road just on the outskirts of town, offers high-quality, bright, and imaginative decanters, glasses, candlesticks, and one-of-a-kind pieces, including an old-fashioned contraption to catch flies. In town, see the delicate porcelain bowls of **Per Rehfeldt** (✉ Kastenievej 8, ☎ 56/48–54–13). Unique, hand-thrown ceramic work is available from and by **Julia Manitius** (✉ Holkavej 12, ☎ 56/48–55–99).

OFF THE
BEATEN PATH **CHRISTIANSØ** – A 45-minute boat ride northeast from Gudhjem will bring you to the historic island of Christiansø. Though it was originally a bastion, the Storetårn (Big Tower) and Lilletårn (Little Tower) are all that remain of the fort, built in 1684 and dismantled in 1855. The barracks, street, and gardens, for which the earth was transported in boats, have hardly changed since that time. They remain under the jurisdiction of the defense ministry, making this a tiny tax-free haven for its 100 inhabitants. Nearby, the rocky, uninhabited island of **Græsholmen** is an inaccessible bird sanctuary—the only place in Denmark where the razorbill and guillemot breed.

Rø Plantage

⑧② *6 km (4 mi) southwest of Gudhjem, 24 km (15 mi) northeast of Rønne.*

Rø Plantation is a new but dense forest that serves as a quiet foil to the hubbub of Gudhjem. A century ago it was a heather-covered grazing area, but after stone dikes were erected to keep the cattle out, spruce, pine, larch, and birch were cultivated. The cool refuge now consists largely of saplings and new growth—the result of devastating storms in the late '50s and '60s.

Outdoor Activities and Sports

GOLF

Rø Golfbane (✉ Spellingevej 3, ☎ 56/48–40–50) has won various European and Scandinavian awards for its natural beauty—and challenges. Its 18 holes are set close to the coastal cliffs, and enjoys views of the sea. It has a pro shop and restaurant.

Østerlars

⑧③ *5 km (3 mi) southeast of Rø Plantage, 22 km (14 mi) northeast of Rønne.*

The standout attraction here is the **Østerlars Kirke.** The largest of the island's four round churches, it was built in about 1150; extensions, including the buttresses, were added later. Constructed from boulders and slabs of limestone, the whitewashed church was part spiritual sanctuary, part fortification, affording protection from enemy armies and pirates. Inside is the island's only painted tympanum, with a faded image of a cross and decorative foliage. Several Gothic wall paintings—including depictions of the Annunciation and Nativity—have survived from the 1300s. ✉ *Gudhjemsvej 28,* ☎ *56/49–82–64.* 🎫 *DKr4.* ☯ *Apr.–mid-Oct., Mon.–Sat. 9–5.*

Svaneke

⑧④ *21 km (13 mi) east of Østerlars, 49 km (31 mi) northeast of Rønne.*

The coastal town of Svaneke, Denmark's easternmost settlement, is an enchanting hamlet of 17th- and 18th-century houses, winding cobbled streets, and a harbor sliced from the rocky earth. Once a fishing village, it is now immaculately preserved and home to a thriving artists' community.

Dining and Lodging

$$ ✕🏨 **Siemsens Gaard.** Built in a 270-year-old merchant house, this U-shape hotel with a gravel-courtyard café overlooks the harbor. The inside is cushy, with Chesterfield sofas below severe black-and-white prints and antiques. The rooms differ, but all are done up in stripped pine and soft colors. The bright, modern restaurant serves French-Danish food, with a menu of 125 options—from club sandwiches to smoked Baltic salmon to smørrebrød. ✉ *Havnebryggen 9, DK–3740,* ☎ *56/49–61–49,* FAX *56/49–61–03. 50 rooms. Restaurant, café, sauna, health club. AE, DC, MC, V.*

$$ 🏨 **Hotel Østersøen.** Across from the harbor, this hotel has a provin-
★ cial facade and a Key West courtyard with palm trees and a pool. Industrial carpets and century-old beams line the modern lobby, and the stark apartments (rented by the week) are appointed with leather sofas, swanky teak dinette sets, and streamlined furniture. The hotel is well suited for families and couples traveling in pairs. ✉ *Havnebryggen 5, DK–3740,* ☎ *56/49–60–20,* FAX *56/49–72–79. 21 apartments. Pool, business services. AE, DC.*

Shopping

Stroll through the ateliers and boutiques in the central Glastorvet in Svaneke. Among them is the studio of **Pernille Bülow** (✉ Glastorvet, Brænderigænget 8, ☎ 56/49–66–72), one of Denmark's most famous glassblowers. Her work is sold in Copenhagen's best design shops. Even if you buy directly from her studio, don't expect bargains—though you may be lucky to find seconds—but do expect colorful, experimental work. **Askepot** (✉ Postg. 5, Svaneke, ☎ 53/99–70–42), whose name means Cinderella, sells handmade leather hats, jackets, shoes, bags, belts, and wallets.

Neksø

⑧⑤ *9 km (5½ mi) south of Svaneke, 48 km (30 mi) northeast of Rønne.*

Neksø (or Nexø) bustles with visitors and locals who shop and live around its busy harbor, lined with fishing boats from throughout the Baltics and Eastern Europe. It might seem like a typical 17th-century town, but it was rebuilt almost completely after World War II, when the Russians bombed it to dislodge stubborn German troops who refused to surrender—three days after the rest of Denmark had been liberated. The Russians lingered on the island until April 1946.

Wander down to the harbor to find, in a mustard-yellow building, the **Neksø Museum** with its fine collection of fishing and local history exhibits. The museum also houses photographs and memorabilia of Danish author Martin Andersen Hansen (1909–55), who changed his last name to Nexø after his beloved town. A complicated and vehement socialist, he wrote, among other works, *Pelle the Conqueror,* set in Bornholm at the turn of the century, when Swedish immigrants were exploited by Danish landowners. The story was turned into an Academy Award–winning film. ✉ *Havnen,* ☎ *56/49–25–56.* 🎟 *DKr10.* ☉ *May–Oct., Tues.–Sun. 10–4.*

Outdoor Activities and Sports

GOLF

The 18-hole **Nexø Golf Club** (☎ 56/48–89–87) is close to the island's best sandy, rock-free beaches.

WINDSURFING

The best windsurfing beaches are on the southern sandy coast, where the winds are strong and the beaches sandy (the shores are rockier north of Neksø). **Windsurfing ved Balke Strand** (☎ 56/95–00–77), 4 km (2½ mi) south of Neksø, offers classes and board rentals.

Shopping

For exquisite **woodwork** see Bernard Romain (✉ Rønnevej 54, Neksø, ☎ 56/48–86–66).

Almindingen

⑧⑥ *23 km (14 mi) west of Neksø, 27 km (17 mi) northeast of Rønne.*

The lush Almindingen, Denmark's third-largest forest, is filled with ponds, lakes, evergreens, well-marked trails, and blooms with lily of the valley in spring. Within it, the oak-lined **Ekkodalen** (Echo Valley)— where children love to hear their shouts resound—is networked with trails leading to smooth rock faces that soar 72 ft high. At the northern edge, near the road to Østermarie, stood one of Bornholm's most famous sights until 1995: seven evergreens growing from a single trunk. The tree fell that year, but pass by, and you might see the remains of its curious trunk.

Outdoor Activities and Sports

HIKING

Check with the tourist board for a map delineating three 4-km (2½-mi) hikes through the Almindingen Forest and several more through its Echo Valley. The *Bornholm Green Guide,* available in shops and tourism offices, offers walking and hiking routes.

Åkirkeby

⑧⑦ *5 km (3 mi) south of Almindingen, 24 km (15 mi) east of Rønne.*

Åkirkeby is the oldest town on the island, with a municipal charter from 1346. The town's church, the **Åkirke,** is Bornholm's oldest and largest, dating from the mid-13th century. Though it is not a round church, both walls and tower were well suited for defense. The altarpiece and pulpit are Dutch Renaissance from about 1600, but the carved sandstone font is as old as the church itself. ✉ *Torvet,* ☎ *56/97–41–03.* ⌦ *DKr5.* ☉ *Mon.–Sat. 10–4.*

Nylars

⑧⑧ *8 km (5 mi) west of Åkirkeby, 9 km (6 mi) east of Rønne.*

Like the Østerlars church, the round **Nylars Kirke** dates from 1150. The chalk paintings from the Old Testament on its central pillar are the oldest on the island, possibly dating from 1250. Even older are the runic stones on the church's porch. Both are of Viking origin. ✉ *Kirkevej,* ☎ *56/97–20–13.* ⌦ *Suggested donation DKr3.* ☉ *Mid-May–mid-Sept., Mon.–Sat. 9–5.*

Bornholm A to Z

Arriving and Departing

BY BUS

A *Gråhund* (Greyhound) No. 866 bus from Copenhagen's main station travels to Dragør, boards a ferry to Limhamn, and then continues to Ystad, where it connects with a ferry to Rønne. Buses depart twice daily, once in the morning and again in late afternoon. Call **Bornholm Bussen** (☎ 44/68–44–00).

The *Bornholmstrafikken* car ferry from Copenhagen's Kvæsthusbro Harbor (near Nyhavn) departs at 11:30 PM year-round and from June through July daily (except Wednesday) at 8:30 AM. The trip takes seven hours. To avoid delays, make reservations. Comfortable sleeping bunks in a massive hall are also available for an extra cost.

The Nordbornholms Turistbureau (North Bornholm Tourist Board, ☎ 56/48–00–01) is the agent for a summer ferry that links Neu Mukran (3½ hours) and Sassnitz (3½ hours) on the island of Rügen in Germany. **Bornholmstrafikken** (☎ 56/95–18–66), a competing company, offers passage aboard the ferry to Neu Mukran (3½ hours), just 5 km (3 mi) from Sassnitz. Prices vary according to the number of people traveling and the size of the vehicle. There is also a boat between Świnoujście, Poland and Rønne (seven hours); call **Polferries** (☎ 48/97–32–1614–0) in Poland. A hydrofoil from Nyhavn goes to Malmö, Sweden, where it connects with a bus to Ystad and a ferry to Rønne. The four-hour voyage runs twice daily, usually in the morning and again in the late afternoon. Call **Flyve Bådene** (☎ 33/12–80–88).

The **airport** is 5 km (3 mi) south of Rønne at the island's southwestern tip. **Mærsk Air** (☎ 56/95–11–11) makes several daily flights only from Copenhagen. **Lufthansa** (☎ 33/37–73–33) flies from Berlin and Hamburg; **Eurowings** (☎ 49/231–924–5306) from Dortmund and Osnabrück.

Getting Around

Biking is eminently feasible and pleasant on Bornholm, thanks to a network of more than 200 km (125 mi) of cycle roads, including an old railway converted to a cross-island path. Rentals of sturdy two-speeds and tandems are available for about DKr50 a day at more than 20 different establishments all over the island—near the ferry, at the airport, and in Allinge, Gudhjem, Hasle, Pedersker (near Åkirkeby), Rønne, Svaneke, and most other towns. Try Bornholms Cykleudlejning (⌧ Nordre Kystevej 5, ☎ 56/95–13–59) or Cykel-Centret (⌧ Sønderg. 7, ☎ 56/95–06–04), both in Rønne.

Though bus service is certainly not as frequent as in major cities, there are regular connections between towns. Schedules are posted at all stations, and you can usually pick one up on board. The fare is DKr8 per zone, or you can buy a klip kort (punch ticket) of 10 klips for DKr64. A 24-hour bus pass costs DKr100. Children 5–11 pay half-price.

There are excellent roads on the island, but be alert for cyclists and occasional leisurely paced cows.

Contacts and Resources

Ambulance, accident, or **fire** (☎ 112). **Bornholm's Central Hospital** (⌧ Sygehusvej, Rønne, ☎ 56/95–11–65). **Rønne Apotek** (Rønne Pharmacy, ⌧ Store Torveg. 12, Rønne, ☎ 56/95–01–30).

Aerial Tours: An aerial tour in a Cessna or Piper plane (20–45 min) covers either the entire coast or the northern tip. Call **Klippefly** (☎ 56/95–35–73 or 56/48–42–01).

BAT Tours: The **BAT** (Bornholm Municipality Traffic Company, ☎ 56/95–21–21) offers some inventive summer tours. All are offered Tuesday through Friday, from mid-July until early August. All begin at the red bus terminal at Snellemark 30 in Rønne at 10 AM and cost DKr100. (You can also buy a 24-hour bus card for DKr100, or a five- or seven-day card for DKr350, good for both the regional buses and the tours.) Tour prices do not include some DKr5–DKr10 admissions or lunch at a herring smokehouse. The five-hour Kunst og håndværk (Arts and Crafts) tour includes stops at glass, pottery, textile, and silver studios. In summer, different studios are visited each day. The Grønne Bus (Green Bus) visits sights that illustrate the ways in which the island's exquisite flora and fauna are being preserved. Bondegårdsbussen (Farm Bus) visits chicken, cow, and pig farms, as well as a "free-range" pig farm, to show the differences in practice and attitude between conventional and progressive farming. The Veteranbus (Veteran Bus), a circa World War II Bedford, connects some of Bornholm's oldest industries, including a clockmaker, water mill, and Denmark's last windmill used for making flour.

Boat Tours: From mid-June to mid-September, boats to the Hellig-domsklipperne (Sanctuary Cliffs) leave Gudhjem at 10:30, 1:30, and 2:30, with extra sailings mid-June to mid-August. Call **Thor Båd** (☎ 56/48–51–65). Boats to Christiansø depart from Svaneke at 10 AM daily year-round; May to September daily at 10:20 from Gudhjem, and at 1 from Allinge; between mid-June and August, an additional boat leaves Gudhjem weekdays at 9:40 and 12:15. Call **Christiansø Farten** (☎ 56/48–51–76) for additional information.

Sightseeing Tours: The **Bornholmrund** (Round Bornholm) bus tour (8½ hours), beginning at 9:30 Tuesday and Thursday, includes Rønne, Hammershus, Allinge, Gudhjem, Østerlars Church, Svaneke, Nexø, Balka, Åkirkeby, and the Almindingen Forest. To make reservations, call the Bornholm tourist board (☞ *below*).

VISITOR INFORMATION

Nordbornholms Turistbureau (North Bornholm Tourist Board, ☎ 56/48–00–01). **Bornholm** (✉ Nordre Kystvej 3, Rønne, ☎ 56/95–95–00.

Allinge (✉ Kirkeg. 4, ☎ 56/48–00–01). **Åkirkeby** (✉ Torvet 2, ☎ 56/97–45–20). **Gudhjem** (✉ Åbog. 9, ☎ 56/48–52–10. **Hasle** (✉ Havneg. 1, ☎ 56/96–44–81). **Nexø,** (✉ Åsen 4, ☎ 56/49–32–00). **Svaneke** (✉ Storeg. 24, ☎ 56/49–63–50).

7 Greenland

HEN ERIC THE RED discovered Greenland (Kalaallit Nunaat in Greenlandic, Grønland in Danish) a thousand years ago, his Norsemen thought they had reached the edge of the world. After it, there was only *Ginnungagap,* the endless abyss.

Greenland still commands awe from the growing number of visitors who venture off the usual Scandinavian path to explore the world's largest island. Measuring more than 1.3 million square km (840,000 square mi), it's larger than Italy, France, Great Britain, unified Germany, and Spain combined. The coastal regions are sparsely populated with about 7,500 Danes and 48,000 Inuit—the indigenous people, whose roots can be traced to the native inhabitants of Canada's Arctic, and further back to the people of Alaska. More than 80% of the land is eternally frozen beneath an ice cap that, at its deepest, reaches a thickness of 3 km (2 mi). If it melted, sea levels around the world would rise nearly 20 ft.

The number of tourists is growing at a enormous rate, from just 3,000 in 1993 to 16,000 in 1996. But relatively speaking, with these few tourists (almost all on package tours), Greenland remains one of the world's least developed regions. By its nature, the region is far more difficult to explore than dwarfed mother Denmark. Travel is possible only by helicopter or coastal boat, since there are few roads and no railroads. However, the southern and western towns—trimmed with building-block red-and-green houses and well-used harbors—have adequate hotels, airfields and helicopter pads, and some summertime ferry service. Man-made luxuries are few, but the rewards of nature are savagely beautiful. Below the Arctic Circle, the draws include Norse ruins, Ice Age–gouged mountains, and jagged fjords. Farther north, dogsleds whip over icy plains, and ferries glide past icebergs as big as city blocks.

Greenland's first inhabitants probably arrived some 4,000 years ago from what is today Canada. Various Inuit peoples continued to migrate to and roam across the island, but current Greenlanders are descendants of a particular Canadian Inuit culture that arrived around AD 1000. Greenland's recorded history began at about the same time, in AD 982, when Eric and his Norse settlers claimed the land, but after 400 years of colonization they mysteriously disappeared. During this period Denmark and Norway were joined under the Danish crown, a union that muddled ownership of Greenland until 1933, when the International High Court awarded Denmark complete sovereignty. (Until 1997, this dual heritage lead every town to have both a Greenlandic and a Danish name; today only the Greenlandic names are used on modern maps.) Geographically isolated and increasingly politically independent, Greenlanders are intent on redefining their ethnic identity in a modern world. They refer to themselves as Inuit, in solidarity with native peoples of Canada, Alaska, and the former Soviet Union, and speak their own language in addition to Danish.

In 1978 Denmark granted Greenland home rule, vesting its tiny Landsting (parliament) in the capital Nuuk/Godthåb with power over internal affairs. Though Denmark continues to devolve power, it still administers foreign policy and provides financial aid to an economy based on fishing, animal husbandry, construction, and tourism.

Since most travelers follow preset routes, towns and sites are arranged south to north in geographic order and not necessarily in the order they would be visited. Perhaps only one major museum or site is noted per village, but there is much more to see in Greenland's changeable nature. Venture along the wooden stairs and boardwalks that connect most private homes and provide inner-village walking paths. Cruise beneath the expanse of an iceberg and listen to it moan. Rise at 3 AM to take a stroll through the sunshine. There is no private property in Greenland—nature is free for all to enjoy, and in Greenlandic fashion, it is best savored slowly. Those who love this island do not move through it at a clip: it's more gratifying to let it move you.

Fishing

Visitors can buy fishing licenses (DKr200) from the local police, major hotels, and tourism offices. Call the local tourist board for details.

Hiking

Hiking in Greenland is unlimited. Keep in mind, however, that it's wiser to join an organized hike with an experienced guide than to attempt a solo expedition, since it's not uncommon for rescue crews to have to go out in search of lost hikers. Organized excursions are available in Nuuk/Godthåb and Narsarsuak for about DKr150 for a half day, DKr300 for a full day. The tourist offices of Qaqortoq/Julianehåb and Sisimiut/Holsteinsborg arrange hikes on request and charge according to the number of participants. For the most popular hiking areas in Greenland, new topographic maps at 1:50,000 are available. In these areas, experienced hikers can find their way without a guide. To cross the polar ice cap or to enter Greenland's national parkland—which is the size of Great Britain and France combined—you must obtain a license. Contact the **Danish Polar Center** (⊠ Strandg. 100H, DK–1401 KBH K, ☎ 32/88–01–00, ℻ 32/88–01–01).

Narsarsuaq

⑧⑨ *4 hrs, 50 min northwest of Copenhagen by plane.*

Narsarsuaq, meaning Great Plain in English, aptly describes the wide, smooth land harboring one of Greenland's largest civilian airports. The town is accessible from Copenhagen, Reykjavík, and Kangerlussuaq only by plane, and from Nuuk/Godthåb by plane and boat—though boats are booked months in advance.

Not far from the edge of town, visitors can take a 10-km (6-mi) boat ride from the Narsarsuaq harbor to an area where icebergs have broken off from a nearby glacier. There they are invited to collect glacial ice for the cocktails served on board.

Also near Narsarsuaq is the point locals call **Hospitalsdalen** (Hospital Valley), a controversial area named for an alleged American hospital where Korean War wounded were said to have been hidden away so as not to weaken morale back home. Though most history books deny the story, many locals swear it's true.

Qaqortoq/Julianehåb

⑨⓪ *6 hrs south of Narsarsuaq by ferry.*

With a population of 3,600, this is the largest town in southern Greenland and one of the loveliest. In the town square you'll see the island's only fountain, surrounded by half-timber and brightly colored houses. Though the oldest building in town is the cooper shop, which dates from 1797, the most interesting is the smithy, from 1871, which now houses the **Julianehåb Museum.** Inside are handmade hunting tools, kayaks, Inuit clothing, and a furnished sod house you can enter. A traditional dwelling, it remained cozy and warm even during the harsh winter. ▨ *Free.* ☉ *Weekdays 11–4.*

Lodging

$$ ⊞ **Hotel Qaqortoq.** Built in 1987, this hotel is among the more mod-
ern on the huge island. Its glass-and-white facade atop a hill overlooks
the surrounding fjord and the picturesque town center. Rooms are sim-
ple but comfortable, all with private bath, TV, and phone. ⊠ *Box 155,
DK–3920,* ☎ *299/3–82–82,* FAX *299/3–72–34. 21 rooms. Restaurant,
bar, billiards. DC, MC, V.*

OFF THE   **HVALSEY CHURCH –** A nice half-day excursion from Qaqortoq is the 14½-
BEATEN PATH   km (9-mi) sailboat ride to the well-preserved Hvalsey Church ruins, site
                 of a well-attended Norse wedding in 1408—the community's last
                 recorded activity before it mysteriously disappeared. As the church is
                 close to a rocky beach, the hardy can opt for a frigid dip.

Qassiarsuk

91 *30 min northwest of Narsarsuaq by boat.*

The main focus of the tiny village of Qassiarsuk is sheep breeding.
Though there are few modern facilities in town, the **Norse ruins** are
fascinating and include, for example, the Brattahlíð—1,000-year-old
ruins of Eric the Red's farm.

The remains of **Tjodhilde Kirke** are especially intriguing: this was touted
as the first Christian church on the North American continent (Green-
land is geographically considered part of North America and politi-
cally thought to be part of Europe). It was from this point that Eric
the Red's son, Leif Ericsson, began the expedition in AD 1000 that took
him to Vinland, somewhere on the coast of North America. The first
Greenlandic Ting (outdoor parliament), fashioned after those in Ice-
land, was also held here at about the same time.

Nuuk/Godthåb

92 *1 hr, 25 min northwest of Narsarsuaq by small plane (15 hrs by ferry),7
hrs east of Ottawa by plane.*

Nuuk/Godthåb, the capital of Greenland, is beautifully situated on a
peninsula between two fjords. It was founded in 1728 by the Norwe-
gian missionary Hans Egede; his harborside home is now the private
residence of the island's home-rule premier.

The city's newest landmark is **Katvaq,** the Greenland Cultural Center
in town center. A triangular-shape construction fronted by a wavy wall—
inspired by the Aurora Borealis—contains spaces for concerts, exhi-
bitions, theater, conventions, and cinema, as well as a café. Its residents
include the Greenland Art School, Nordic Institute on Greenland, and
the Groenlandica Collection, a modern lending library with what is
thought to be the largest collection of literature on the Arctic regions.
⊠ *Skibshavnsvej,* ☎ *299/2–33–00.* ▣ *Free.* ☉ *Weekdays, 10–9:30,
weekends 1:30–9:30.*

The centrally located **Landsmuseet** (National Museum) has a good per-
manent display of kayaks, costumes, and hunting weapons, an art ex-
hibit, and the five 15th-century mummies of Qilakitsoq, one of
Greenland's archaeological treasures. Among the most striking are a
woman and child so well preserved that even their 500-year-old clothes
are in pristine condition. ⊠ *Hans Egede Vej 8,* ☎ *299/2–26–11.* ▣
Free. ☉ *Tues.–Sun. 1–4.*

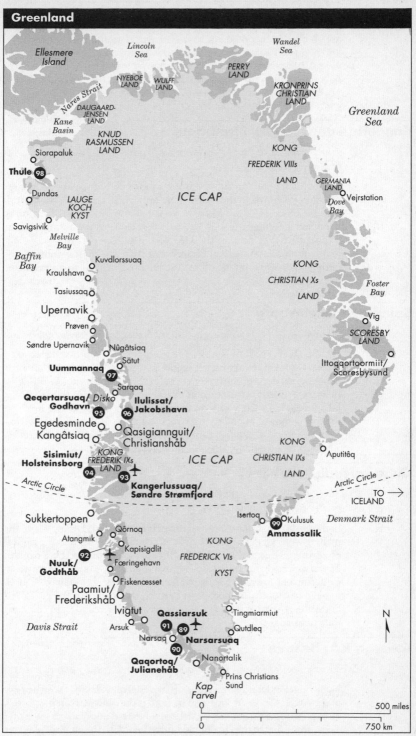

Greenland

Ellesmere
Island

Lincoln
Sea

Wandel
Sea

NYEBOE
LAND

WULFF
LAND

PERRY
LAND

KRONPRINS
CHRISTIAN
LAND

Nares Strait

DAUGAARD-
JENSEN
LAND

*Kane
Basin*

KNUD
RASMUSSEN
LAND

*Greenland
Sea*

Siorapaluk

Thule 98

Dundas

LAUGE
KOCH
KYST

ICE CAP

KONG

FREDERIK VIIIs

LAND

GERMANIA
LAND

Vejrstation

*Dove
Bay*

Savigsivik

*Melville
Bay*

*Baffin
Bay*

Kuvdlorssuaq

Kraulshavn

Tasiussaq

KONG

CHRISTIAN Xs

LAND

*Foster
Bay*

Upernavik

Prøven

Søndre Upernavik

Nûgâtsiaq

Sátut

Vig

*SCORESBY
LAND*

Uummannaq 97

Sarqaq

Ittoqqortoormiit/
Scoresbysund

**Qeqertarsuaq/
Godhavn** 95

Disko

**Ilulissat/
Jakobshavn** 96

Egedesminde
Kangâtsiaq

Qasigiannguit/
Christianshåb

KONG

CHRISTIAN IXs

ICE CAP

Aputitêq

**Sisimiut/
Holsteinsborg** 94

KONG
FREDERIK IXs
LAND

93 ✈

LAND

- - *Arctic Circle*

**Kangerlussuaq/
Søndre Strømfjord**

Arctic Circle - -

TO →
ICELAND

Sukkertoppen

Isertoq

99 Kulusuk

Denmark Strait

Ammassalik

Atangmik

Qôrnoq

Kapisigdlit

92 ✈

Fœringehavn

KONG

FREDERICK VIs

KYST

**Nuuk/
Godthåb**

Fiskenœsset

Paamiut/
Frederikshåb

Ivigtut

Qassiarsuk

Tingmiarmiut

Davis Strait

Arsuk

91 89 ✈

Qutdleq

Narsaq

Narsarsuaq

90

Nanortalik

**Qaqortoq/
Julianehåb**

Prins Christians
Sund

*Kap
Farvel*

N

0   500 miles

0   750 km

Dining and Lodging

$$$$ ✕▥ **Hotel Hans Egede.** This hotel is the largest in Greenland. The rooms
are plain and functional but have such extras as minibars, TVs, VCRs,
and phones. The sixth-floor Sky Top Restaurant, known for its lovely
view of the fjords and its inventive nouveau Greenlandic menu, pre-
pares local fish employing French methods. ⊠ *Box 289, DK–3900,*
☏ *299/2–42–22,* ℻ *299/2–44–87. 108 rooms. Restaurant, pub, dance
club, meeting rooms. DC, MC, V.*

Kangerlussuaq/Søndre Strømfjord

⑨③ *1 hr northeast of Nuuk/Godthåb by plane, 4 hrs, 20 min northwest
of Copenhagen by plane.*

Kangerlussuaq/Søndre Strømfjord is at the head of one of the longest
and deepest fjords in the world. The airport, Greenland's most vital,
lies just 25 km (15½ mi) from the ice cap. Until World War II, nobody
lived here permanently, but Greenlanders came in the spring to hunt
reindeer. During the war, the U.S. Air Force chose its dry, stable climate for an air base, called Bluie West Eight. The military moved out
in the fall of 1992, selling all the facilities to the local government for
the sum of $1.

Sisimiut/Holsteinsborg

⑨④ *40 min west of Kangerlussuaq/Søndre Strømfjord by helicopter.*

On the Davis Strait, this hilltop town is full of Danish-style wooden
houses—a local luxury, as all wood is imported. A favorite area for
dogsledging, during which you are pulled by a team of rabid wolf-dogs;
they are harnessed in a fan shape rather than a straight line, so if one
falls through the ice, you won't all plummet to an icy death. It is also
the southernmost boundary for walrus hunting; the walrus, though extremely rare, is a popular game animal because of its valuable tusks.
The Greenlandic name Sisimiut means Burrow People.

Qeqertarsuaq/Godhavn

⑨⑤ *1 hr, 20 min west of Illulissat by helicopter (8 hrs, 30 min by coastal
boat; reserve far in advance).*

In the Disko Bugt (Bay) is the island of Qeqertarsuaq/Disko, where the
main town is Qeqertarsuaq/Godhavn. Until 1950 this was the capital
of northern Greenland; Nuuk/Godthåb served as the southern capital.
The task was divided because it was too difficult to rule the entire island from one town. Accessible by helicopter and ship, Godhavn is often
booked to capacity by European tourists; they come for the organized
dogsledging trips, as this is the only area in Greenland with summertime dogsledging.

Ilulissat/Jakobshavn

⑨⑥ *45 min north of Kangerlussuaq/Søndre Strømfjord by plane.*

In the center of Disko Bay is Ilulissat/Jakobshavn, 300 km (185 mi) north
of the Arctic Circle. At the tip of its fjord is the Northern Hemisphere's
most productive glacier, calving 20 million tons of floes each day—equivalent, according to the Greenland tourist board, to the amount of water
New York City uses in a year. For a humbling experience, take one of
the helicopter tours encircling the glacier. A violent landscape of float-
ing ice giants and dazzling panoramas, it's been inhabited by the Inuit
for as long as 4,000 years. The town was founded in 1741 by a Dan-

ish merchant, Jakob Severin. Today the largest industry is shrimping, though in the winter dogsledgers fish for halibut along the fjord.

Visit the **Knud Rasmussens Fødehjem** (boyhood home of Knud Rasmussen); this Danish-Greenlandic explorer (1879–1933) initiated the seven Thule expeditions, which enhanced the knowledge of Arctic geography and Inuit culture. At the museum you can follow his explorations through photographs, equipment, and clothing. ⊠ *DKr20.* ☉ *Daily 10–4.*

Dining and Lodging

$$$ ✕⛏ **Hotel Arctic.** This modern hotel, divided into two low-lying red buildings, is in the mountains on the edge of town, and provides views of the ice fjord and the mountains. Rooms are simple, with bathroom, phone, radio, and TV. The main dining room has panoramic views of the iceberg-filled harbor and serves fine beef and fish dishes. ⊠ *Box 1501, DK–3952,* ☎ *299/4–41–53,* FAX *299/4–39–24. 40 rooms. Restaurant, sauna, billiards, meeting rooms. AE, DC, MC.*

$$$ ✕⛏ **Hotel Hvide Falk.** The compact rooms in this central, moderate-size, two-story building are furnished with TVs and small desks, and have magnificent views of the icebergs and the Disko Mountains. The restaurant, which specializes in seafood—especially herring, cod, and salmon—looks out over the bay and its looming icebergs. The director of the hotel, Lars Rasmussen, is explorer Knud Rasmussen's grandson. ⊠ *Box 20, DK–3952,* ☎ *299/4–33–43,* FAX *299/4–35–08. 27 rooms. Restaurant. DC.*

Uummannaq

⑨ *55 min north of Ilulissat/Jakobshavn by helicopter.*

The inhabitants of the town of Uummannaq, on the island of the same name, maintain Greenlandic traditions in step with modern European life. Ranging from hunters to linguists, they are as apt to drive dogsleds as they are four-wheel drives. The town lies beneath the magnificent hues and double humps of the granite Uummannaq Mountain, 3,855 ft high. Because the village is also perched on uneven stone cliffs, housing largely consists of brightly painted, freestanding cottages rather than the ugly Danish barracks that line some of the larger towns.

The **Uummannaq Museum** will give you a good overview of life on the island, with photographs and costumes of local hunters and displays on the now-defunct mines of the area. Exhibits also detail the doomed 1930 expedition of German explorer Alfred Wegener, and there is also a bit on the Qilakitsoq mummies (☞ Nuuk/Godthåb, *above*), found in a nearby cave in 1977. ⊠ *Uummannaq Museum,* ☎ *299/4–81–04.* ⛏ *Free.* ☉ *Weekdays 8–4.*

The **Uummannaq Church,** dating from 1937, is the only stone church in Greenland and is made from local granite. Next door to it are three sod huts, typical Inuit dwellings until just a couple of decades ago.

Though there is plenty of **dogsledging** north of the Arctic Circle, the trips that set forth from Uummannaq are the most authentic, as local hunters drive; they are also the most gentle, since the terrain here is especially smooth. Visitors sit comfortably in heavy, fur-lined sleighs that tear across the frozen fjord in the hands of experienced Inuit drivers. Trips can be arranged at the Hotel Uummannaq and range from a few hours to several days of racing through the terrifying beauty of the landscape and sleeping in the shadows of towering icebergs.

Dining and Lodging

$$ ╳▥ **Uummannaq Hotel.** This natty harborside hotel and brand-new extension offer bright, compact rooms with white, Danish-designed furniture. The fine restaurant serves local specialties, including polar bear, caribou, seal, and plenty of fish. ⊠ *Box 202, DK–3961,* ☎ *299/4–85–18,* ☎ *299/4–82–62. 22 rooms, 10 in a nearby annex. Restaurant, bar. AE, MC, V.*

Thule

🕘 *2 hrs, 40 min north of Uummannaq by passenger-cargo plane, 1 hr, 45 min north of Kangerlussuaq/Søndre Strømfjord by plane.*

The northern reaches of Greenland are sparsely populated, with few hotels. The American air base at Thule, used for monitoring the Northern Hemisphere, is difficult to visit, but check with the Danish Ministry of Foreign Affairs in Copenhagen (⊠ ☎ 33/92–00–00) or the Royal Danish Embassy in Washington, DC (⊠ 3200 Whitehaven St. NW 20008-3683, ☎ 202/234–4300, ☎ 202/328–1470).

Ammassalik

🕘 *2 hrs west of Reykjavík by plane, connecting via helicopter from Kulusuk.*

Much of the east coast is empty. The most accessible towns are Ammassalik and Kulusuk, a tiny village slightly farther northeast. Both towns welcome most of Greenland's visitors, day-trippers from Iceland. Though tours, arranged through Icelandair, are usually short—often just day trips—they are very well organized, offering an accurate (and relatively affordable) peek at Greenlandic culture and the natural splendor of the Arctic.

Lodging

$$ ▥ **Hotel Angmagssalik.** Perched on a mountain, with a lovely view of the town and harbor, this hotel is decorated with a simple wood interior, both in the guest rooms and common areas. ⊠ *Box 117, DK–3900,* ☎ *299/1–82–93,* ☎ *299/1–83–93. 30 rooms, 18 with shower. Restaurant, bar. AE, DC, MC, V.*

Greenland A to Z

Arriving and Departing

BY PLANE AND HELICOPTER

The main airport in Greenland is **Kangerlussuaq/Søndre Strømfjord.** International flights also arrive less frequently into **Narsarsuaq** for those who are destined for south Greenland. **Kulusuk** is the main airport for the east coast. **Nuuk** and **Ilulissat** also serve as domestic airports.

Helicopters and small planes connect small towns. Because of Greenland's highly variable weather, delays are frequent. As with all arrangements in Greenland, confirm all flights, connections, and details with your local travel agent or airline representative before you leave home.

The most common points of departure for Greenland are Denmark and Iceland. If you're going by way of **Iceland,** Icelandair (☎ 354/505–0300) has flights from New York, Baltimore, Fort Lauderdale, and Orlando to Keflavík, Iceland, daily in summer, and **Greenlandair** (Grønlandsfly in Danish) makes three flights a week between Keflavík and Narsarsuaq in summer and winter. It's more expensive to go by way of **Copenhagen** with SAS (☎ 32/33–68–48), which flies seven times a week in summer to Kangerlussuaq/Søndre Strømfjord. Connections are also

available through **Canada,** where you can catch an early morning
flight from Ottowa to Frobisher Bay on Baffin Island, then cross the
Davis Strait to Kangerlussuaq/Søndre Strømfjord on **Firstair** (☎ 613/
839–8840).

Getting Around

BY BOAT

The most beautiful passage between towns is by water. Every town has
a harbor, where private boats can be hired for connections or excursions. Some cruise and coastal boats, as well as the privately-owned
Disko, which plies the waters of the west coast, and the M/S *Ioffe,* which
sails around the east and south coasts, make frequent stops. You can
only reserve through a travel agency. Boat voyages, including luxury
cruises, are also available from Canada's Frobisher Bay, Norway's
Svalbard (archipelago), and Iceland. Contact **KNI Service** (✉ Box 608,
DK–3900 Nuuk, ☎ 299/2–52–11, FAX 2–32–11) or Greenland Travel
in Copenhagen (☎ 33/13–10–11).

BY PLANE AND HELICOPTER

Greenlandair is the only airline licensed for domestic flights on the island. Its modest fleet of helicopters and small planes is booked year-
round, so make reservations well in advance.

Contacts and Resources

EMERGENCIES

Every community has its own fire, ambulance, and police numbers and
dentist and doctor, all of which you may reach through your hotel. The
best way to handle emergencies is to avoid danger in the first place.
Don't take risks, ask for advice, and give your travel agent and hotel
your itinerary so that they can reach you in case of emergencies—or
if you don't show up when you're due.

Hospital: Sana Dronning Ingrids Hospital (✉ DK–3900 Nuuk, ☎ 299/
2–11–01).

GUIDED TOURS

On-the-spot excursions are available in most towns and range from
about DKr250 for a half-day to DKr600 for a full day, more for
dogsledging, boat, and helicopter trips. Because transportation and accommodations are limited, have all details of your trip—connections,
accommodations, sightseeing, and meals—arranged by an experienced
travel agent, tour organizer, or airline. (It's also helpful to bring a copy
of your tour contract and all confirmations.)

Tour packages range from one- to four-day east-coast excursions from
Reykjavík by Icelandair to monthlong excursions, which can include
sailing, hiking, hunting, dogsledging (February to May), whale sa-
faris, and iceberg-watching.

United States: Bennett of Scandinavia (✉ 270 Madison Ave., New York,
NY 10016, ☎ 800/221–2420). **Eurocruises** (✉ 303 W. 13th St., New
York, NY 10014, ☎ 800/688–3876). **Icelandair** (✉ Symphony Woods,
5950 Symphony Woods Rd., Columbia, MD 21044, ☎ 800/223–
5500). **Quark Expeditions** (✉ 980 Post Rd., Darien, CT 06820, ☎ 203/
656–0499). **Scanam** (✉ 933 Hwy. 23, Pompton Plains, NJ 07444, ☎
800/545–2204). **Scantours Inc.** (✉ 1535 6th St., Suite 209, Santa Monica, CA 90401, ☎ 800/223–7226). **Travcoa** (✉ 4000 McArthur Blvd.
E, Suite 650, Newport Beach, CA 92660, ☎ 714/476–2800).

Canada: Marine Expeditions Inc. (✉ 30 Hazelton Ave., Toronto, Ontario
M5R 2E2, ☎ 416/964-9069). **Pedersen World Tours** (✉ 15 Wertheim
Ct., Suite 402, Richmond Hill, Ontario L4B 3H7, ☎ 416/882–5470).

In Denmark, contact **Arctic Adventure** (⊠ Reventlowsg. 30, DK–1651 KBH V, ☎ 33/25–32–21). **Greenland Travel** (☞ Visitor Information, *below*) also operates out of Denmark.

LATE-NIGHT PHARMACIES

If you are taking medication, bring enough to last throughout your visit. In emergencies, the local hospital can fill prescriptions.

VISITOR INFORMATION

There is a tourism office in almost every town, but brochures, maps, and specific information may be limited. Call ahead for an exact street address (a 299 access code must be dialed before all phone numbers when calling from outside Greenland).

Ammassalik (⊠ Box 120, DK–3913 Ammassalik, ☎ 299/1–82–77, FAX 299/1–80–77). **Ilulissat/Jakobshavn** (⊠ Box 272, DK–3952 Ilulissat, ☎ 299/4–43–22, FAX 299/4–39–33). **Kangerlussuaq/Søndre Strømfjord** (⊠ Box 49, DK–3910, Kangerlussuaq, ☎ 299/1–10–98, FAX 299/ 1–14–98). **Nuuk/Godthåb** (⊠ Box 199, DK–3900 Nuuk, ☎ 299/2–27–00, FAX 299/2–27–10). **Nielsen Travel** (⊠ Box 183, DK–3920 Qaqortoq, ☎ 299/3–89–13, FAX 299/3–89–87). **Qasigiannguit/Christianhåb** (⊠ Hotel Igdlo, Box 160, DK–3951 Qasigiannguit, ☎ 299/4–50–81, FAX 299/4–55–24). **Qeqertarsuaq/Godhavn** (⊠ Box 113, DK–3953 Qeqertarsuaq, ☎ 299/4–71–96, FAX 299/4–71–98). **Sisimiut/Holsteinsborg** (⊠ Box 65, DK–3911 Sisimiut, ☎ 299/1–48–48, FAX 299/ 1–56–22). **Uummannaq** (⊠ c/o Hotel Uummannaq, Box 202, DK–3961 Uummannaq, ☎ 299/4–85–18, FAX 299/4–82–62).

In Copenhagen, **Greenland Travel** (⊠ Gammel Mønt 12, ☎ 33/13–10–11) has a helpful and knowledgeable staff. **Greenland Tourism** (⊠ Pilestr. 52, ☎ 33/13–69–75) is another reliable Copenhagen-based operation.

8 The Faroe Islands

THE 18 FAROE ISLANDS (Føroyar in Faroese; Færøerne in Danish) lift up out of the North Atlantic in an extended knuckle of a volcanic archipelago. All but one are inhabited, by 43,700 people and 70,000 sheep. The native Faroese live by fishing, fish farming, and shepherding, and carefully maintain their refreshingly civilized pace of life.

Situated 300 km (188 mi) northwest of Scotland, 430 km (270 mi) southeast of Iceland, and 1,300 km (812 mi) northwest of Denmark, the fjord-chiseled islands support little vegetation besides a bristle of short grasses and moss. The climate is oceanic: humid, changeable, and stormy, with surprisingly mild temperatures—52°F in the summer, and 40°F in the winter—and a heavy annual rainfall of 63 inches.

Of their 1,399 square km (540 square mi), only 6% is fertile, the rest rough pasture—an Eden for 70 breeding and 120 migratory species of birds, among them thousands of gannets, auks, and puffins. Beneath azure skies and rugged, mossy mountains, villages of colorful thatched houses cling to hillsides while large trawlers and small fishing boats stream in and out of their harbors. Religious and proud, the Faroese have built churches in nearly every settlement.

Catholic monks from Ireland were the first to settle the islands, but they died out and were replaced by Norwegian Vikings, who settled the land about AD 800. It was here that the *Løgting* (parliament) met for the first time in AD 900 in Tórshavn—where it still meets. Under the Danish crown, the islands have had a home-rule government since 1948, with their own flag and language. The roots of the Faroese language are in Old West Norse. Most people speak English, but a Danish dictionary can be helpful to the visitor, as Danish is the second language.

It's difficult for visitors to understand the isolation or the practical relationship the Faroese have with the natural world. Dubious outsiders, for example, accuse locals of cruelty during the traditional pilot-whale harvests. An essential foodstuff, the sea mammals are killed in limited numbers to reduce the islands' dependence on imported meat. The profit factor is eliminated: whale meat is not sold—it's given away to the townspeople in equal portions on a per capita basis. The hunt is also an important social bond involving both the young and the old.

In 1993 the islands plunged into a severe depression, with unemployment, formerly an unknown phenomenon, surging from less than 3% to more than 20%. Toward the end of 1996, however, unemployment was pushed back down to 8% as the numbers of cod surrounding the islands mysteriously tripled (scientists and biologists are at a loss to explain why). Tourism is also a part of this brighter picture, and is increasing at a rate of 10% to 15% yearly. Though there appears an upward trend, there is also some fear: large international oil companies believe there is oil in the region. If they strike it rich, the islands could get out of their financial difficulties and return the DKr4 billion they currently owe Denmark. But many people fear that the black gold will irrevocably change the face of their islands.

Tórshavn on the island of Streymoy makes for a good touring base; spend one night in Klaksvík on the island of Borðoy. The very efficient bus and connecting boat service is the best way to travel between towns (☞ The Faroe Islands A to Z, *below*).

Tórshavn

1,343 km (839 mi) northeast of Copenhagen, 2 hrs, 15 min by plane.

Most visitors who arrive on the Faroe Islands by plane begin their explorations on the largest and most traveled island of Streymoy, which, though carved by sheer cliffs and waterfalls, has good roads and tunnels. On the northern end of the island are bird sanctuaries and a NATO base. On its southeastern flank is one of the world's tiniest capitals, Tórshavn, named for the Viking god Thor. Centrally located among the islands, Tórshavn has a population of 16,000. A Viking parliament was founded here in about AD 1000, but it did not have any real legislative power until 1948. St. Olav's Day, July 29, is named for the Norwegian king who brought Christianity to the islands. Celebrations include rowing competitions and group dances in the form of a chain—a sort of North Atlantic ring dance.

The rugged **Tinganes** is a small peninsula between the east and west bays that was the site of both the old trading post and the meetings of the local parliament (*tinganes* means "assembly place"). Here you can see some of the town's oldest buildings, dating from the 17th and 18th centuries, and some old warehouses, which today house the government offices. At the end of the docks is **Skansin,** a fort built in 1580 by Magnus Heinason to protect the town against pirate attacks. After many reconstructions, it reached its present shape in 1790 and was used as the Faroe headquarters of the British Navy during World War II. Two guns from that period remain.

Down from the Tinganes is Old Main Street, lined with small 19th-century houses and crossed by twisting streets. You'll come to the slate **Havnar Kirkja** (Tórshavn's Church), rebuilt many times in its 200-year history. Inside is a model of a ship salvaged from an 18th-century wreck, the ship's bell, and an altarpiece dating from 1647.

There are very few trees on the islands. **Tórshavn Park,** a walk up Hoyviksvegur, used to be the pride of the town—it was a rare cultivated oasis of green trees in a land where storms and strong winds flatten tall vegetation. Planted around the turn of the century, the park thrived until 1988, when a storm virtually destroyed it.

Standing atop a hill, **Kongaminnið** (King's Memorial) commands a good view of the old town. The basalt obelisk commemorates the visit of King Christian IX in 1874. ✉ *Norðrari Ringvegur, just off R. C. Effersøes Gøta.*

At the northern tip of Tórshavn is the modern **Norðurlandahúsið** (Nordic Culture House), built in 1983. It hosts an international jazz festival in mid-August and theater and concerts throughout the year. ✉ *Norðrari Ringvegur,* ☎ *298/17900.* ⊙ *Call for event schedules.*

Dining and Lodging

$$$ ✕▥ **Hotel Föroyar.** Five minutes from Tórshavn center, this hotel has a view of the Old Town. The rooms all have TVs, refrigerators, and phones, and there's a good restaurant with island specialties. ✉ *Oyggjarvegur, FR–110,* ☎ *298/17500,* ⓕ *298/16019. 216 beds. Restaurant. AE, DC, MC.*

$$$ ✕▥ **Hotel Hafnia.** Close to the pedestrian streets of town, this modern business hotel offers a good buffet and big-city ambience. The rooms vary in size, but all are comfortably appointed with TVs, telephones, desks, and private showers. The restaurant serves Faroese seafood, including local cod and flounder. ✉ *Áarvegur 4, FR–110,* ☎ *298/11270,* ⓕ *298/15250. 76 beds. Restaurant. AE, DC, MC.*

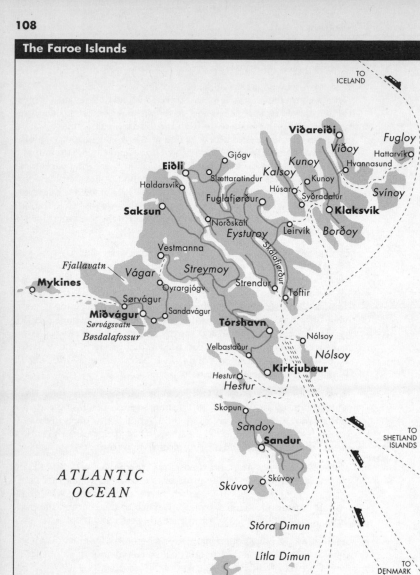

TO ICELAND

Viðareiði

Fugloy

Gjógv

Viðoy

Hattarvík

Kunoy

Hvannasund

Eiði

Kalsoy

Slættaratindur

Kunoy

Haldarsvík

Húsar

Svínoy

Fuglafjørður

Syðradalur

Saksun

Klaksvík

Norðskáli

Eysturoy

Leirvík

Borðoy

Vestmanna

Skálafjørður

Fjallavatn

Vágar

Streymoy

Mykines

Oyrargjógv

Strendur

Sørvágur

Miðvágur

Sandavágur

Tóftir

Sørvágsvatn

Tórshavn

Bøsdalafossur

Nólsoy

Velbastaður

Nólsoy

Kirkjubøur

Hestur

Hestur

Skopun

Sandoy

TO SHETLAND ISLANDS

Sandur

ATLANTIC
OCEAN

Skúvoy

Skúvoy

Stóra Dimun

Lítla Dímun

TO DENMARK

N

Tvøroyri

Suðuroy

TO DENMARK

Vágur

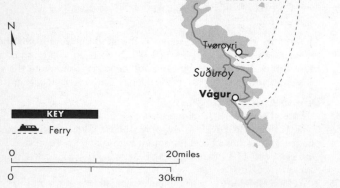
0   20miles

0   30km

$$ ☷ **Skansin Guesthouse.** Hard times have forced owner Frantz Restorff to close part of his guest house, but the rest of it, where he and his wife live, remains open to guests, who will experience typical Faroese hospitality within the modesty and personality of this private home. Filled with their belongings—a watercolor of a family-owned island, family photos, a collection of old records—the house is familiar and cozy. The Restorffs serve a generous breakfast (included in the room rate) and offer expert advice and assistance in planning activities. Guests have use of the kitchen. ✉ *Jekaragøta 8, Box 57, FR–110 Tórshavn,* ☎ *298/ 12242,* ℻ *298/10657. 22 beds. No credit cards.*

$$ ☷ **Youth Hostel Tórshavn.** Open as a hotel from July to September, this summer-only hotel is a school during the winter. ✉ *Vesturgøta 15, FR– 1100,* ☎ *2998/18900,* ℻ *298/15707. 100 beds. AE, DC, MC. Closed Oct.–June.*

$ ☷ **Tórshavnar Sjómansheim.** In the middle of Tórshavn, this modest hotel caters to those who need only a bed to be happy. Rooms are clean and basic, with dark hand-me-down furniture. The restaurant serves one special of the day, ranging from beef stew to—if there is a catch— whale. ✉ *Tórsgøta 4, FR–1100,* ☎ *298/13515,* ℻ *298/13286. 55 beds. Restaurant. No credit cards.*

OFF THE
BEATEN PATH

BOAT TRIP FROM VESTMANNA – You can take a bus from Tórshavn to Vestmanna (40 km/25 mi north of Tórshavn), where a boat takes you through narrow channels from which you can see sheep grazing atop sheer cliffs. In the spring the sheep are hoisted up the 2,310 ft with ropes, and in the fall they are caught and brought back down—apparently this process makes them taste better. Double-check the bus schedule before you leave to avoid geting stranded. Contact Aldan Tourist Information in Tórshavn (☞ The Faroe Islands A to Z, *below*).

Kirkjubøur

13 km (8 mi) south of Tórshavn.

From Tórshavn, a bus takes you to the outskirts of Kirkjubøur, from which you will have to walk a mile—through fields grazed by ponies and sheep—to the tiny town populated by 60 (ask the tourist office in Tórshavn for detailed directions). The townsfolk live in black houses with red window frames and green grass roofs perched on hillsides around the tiny, often fog-shrouded harbor. At the southern tip of the island, the town was the Faroes' spiritual and cultural center from 1269 to 1308.

A particularly ambitious priest, Bishop Erland, built a cathedral in the town in the 13th century—there is some controversy over whether or not it was ever completed—and the ruins of the Gothic **Magnus Cathedral** still stand. Inside the church is a large stone tablet engraved with an image of Christ on the cross, flanked by the Virgin Mary and Mary Magdalene, and an inscription to St. Magnus and St. Thorlak. During restoration work in 1905, the tablet was removed to reveal well-preserved relics of the saints. In 1538, after the Reformation, the episcopal see was dissolved and with it the town's power.

Just next door to the Magnus Cathedral is the restored **St. Olav's Church,** which dates from 1111 and is now the only church from that time still in use. Most of its sculptures have been removed to Copenhagen, leaving little to see, but there's a hole in the north wall that once allowed lepers standing outside to watch the mass and receive the Eucharist. The altarpiece is the work of the most famous painter of the islands, Sámal Mikines.

Near the church is a farmhouse, the **Roykstovan.** Legend has it that the lumber for the building came drifting to the town, neatly numbered and bundled, from the Sogne Fjord in Norway. Inside are the traditional Faroese one-main-room living quarters and a dozen other rooms. It's been in the same family for the last 16 generations, and it is here that foreign dignitaries are welcomed to the town.

Saksun

30 km (18 mi) northwest of Tórshavn.

Among the fjords slicing the northern end of Streymoy is the tiny town of Saksun, one of the most popular excursions on the island. Set around a pastoral lake in the midst of a deep valley are scattered sod-roof houses with lovely views. The town also swarms with great skuas, large brown seabirds prone to low dives. As you unwittingly near their nests, you will certainly notice their cantankerous presence.

Eiði

52 km (32 mi) northwest of Tórshavn.

The island of Eysturoy, just east of Streymoy, is connected to the latter by bridge and buses. The center of activity is the town of Eiði, which lies to the northwest in a spectacular landscape. Looking northwest, you can see two 250-ft cliffs, a part of local mythology: one night an Icelandic giant and his wife came to carry the islands to Iceland, but she dropped them, giving the islands their cracked geography. Once the sun rose, the giants were petrified and transformed into the bluffs.

Due east of Eiði is the islands' highest point, the 2,910-ft **Slættaratindur** mountain. On the shores of the southern **Skálafjørður,** the longest fjord in the archipelago, the majority of the island's 10,500 people live.

Lodging

$$ 🏨 **Hotel Eiði.** Perched on a hilltop in a village near the sea, about an hour by bus from Tórshavn, this slightly dated hotel is small and clean, with TVs and refrigerators in all rooms. ⊠ *FR–470 Eiði,* ☎ *298/23456,* 🅵🅰🆇 *298/23200. 28 beds. Restaurant. DC, MC, V.*

$ 🏨 **Gjáargarður.** This youth hostel, built in traditional Faroese style, has a prime position on the north end of the island, near the ocean and the mountains. ⊠ *FR–476 Eiði,* ☎ *298/23171,* 🅵🅰🆇 *298/23505. 100 beds. No credit cards.*

Klaksvík

35 km (22 mi) northeast of Tórshavn.

The island of Borðoy is accessible by boat from eastern Eysturoy. On its southwest coast, nearly divided by two fjords, Klaksvík is the Faroes' second-largest town and most important fishing harbor; its fleet of sophisticated boats harvests cod, haddock, herring, and other fish. Within this scattering of islands, Borðoy, Viðoy, and Kunoy are connected by causeways. The other three islands, Fugloy, Svinoy, and Kalsoy, are accessible by passenger boat or helicopter.

Within Klaksvík, the baptismal font in the **Christianskirkjan** (Christian's Church) is a piece of carved granite thought to have been used in pagan rituals in Denmark 4,000 years ago. Suspended from the church roof is a 24-ft boat used by a former vicar to visit nearby towns; the boat—common in Danish churches—is a symbol that God is watching over the village fishermen.

Lodging

$$ ⊞ **Klaksvíkar Sjómansheim.** Sheep graze on the front lawn of this big, white hotel; the back overlooks the colorful harbor. The staff is cheery and helpful, and rooms—request one with a harbor view—offer no-frills comfort; showers and toilets are in the hallways, but sinks are in the rooms. The restaurant serves generous portions of the homemade special of the day. ✉ *Vikavegur 39, FR–700 Klaksvík,* ☎ *298/55333. 34 rooms. No credit cards.*

$ ⊞ **Youth Hostel and Guest House Ibuð.** This youth and family hostel, the only one on the northern islands, is in a former hotel, built in 1945. It is near a ferry slip and surrounded by hiking trails. ✉ *Garðavegur 31, FR–700 Klaksvík,* ☎ *298/55403 or 298/57555. 28 youth hostel beds, 8 guest house beds. No credit cards.*

Viðareiði

18 km (11 mi) north of Klaksvík.

The island of Viðoy is among the wildest and most beautiful of the islands, with mountains of 2,800 ft and sheer cliffs plunging into extremely rough, unnavigable waters. Amazingly, 600 people live here, many in the town of Viðareiði. Cape Enniberg, at its northernmost tip, reaches 2,460 ft; it's the world's highest cape rising directly from the sea. From the town of Viðareiði you can take a boat tour (call Tora Tourist Travel; ☞ The Faroe Islands A to Z, *below*) to see many seabirds nesting on cliff walls, including kittiwakes and puffins—endearing little black-and-white birds with enormous orange beaks. The Faroese have a remarkable relationship with the puffins, harvesting them by the thousands for food and yet not endangering their numbers.

Lodging

$ ⊞ **Hotel Norð.** In a small town of 300 inhabitants on the northern end of the island, this simple business hotel has beautiful surroundings and great bird-watching. ✉ *FR–750 Viðareiði,* ☎ *298/51061,* ℻ *298/ 51144. 20 beds. No credit cards. Closed Oct.–May.*

Miðvágur

18 km (11 mi) west of Tórshavn.

Vágar, the third-largest island, takes its name from its fjords, and it is cut by three of them, as well as by the Fjallavatn and Sørvágsvatn lakes, the last of which is fed by the Bøsdalafossur, a 100-ft waterfall. The main town here is Miðvágur, an excellent perch for auk- and gannet-watching.

Lodging

$$ ⊞ **Hotel Vágar.** A standard small hotel, this one is modern. ✉ *FR–380 Sørvágur,* ☎ *298/32955,* ℻ *298/32310. 50 beds. Restaurant. AE, DC, MC.*

Mykines

48 km (30 mi) west of Miðvágar (1 hr, 15 min by boat, 15 min by helicopter).

It's rough sailing to the tiny atoll of Mykines and only manageable when weather permits. In the town of the same name, population 15, the few dwellings are roofed with sod. The town was sited here to be close to the **Mykineshólmur,** an islet swarming with thousands of puffins, which are harvested for food. You can get here by traversing the island northward on foot about 2 km (1¼ mi) from the boat landing in Søvágur.

Sandur

25 km (16 mi) south of Tórshavn, 16 km (10 mi) south of Klaksvík.

Sandoy, the fifth-largest island, lies to the south. Relatively fertile, it's named for the sandy white beaches of the town of Sandur, on its bay. Sheep graze on green hills, and the lakes north and west of town swell with auks, purple sandpipers, and great skuas. This is great walking or biking country; bike rentals are available in town.

Vágur

64 km (40 mi) south of Tórshavn.

The southernmost island, Suðuroy, is milder than the others, with cultivated green fields at its center and mountains along the coast. Ferries from Tórshavn dock either in Vágur or the quieter village of Tvøroyri.

Lodging

$$ ⊞ **Hotel Tvøroyri.** In the middle of town, this old hotel has simple, clean rooms and minimal service. ⊠ *FR–800 Tvøroyri,* ☎ *298/71171,* FAX *298/72171. 21 beds. AE.*

$ ⊞ **Hotel Bakkin.** This plain lodging is usually booked by fishermen and local workers. ⊠ *FR–900 Vágur,* ☎ *298/73961. 18 beds. No credit cards.*

The Faroe Islands A to Z

Arriving and Departing

BY FERRY
There is frequent ferry service to all islands, with the most remote areas served by helicopter as well. Once a week in summer there are car ferries from Esbjerg (33 hours) to Tórshavn. Call **DFDS** (☎ 33/11–22–55). Year-round ferries depart from Hirtshals, Jylland on Friday and arrive in Tórshavn on Monday (48 hours), and there are regular connections to and from Aberdeen. Call **Faroeship** (☎ 39/29–26–88) for more information.

BY PLANE
SL Visitor Cards are sold at airports (☞ Getting Around, *below*). Delays due to heavy fog are common. **From Copenhagen** there are daily connections to the western island of Vágar that take about two hours. From there, count another 2½ hours to get to Tórshavn by bus and ferry. For reservations on either **Danair** or **Atlantic Airways,** call SAS (☎ 32/32–68–68) in Copenhagen or Flogfelag Føroya (☎ 298/32755) in the Faroe Islands. **Mærsk Air** (☎ 32/31–45–45 in Copenhagen; ☎ 298/11025 in Tórshavn) flies year-round between Copenhagen and Billund, on Jylland, and the Faroe Islands, with other connections available from Amsterdam, Brussels, Frankfurt, London, Paris, and Stockholm. Two weekly flights are also available from **Reykjavík** (☎ 912–5100) on **Icelandair,** which also flies once a week, in the summer, from Glasgow to the Faroes and on to Iceland.

Getting Around

BY BUS, FERRY, AND HELICOPTER
The main islands are connected by regular ferries; smaller ones are linked by mailboat and helicopter. The **SL Visitor Card** is a good value for exploring the islands; it affords free passage on all SL (the local transportation company) buses and ferries. Be sure to buy the card at the airport (or from your travel agent) to pay for the trip to Tórshavn. It costs DKr385 for four days, DKr600 for seven days, DKr900 for 14 days; it's half-price for children under 13, free for those under 7 years old. For ferries, call **Strandfaraskip Landsins** (☎ 298/14550, FAX /298/

16000) in Tórshavn. **Helicopter Service** (☎ 298/33410) is available in Vagar. In towns, and between islands that are connected by bridges, there is regular bus service. For schedules and reservations, call **Bygdaleiðir** (☎ 298/14550) in Tórshavn.

BY CAR

Driving laws are the same as in Denmark. Car rentals are available in Tórshavn and at Vagar Airport. A network of two-lane asphalt roads has been built between towns, using tunnels and bridges. The roads are best on the nine main islands. Speed limits are 50 kph (30 mph) in urban areas, 80 kph (50 mph) outside. Once outside towns, beware of untethered animals.

Contacts and Resources

EMERGENCIES

Ambulance, fire, police (☎ 000).

Pharmacy: Tórshavn (✉ by SMS shopping center, ☎ 298/11100). **Klaksvik** (✉ Klaksvíksvegur, ☎ 298/55055. **Tvøroyri Pharmacy** (☎ 298/71076).

GUIDED TOURS

In addition to the local tours offered by many hotels, two main tour operators on the islands, **Kunningarstovan** (✉ Vaglid, Tórshavn, ☎ 298/15788) and **Tora Tourist Travel** (✉ N. Finsensgøta, Tórshavn, ☎ 298/15505), offer angling, city, and bird-watching tours.

Bird-Watching–Cave Tours: Tora Tourist Travel runs tours to Vestmanna Birdcliffs Tour (six hours), which includes a look at bird colonies and nearby caves.

Boat–Fishing Tours: Tours of Nolsoy and Hestur (Kunningarstovan) leave from Tórshavn harbor and include coastal sailing through the Kapilsund strait and along Hestur's west coast to see puffins and other seabirds. The three-hour trips are aboard the 50-year-old wooden schooner *Nordlys* (*Northern Light*), and guests may even get a chance to do some fishing.

Sightseeing Tours: Tora Tourist Travel organizes a tour to Gjógv, the northernmost village on Eysturoy (five hours), including a view of mountains and a local village.

VISITOR INFORMATION

The helpful brochure *Around the Faroe Islands,* is published by the tourist board. In Copenhagen, call the **Faroese Government Office** (✉ Højbropl. 7, ☎ 33/14–08–66). The **Danish Tourist Board** (branches in Denmark and abroad) can also supply information.

Klaksvík Tourist Information (✉ N. Palsgøta, FR–700 Klaksvík, ☎ 298/56939). **Aldan Tourist Information** (✉ Reyngøta 17, FR–100 Tórshavn, ☎ 298/19391).

9 Portraits of Denmark

Denmark at a Glance: A Chronology

The Utterly Danish Pastries of Denmark

Tivoli

Books and Videos

DENMARK AT A GLANCE: A CHRONOLOGY

ca. 10,000 Stone Age culture develops in Denmark.

ca. 2,000 Tribes from southern Europe, mostly Germanic peoples, migrate toward Denmark.

ca. 500 Migration of Celts across central Europe impinges on Denmark's trade routes with the Mediterranean world. Trade becomes less economically crucial because of the growing use of abundant iron.

ca. 770 The Viking Age begins. For the next 250 years, Scandinavians set sail on frequent expeditions stretching from the Baltic to the Irish seas, and even to the Mediterranean as far as Sicily, employing superior ships and weapons and efficient military organization.

830 Frankish monk Ansgar makes one of the first attempts to Christianize Sweden and builds the first church in Slesvig, Denmark.

1016–35 Canute (Knud) the Great is king of England, Denmark (1018), and Norway (1028).

1070 Adam of Bremen composes *History of the Archbishops of Hamburg-Bremen,* the first important contemporary source for Danish history.

1169 King Valdemar, who was acknowledged as the single king of Denmark in 1157 and undertook repeated crusades against the Germans, captures Rugen and places it under Danish rule, signifying the beginning of the Danish medieval empire. It culminates in 1219 when Valdemar marches to Estonia and builds a fortress at Ravel. In 1225, Valdemar, after being kidnapped by a German vassal, is forced to give up all his conquests, except for Rugen and Estonia, in exchange for freedom.

1282 At a meeting of the Hof, or Danish Parliament, Danish king Erik Glipping signs a coronation charter that becomes the first written constitution of Denmark.

1370 The Treaty of Stralsund gives the north German trading centers of the Hanseatic League free passage through Danish waters and full control of Danish herring fisheries for 15 years. German power increases throughout Scandinavia.

1397 The Kalmar union is formed as a result of the dynastic ties between Sweden, Denmark, and Norway, the geographical position of the Scandinavian states, and the growing influence of Germans in the Baltic. Erik of Pomerania is crowned king of the Kalmar Union.

1479 University of Copenhagen is founded.

1520 Christian II, ruler of the Kalmar Union, executes 82 people who oppose the Scandinavian union, an event known as the "Stockholm bloodbath." Sweden secedes from the Union three years later. Norway remains tied to Denmark and becomes a Danish province in 1536.

1534 Count Christoffer of Oldenburg and his army demand the restoration of Christian II as king of Denmark, initiating civil war between supporters of Christian II and supporters of Prince Christian (later King Christian III).

1611–16 The Kalmar War: Denmark wages war against Sweden in hopes of restoring the Kalmar Union.

1611–60 Gustav II Adolphus reigns in Sweden. Under his rule, Sweden defeats Denmark in the Thirty Years' War and becomes the greatest power in Scandinavia as well as northern and central Europe.

1660 Peace of Copenhagen establishes modern boundaries of Denmark, Sweden, and Norway.

1754 Royal Danish Academy of Fine Arts is established.

1762 The duke of Gottorp becomes czar of Russia and declares war on Denmark. Catherine, the czar's wife, overrules her husband's war declaration and makes a peaceful settlement.

1801–14 The Napoleonic wars are catastrophic for Denmark economically and politically: the policy of armed neutrality fails, the English destroy the Danish fleet in 1801, Copenhagen is devastated at the bombardment of 1807, and Sweden, after Napoléon's defeat at the Battle of Leipzig, attacks Denmark and forces the Danish surrender of Norway. The Danish monarchy is left with three parts: the Kingdom of Denmark and the duchies of Schleswig and Holstein.

1849 Denmark's absolute monarchy is abolished and replaced by the liberal June Constitution, which establishes freedom of the press, freedom of religion, the right to hold meetings and form associations, and rule by Parliament with two elected chambers as well as the king and his ministers.

ca. 1850 The building of railroads begins in Scandinavia.

1864 Denmark goes to war against Prussia and Austria; the hostilities end with the Treaty of Vienna, which forces Denmark to surrender the duchies of Schleswig and Holstein to Prussia and Austria.

1914 At the outbreak of World War I, Germany forces Denmark to lay mines in an area of international waters known as the Great Belt. Because the British fleet makes no serious attempts to break through, Denmark is able to maintain neutrality.

1917 Danish writer Henrik Pontoppidan is awarded the Nobel prize for literature.

1918 Iceland becomes a separate state under the Danish crown; only foreign affairs remain under Danish control. Sweden, Denmark, and Norway grant women the right to vote.

1920 Scandinavian countries join the League of Nations.

1929–37 The first social democratic governments take office in Denmark, Sweden, and Finland.

ca. 1930 The Great Depression causes unemployment, affecting 40% of the organized industrial workers in Denmark.

1939 Denmark and the other Nordic countries declare neutrality in World War II.

1940 Germany occupies Norway and Denmark.

1949 Denmark, Norway, and Iceland become members of NATO. Sweden and Finland decline membership.

1952 The Nordic Council, which promotes cooperation among the Nordic parliaments, is founded.

1972 Sweden, on the basis of its neutral foreign policy, and Norway decline membership in the EU; Denmark becomes a member in 1973. Queen Margarethe II ascends the throne of Denmark.

1982   Poul Schluter becomes Denmark's first Conservative prime minister since 1894.

1989   Tycho Brahe Planetarium opens in Copenhagen; and Denmark becomes the first NATO country to allow women to join front-line military units. Denmark becomes the first country in the world to recognize marriage between citizens of the same sex.

1991   The Karen Blixen Museum, in Rungstedlund, Denmark, is founded.

1992   Denmark declines to support the Maastricht Treaty setting up a framework for European economic union. Denmark wins the European Soccer Championships.

1993   Denmark is the president of the EU for the first half of 1993. In a second referendum, the country votes to support the Maastricht Treaty, as well as its own modified involvement in it. Tivoli celebrates its 150th year, Legoland celebrates its 25th birthday, and the Little Mermaid turns 80. Denmark also commemorates the 50th anniversary of the World War II rescue of Danish Jews, in which they were smuggled into Sweden.

1995   The 50th anniversary of the end of World War II in Europe is celebrated, especially in Denmark and Norway, where May 5 marks the end of the German occupation.

1996   Copenhagen is fêted as the Cultural Capital of Europe.

1997   Copenhagen's venerable Carlsberg Brewery, one of the largest supporters of the arts in Denmark, celebrates its 150th anniversary.

THE UTTERLY DANISH PASTRIES OF DENMARK

IBELIEVE above and beyond every gastronomic specialty a country offers, there is one, just one, perfect, delicious bit or bite or drop of something or another that sums up everything the country is and ever has been. As a transplanted American living in Denmark, I long thought the country's perfect bite was the *smørrebrød,* or open-face sandwiches: they are practical, well designed, and small—in essence everything Denmark is. Over time, however, I have revised my theory. Today, I believe that divine bite can be found in the pastries, the Danish pastries.

Take a stroll through Copenhagen, and before long, you'll have to make an effort to pass up the bakeries, to steel yourself not to try one of the flaky sweets. But then again, why should you? A Danish is effortlessly elegant, unobtrusively hedonistic, and often packed with a surprise—an edible metaphor of the Danish experience.

Imagine this: you are walking through Copenhagen, and you happen to meander off Strøget, the store-crammed and remarkably congested pedestrian spine. Immediately, you notice the pace of the city slows. Antique shops sidle up to cafés while, a block away, rows of half-timbered houses lined with thick squares of convex windows wiggle to nowhere. At the tip of Gammel Strand, literally the old beach, you spy a lone fisherwoman in worn shawls and head scarves hawking live eel and smoked herring. You wind back to the more-than-150-year-old La Glace, purported to be the oldest confectionery shop in Copenhagen. Decorous ladies in aprons serve you a dainty china pot of coffee and light, crisp, and exceedingly Danish, pastries.

Not just any sweets these—not French, nor Austrian—and certainly not those suspicious-looking pillows of white dough injected with Red Stuff you chance to order in the United States, but the real McCoy, made in the same way since the 19th century. It makes me wonder why the Danes

don't lay claim to the name, and insist upon it as an *appellation d'origine.*

THE FIRST TIME I had a Danish pastry, at the source, was 14 years ago, when the Dane of my affections (my husband today) introduced me to Copenhagen. A late night of debauchery had turned into an early morning amble, when Jesper and his best friend, Jan Erik, assured me that pastries would cure all of our ails. Though most bakeries don't open until 6 AM, Jan Erik went to a side door and rapped on its top window. Shady conversation with a young, flour-dusted blade ensued, and paper bags and cash were quickly exchanged. (I was never clear if it was law or legend, but in those days, most Danes believed the police enforced regular shopping hours.) Prize in hand, we strolled to Peblinge Sø, one of the city's lakes, where we sat on a bench, drank from a carton of milk, and ate several flaky pastries topped with nuts and sugar icings and filled with marmalades and creams. As the sun rose, defining the ducks, swans, and an occasional heron, I felt enormously happy just to be there.

Those who record such events mark the birth of the Danish pastry sometime at the end of the 19th century, when Danish bakers went on strike, demanding money rather than room and board as payment for their work. Their employers replaced them with Austrian bakers, who brought with them the mille-feuille, or puff pastry, which they learned to make from the French. Once the Danes were back at work, they adopted the continental dough, making it their own by adding yeast and sweet fillings.

It was a tradition at the time (and to a lesser degree today) for Danish bakers to travel abroad to add to their repertoire. This pastry cross-pollination helps explain why the yeast-risen puff pastry is called *Kopenhagener Geback,* literally "Copenhagen bread," in Austria, and Danish pastry in America. Ironically, the yeast-risen pastries are still called *wienerbrød,* or Vienna bread, in Denmark.

What makes Danish pastries special is the production process, which for most bakers is still done by hand. Essentially, the dough—milk, flour, eggs, butter, sugar, and yeast—is made, then chilled. It is then rolled into a rectangle, and, unapologetically, a slab of margarine or butter is put on the center third. The two ends of the dough are folded over the butter, and the process is repeated three times, until there are 27 layers in all.

Once the dough has been rolled and chilled, it is finally shaped into pretzel forms (called *kringle*), as well as braids, squares, triangles, fans, combs, swirls, pinwheels, horns, crescents, and wreaths, and filled with *remonce,* the stupefyingly rich butter, sugar, and nut (or marzipan) combination. The word remonce only sounds French; since it was very fashionable in 19th-century Denmark to give things French-ified names, a Danish baker is said to have invented the word. Ask for it in Paris, and, no doubt, you will be met with bewilderment.

In addition to the remonce, Danish bakers also fill their pastries with raisins, fruit compotes, and vanilla and—to a lesser degree—chocolate custards. As Gert Sørensen, the chief baker and owner of Konditoriet in Tivoli, says "The final product should be crisp on the outside, juicy on the inside."

He should know: as one of the country's most respected pastry chefs, he has been educating and enlightening generations of young pastry stars. In fact, not just anyone can be a *konditor,* as they are known in Denmark. The rigorous education takes three years and seven months, and entails basic economics as well as an apprenticeship at a bakery, making wienerbrød daily. Danes are happy to consume the schoolwork, and do so at breakfast, after lunch, or with their afternoon coffee, especially on the weekends. Copenhagen alone boasts more than 150 of Denmark's 1,400 bakeries, the latter pulling in the equivalent of $727 million annually, about 20 percent of which is attributable to wienerbrød. At an average cost of 5 kroner (roughly 91 cents), I figure that's close to 30 million pastries a year.

Trying to pick the best of Copenhagen's—let alone Denmark's—pastries is like hunting down France's best truffle. Though Denmark's pastry chefs participate in a number of national and international pastry contests (and consistently rank among the world's best), nearly every Dane has found a bakery within a five-minute cycling radius of home that they claim to be the best in the land. My own allegiance is to the bakery named Bosse, in the neighborhood of Østerbro. I often find my bed-headed self wandering there on Saturday morning to buy a bagful of pastries with names like rum snail, marzipan horn, and my husband's favorite, a rum ball, essentially the sausage of pastries, all the leftover bits rolled together and often covered with chocolate sprinkles. My own favorites include the *spandauer,* a flat swirl of dough, centered with vanilla custard, and the marzipan horn, a crispy twirl of pastry rolled up with remonce. Even though these may not be the finest pastries in town, they are the genuine article, and uncommonly Danish.

But, there's much more to Danish pastries than wienerbrød. At La Glace the windows display delicate special-occasion cakes like those for baptisms, trimmed with marzipan pacifiers, cradles, and dolls. From her original 1920 pink, green, and gold tea room, proprietor Marianne Stagetorn Kolos explains that most guests come for her layer cakes, like the best-selling *Sportskage,* a mound of macaroons, whipped cream, and caramel chunks created and named for a play performed at the nearby Folketeatret in 1891. It's a Danish custom to name confections for events and personalities, but there was a time when ordering a miniature Sarah Bernhardt, a chocolate-truffle-covered macaroon named for the French actress, was an act of courage. During World War II, resistance fighters and sympathizers recognized one another by ordering the pastry as a "radio macaroon," since it resembles an old-fashioned radio knob. The name stuck.

Close by, on a quiet cobblestoned courtyard, is the Kransekagehuset, where confectioner Jørgen Jensen makes the marzipan cakes compulsory at any Danish wedding. Using 1 kilogram marzipan to 400 grams sugar to 200 grams egg whites, Jensen molds the dough into rings of varying sizes. Once baked, they are fashioned into cones or cornucopias, squiggled with white icing, decked with paper decorations, or filled with wrapped candies.

I know the *kransekage* intimately. At our wedding years ago, Jesper and I split the difference in our Italian-Armenian-American-Danish backgrounds, and ordered two cakes, one of which was a kransekage laced with Danish and American flags, and tiny, shiny-paper firecrackers that made a polite, little bang.

"It's something special," smiles Jensen. "It's something very Danish."

— By Karina Porcelli

TIVOLI

AWOMAN IS TELLING ME about her life and her travels in a poetic English that, I am sure, despite being a native English speaker, I will never master.

"I came to Tivoli for the first time when I was five," she says in a lilting Danish accent. "My parents made me take a nap first, because they said it would be like the fairy-tales."

Erna Wahlin stretches her feet and points them high in the purple evening air. She sits next to Elly Larsen, two years her junior, at 86 years old. The downy-haired octogenarians prattle on about the quality of the coffee, the flakiness of the pastries, the way young people dress, and the magic of their beloved Tivoli.

Behind them, thousands of green, yellow, and purple lights twinkle as the first bulbs of the evening blink. The air fills with a gushing waltz that dissolves to the squeals of children as they are flung skyward in Ferris wheels and motorized swans. Coifed teens bound towards a ride, nearly toppling an elderly couple in mid-smooch. A young couple pushes a baby carriage, adangle with paper cocktail umbrellas, toward the Peacock Theater, and teenagers romance awkwardly in the corners of the Japanese Garden.

Tivoli's innocence is catching, especially on sunny days when Danes and tourists flock to its neat lanes and flower gardens to enjoy an old-fashioned amusement park with nothing Disneyesque about it. In the Copenhagen scheme of things—where mothers park baby carriages (contents snoozing) outside bakeries, where businessfolk talk on mobile phones while cycling to work, and where blonds-like-only-Scandinavians-can-be blonds drink Carlsberg in public parks—Tivoli fits right in. It shares a chicken-and-egg relationship with the capital: which came first? Tivoli or Copenhagen's quixotic ways?

Tivoli still blurs the line between formal European garden and old-time amusement park. In April, when the soggy northern winter retreats and the days lengthen in hyper-speed succession, the Danes are ready to throw off the chill and celebrate. It is time for Tivoli. In the relatively short five-month season, more than four million people come through the gates—an impressive figure considering the population of Denmark just hovers over five million.

Though the number of visitors has grown, the park has not changed radically since the 19th century, when Danish architect George Carstensen persuaded King Christian VIII to let him build an amusement park. He argued the park would be an opiate for people of all classes and backgrounds, and "when people amuse themselves, they forget politics."

TIVOLI WAS ORIGINALLY BUILT on the edge of Copenhagen's fortifications, among cows and countrysides. As the city was still scarred by the bloody battles between Denmark and England (it was here Lord Nelson turned his famous blind eye, and bombed Copenhagen to bits), the park rose up like an apparition. It sprouted quirky Oriental and Moorish architecture inspired by Carstensen's privileged childhood in Algiers, where his father had been Danish Consul General.

On August 15, 1843, the day Tivoli officially opened, most visitors were enchanted by the exotic park, including Hans Christian Andersen, so inspired he wrote his tale, *The Nightingale*. Others, including the press, thought Carstensen foolish to encourage the social classes to mix. Danish history recalls Carstensen a braggart—a condition even modern Danes dislike. As his popularity declined, Carstensen decided to test his political and entrepreneurial talents abroad, but, eventually returned to Copenhagen bankrupt. The story goes he was not recognized when he returned to the gardens he founded, and had to enter through the turnstiles a paying visitor.

Unlike many famous amusement parks around the world, Tivoli is not in a dislocated expanse, far from the city. Rather, it is the heart of the city. The main entrance on Vesterbrogade welcomes visitors with a grand arched portal and shaded walking paths. They lead to more than 20 verdant acres, punctuated throughout with flower-trimmed fountains, covered stages, and outdoor pavilions. Not including the independently run Jazzhus Slukefter and Vise Vers Huset, a bar featuring folk music, seven separate venues offer entertainment. Performances range from children's theater to classical concerts featuring luminaries like violinist Anne-Sophie Mutter, flutist Jean-Pierre Rampal, and Denmark's own musical jester Victor Borge.

Any self-respecting amusement park has rides, and Tivoli is no exception. Its 28 rides are settled unobtrusively along its perimeter, and have always been a part of the whole, rather than a central, attraction. The roller coaster existed at Carstensen's time, along with a freak show and shooting gallery, but all of that has disappeared, and the roller coaster is, thankfully, a newer model from 1914. The rides have been built over the years—all with benign names like "The Wild Swans" and "Tubs Ahoy"—to take passengers on mildly butterfly-inducing flights. Though other parks tout coiled innards of gut-wrenching, scream-spewing, warp-speed chaos, children and roller-coaster buffs seem perfectly happy at Tivoli.

When it comes to eating and drinking, the Danes enjoy their food, whether it be a five-course meal or a paper bag of hand-picked Gummy Bears. At last count, 30 sit-down restaurants trimmed the park, plus dozens of sausage stands and candy counters for grazing. I have a weakness for the ice-cream cones: freshly baked waffles rolled and filled with triple-scoops of rich ice cream, a dollop each of strawberry jam and whipped cream, topped with the world's largest chocolate-covered marshmallow.

AS WITH MANY THINGS Danish, there is a sense of poignancy in Tivoli. If one buys 50 season passes over the course of so many years, management will provide them season passes for the rest of their life. Carefully dressed pensioners in fine hats and heavy shoes walk as they lean against each other, then collapse on shaded benches.

Two fine ladies sip coffee and share a cigar. A grandfather and grandson totter in parallel infirmity towards a photographer, and offer compositional advice. Tivoli is their park, and Danes young and especially old, lay claim to it. I raise a *skal* to a man celebrating his 70th birthday.

"Have you heard they have opened a Tivoli in Japan?" I ask. He scoffs, and takes a long draw of his beer. "Tivoli is Denmark," he says. "How can you translate that?"

Insubordination and an astringent sense of humor, especially in the face of foreign authority, have always been Danish attributes. During World War II when the Nazis demanded Jews wear identifying stars, the Danish king, Christian V, put one on first, his loyal subjects quickly following suit. Later when Denmark's resistance was growing in bravery and infamy, the Germans retaliated by striking Tivoli, destroying its most characteristic buildings. Quietly defiant, the Danes built a tent Tivoli within the week, and resumed their promenades.

Things are more peaceful these days, but it appears the pace of modern life does not enter these gates. In a country where personal income tax exceeds 50 percent, and most shops close at 5:30 PM Monday through Thursday, commerce is secondary to the process of life. When Michael Jackson visited the park in the early '90s, local legend says he asked to buy it, but was politely told it was not for sale. While Tivoli glitters with fine restaurants and silver and porcelain boutiques, there are no rabid barkers waving cotton candy, no oily hucksters pushing the arcade games. Tivoli employees, Danish or not, are uniformly neat, polite, and available when needed. Rides are exhilarating, but really, there isn't a hell-raiser in the place.

The gardens enchant even those whose botanical knowledge barely differentiates between trees and grass. Radiant roses face violet thistle, Dutch tulips bow to a dapple of daisies. Their numbers astound: the park contains 864 trees and 400,000 flowers, including 65,000 tulips and 55,000 narcissi. In a single year, upwards of 135,000 new bulbs are planted. Despite their quantity, subtlety is key. The trees, including sprays of willow and bamboo, thrive in natural splendor, and are not carved into obtuse topiaries. Understatement, again, is everything.

LIFE IS NOT A PROBLEM TO BE solved, but a reality to be experienced," said Søren Kierkegaard, Denmark's famed existentialist, in a rare moment of levity. So true, my Danish husband Jesper agrees, before hopping atop a giant, red plastic fish. This is the Tivoli of the weird. I have brought a group of American and British friends to visit the park, and Jesper is telling them about the now defunct flea circus of his childhood, when an old man trained a pack of infinitesimal acrobats to fling themselves across a tiny trapeze. Our friends eye him suspiciously as they stroll to one of 20 arcades, "Det Muntre Kokken," or the Crazy Kitchen, where mild-mannered men and women take out their frustrations by hurling, pitching, launching, slinging, heaving, lobbing, and slamming white tennis-size balls into hundreds of real porcelain dishes.

Nearby, in placid Lake Tivoli, elegant black New Zealand swans and plebeian ducks paddle to their huts, but, this being Denmark, some wade to their pink summer duck villa. More than mere waterfowl, these lucky ducks have few worries, though I reconsider when my three-year-old daughter begins to feed them bits of a leftover pastry. There is an altercation: a giant carp two feet long—it's mouth an alarming "O"— raises its huge head out of the water and displaces a perplexed mallard.

Then it is show time at the Peacock Theater, where pantomime in the Italian tradition of commedia dell'arte, is complete with Pierrot, harlequin, Cassandra, and Columbine. Only Pierrot may speak, a result of an accident sometime around the turn of the century, when a dancer's skirt caught fire, and the audience demanded an explanation. As is typical in Denmark, the experience turned into ritual, which survives today. At the end of the performance, children on grown-up shoulders plead a few words from the elegant joker, and reward with a hearty hurrah.

Night-time transforms Tivoli into a delicate pattern of illuminated curlicues and brightly lit archways. Electric dragonflies flutter atop the lake, and weeping willows twined with white lights tremble. Denmark is the only country outside the United States to celebrate American Independence Day, and Tivoli's midnight fireworks are decidedly not big bang, but delicate twists of gold and silver. The Barfoed fireworks family has been illuminating the park since it opened more than 150 years ago, and will do so again this year, as the sixth generation volleys just enough magic into the dusky sky. White bouquets of light rise and fall and boom, then wink to black. The audience oohs and aahs, and leaves Tivoli wanting just a little bit more.

— By Karina Porcelli

BOOKS AND VIDEOS

Books

A History of the Vikings (Oxford University Press, 1984) recounts the story of the aggressive warriors and explorers who during the Middle Ages influenced a large portion of the world, extending from Constantinople to America. Gwyn Jones's lively account makes learning the history enjoyable.

Excellent reading on Denmark includes the works of Karen Blixen (Isak Dinesen) set in Denmark; *Pelle the Conqueror* (volumes I and II) by Martin Andersen Nexø (a novel about a young Swedish boy and his father who work on a stone farm in Bornholm under hateful Danish landowners); *Laterna Magica* by William Heinesen (a novel of the Faroe Islands by perhaps Denmark's greatest writer since Karen Blixen); and the satirical trilogy by Hans Scherfig—*Stolen Spring, The Missing Bureaucrat,* and *Idealists.* Wallace Stegner's novel *The Spectator Bird* follows a man's exploration of his Danish heritage. Peter Høeg's acclaimed novel *Smilla's Sense of Snow* is a compulsive page-turner that paints a dark and foreboding picture of Copenhagen and the waters around Greenland; the movie version debuted in 1997. Fjord Press (Box 16349, Seattle, WA 98116, ☎ 206/935–7376, FAX 206/938–1991) has one of the most comprehensive selections of Danish fiction in translation of any publisher in the United States.

Films of Interest

Babette's Feast, which won the Oscar for the best foreign film of 1987, was produced in Denmark. Danny Kaye starred in the 1952 film *Hans Christian Andersen.* In fact, his crooning of "Wonderful Copenhagen" became Denmark's official tourism slogan. Disney's *The Little Mermaid* is a great way to get your kids interested in Andersen's fairy tales.

DANISH VOCABULARY

English	Danish	Pronunciation

Basics

English	Danish	Pronunciation
Yes/no	Ja/nej	yah/nie
Thank you	Tak	tak
You're welcome	Selv tak	**sell** tak
Excuse me (to apologize)	Undskyld	**unsk**-ul
Hello	Hej	hi
Goodbye	Farvel	fa-**vel**
Today	I dag	ee **day**
Tomorrow	I morgen	ee **morn**
Yesterday	I går	ee **gore**
Morning	Morgen	**more**-n
Afternoon	Eftermiddag	**ef-tah**-mid-day
Night	Nat	nat

Numbers

1	een/eet	een/eet
2	to	toe
3	tre	treh
4	fire	fear
5	fem	fem
6	seks	sex
7	syv	syoo
8	otte	**oh**-te
9	ni	nee
10	ti	tee

Days of the Week

Monday	mandag	man-day
Tuesday	tirsdag	**tears**-day
Wednesday	onsdag	**ons**-day
Thursday	torsdag	**trs**-day
Friday	fredag	**free**-day
Saturday	lørdag	**lore**-day
Sunday	søndag	**soo**(n)-day

Useful Phrases

Do you speak English?	Taler du engelsk?	te-ler doo in-galsk
I don't speak Danish.	Jeg taler ikke Dansk.	yi tal-ler **ick** Dansk
I don't understand.	Jeg forstår ikke.	yi fahr-store **ick**
I don't know.	Det ved jeg ikke.	deh **ved** yi ick
I am American/British.	Jeg er amerikansk/britisk.	yi ehr a-mehr-i-**kansk**/ bri-**tisk**
I am sick.	Jeg er syg.	yi ehr **syoo**

Please call a doctor.	Kan du ringe til en læge?	can **doo** rin-geh til en lay-eh
Do you have a vacant room?	Har du et værelse?	har **doo** eet va(l)r-sa
How much does it cost?	Hvad koster det?	va cos-ta **deh**
It's too expensive.	Det er for dyrt.	deh ehr **fohr** dyrt
Beautiful	Smukt	smukt
Help!	Hjælp	yelp
Stop!	Stop	stop
How do I get to . . .	Hvordan kommer jeg til . . .	vore-**dan** kom-mer yi til
. . . the train station?	banegarden	**ban** eh-gore-en
. . . the post office?	postkontoret	**post**-kon-toh-raht
. . . the tourist office?	turistkonoret	too-**reest**-kon-tor-et
. . . the hospital?	hospitalet	hos-peet-**tal**-et
Does this bus go to . . . ?	Går denne bus til . . . ?	**goh** den-na boos til
Where is the W.C.?	Hvor er toilettet?	vor **ehr** toi-le(tt)-et
On the left	Til venstre	til **ven**-strah
On the right	Till højre	til **hoy**-ah
Straight ahead	Lige ud	**lee** u(l)

Dining Out

Please bring me . . .	Må jeg få . . .	mo yi foh
menu	menu	me-**nu**
fork	gaffel	gaf-**fel**
knife	kniv	kan-**ew**
spoon	ske	skee
napkin	serviet	serv-**eet**
bread	brød	brood
butter	smør	smoor
milk	mælk	malk
pepper	peber	**pee**-wer
salt	salt	selt
sugar	sukker	**su**-kar
water/bottled water	vand/Dansk vand	van/dansk van
The check, please.	Må jeg bede om regningen.	mo yi bi(d) om **ri**-ning

INDEX

A

Aalborg, 78–80
Adventure tours, xxxi
Ærøskøbing, 67–68
Åholm Automobile Museum, 54
Air travel, xii–xiv
airlines, xii
Bornholm, 93
with children, xv–xvi
Copenhagen, 39–40
Faroe Islands, 112
Fyn, 68
Greenland, 102–103
Jylland, 81
Sjælland, 56
Airports, xiv
Åkirke, 92
Åkirkeby, 92
Ålholm Slot, 54
Allinge, 88–89
Almindingen, 92
Amager Museum, 38
Amalienborg, 17, 26–27, 29–30
Amalienborg Museum, 17
Amalienhaven, 17
Ammassalik, 102
Andersen, Hans Christian, 14, 17, 19, 53, 61, 62, 69
Arbejdermuseet, 20
Århus, 76–77
Assens, 64
ATMs, xxv

B

Ballet, 33
Bars
Copenhagen, 31
Fyn, 63
Jylland, 77
Beaches, 4
Bornholm, 85
Copenhagen, 34
Sjælland, 53
Better Business Bureau, xvi
Bicycling, xxvi–xxvii, 4–5
Bornholm, 93
Copenhagen, 34, 40, 42
Fyn, 59, 68
Jylland, 82
Sjælland, 45
tours, xxxi, 42
Billund, 74
Bird watching, 113
Blixen, Karen, 14, 45–46
Boat tours
Bornholm, 94
Copenhagen, 42
Faroe Islands, 109, 113
Fyn, 62
Greenland, 103
Sjælland, 56
Boating, 5

BonBon Land, 55
Books, 124
Bornholm, 4, 84–94
the arts, 86, 88
beaches, 85
emergencies, 93
guided tours, 93–94
hotels, 86, 88–89, 90, 91
nightlife, 86, 88
pharmacies, 93
restaurants, 86, 91
shopping, 87, 89, 90, 91, 92
sightseeing, 85–92, 94
sports, 85, 86–87, 90, 91–92
transportation, 92–93
visitor information, 94
Bornholm Kunst Museum, 89
Bornholm Museum, 86
Børsen, 10–11
Botanisk Have, 20
Brandts Klædefabrik, 62
Brewery, 20–21
Budolfi Kirke, 78–79
Bus travel, xiv
Bornholm, 92, 93
Copenhagen, 40
Faroe Islands, 112
Fyn, 68–69
Jylland, 82
Business hours, xxvi
By Museum, 48

C

Cafés, 31
Cameras, camcorders and computers, xiv
Camping, xxiii–xxiv, 88–89
Canoeing
Jylland, 71
Sjælland, 45, 55
Car rentals, xiv–xv, 41
Car travel
Bornholm, 93
Copenhagen, 39, 41
driving, xix–xx
Faroe Islands, 113
Fyn, 68, 69
Jylland, 81, 82
Sjælland, 55–56
Carl Nielsen Museum, 61
Carlsberg Bryggeri, 20–21
Carlsberg Museum, 21
Carmelite Kloster, 48
Castles, 6
Copenhagen, 10, 11, 16, 17, 20, 21–22
Fyn, 59, 61, 66–67
Sjælland, 46–48, 48–49, 53, 54, 57
Charlottenborg, 16, 17
Children, traveling with, xv–xvi
Christiania, 11
Christiansborg Slot, 6, 10, 11, 23, 26, 28–29
Christianshavn, 10, 11

Christianskirkjan, 110
Christiansø, 90
Chronology of Denmark, 115–117
Churches, 6
Bornholm, 90, 92
Copenhagen, 10, 14–15, 16, 17, 18, 19, 23
Faroe Islands, 109, 110
Fyn, 62
Greenland, 98, 101
Jylland, 73, 74–75, 78–79, 80
Sjælland, 48, 50, 52
Climate, xxxiii–xxxiv
Consumer protection, xvi
Convent, 48
Copenhagen, 4, 8–43
the arts, 33
car rentals, 41
casino, 31–32
Christianshavn, 10, 11
climate, xxxiv
currency exchanges, 41
doctors and dentists, 41
embassies, 41–42
emergencies, 41–42
English-language bookstores, 42
excursions, 38–39
guided tours, 42–43
hotels, 24–25, 28–31
Istedgade district, 20, 21
Kongens Nytorv, 16, 18
nightlife, 31–33
Nyboder, 19
Nyhavn, 16, 19
pharmacies, 43
Rådhus Pladsen, 15, 23, 26, 28–29
restaurants, 18, 23–28
shopping, 21, 35–38
sightseeing, 9–23
sports, 34–35
Strøget district, 10, 15, 23, 26, 28–29
taxis, 41
transportation, 39–41
travel agencies, 43
Vesterbro area, 20, 23, 28, 30–31
visitor information, 43
Costs, travel, xxv
Cruising, xxxi
Currency exchange, xxv–xxvi, 41
Customs, xvi–xvii

D

Dancing and discos
Copenhagen, 32
Jylland, 77, 80
Danish design, 5
Danish pastries, 118–120
Danish vocabulary, 125–126
Danmarks Grafiske Museum, 62

Dansk Presse Museum, 62
Den Fynske Landsby, 62
Den Gamle Gård, 64
Den Lille Havfrue, 17–18
Disabilities and accessiblity,
  xviii
Discounts, xviii–xix
hotel, xxiv
travel, xv, xxi, xxxii
Dogsledging, 100, 101
Domkirke (Viborg), 78
Døndalen Forest, 89
Dragør, 38
Dragør Museum, 38
Driving, xix
Duties, xvi–xvii
Duus Vinkælder, 78, 80

E

Ebeltoft, 77–78
Egeskov Slot, 66
Eiði, 110
Ekkodalen, 92
Eksperimentarium, 38
Electricity, xx
Emergencies, xx
Bornholm, 93
Copenhagen, 41–42
Faroe Islands, 113
Fyn, 69
Greenland, 103
Jylland, 82
Sjælland, 56
Erichsens Gård, 86

F

Fåborg, 64–65
Fåborg Museum for Fynsk
  Malerkunst, 65
Falster, 53–54
Fanø, 74
Fårevejle Kirke, 50
Farm vacations, xxiv
Faroe Islands, 4, 105–113
emergencies, 113
guided tours, 113
hotels, 107, 109, 110, 111,
  112
pharmacies, 113
restaurants, 107, 109
sightseeing, 107, 109–112,
  113
transportation, 112–113
visitor information, 113
Ferries, xx–xxi
Bornholm, 93
Copenhagen, 39
Faroe Islands, 112
Fyn, 68
Jylland, 81
Festivals and seasonal
  events, 7
Jylland, 76, 77
Sjælland, 50
Film, 33
Fishing, xxvii, xxxi
Bornholm, 85
Faroe Islands, 113
Fyn, 67

Greenland, 97
Jylland, 71
Sjælland, 45
Fjords, 100
Flaskeskibssamlingen, 67–68
Folketinget, 11
Fredensborg Slot, 48–49
Frederiksberggade, 15
Frederiksborg Slot, 49
Frigate Jylland, 77–78
Frihedsmuseet, 17, 18
Frilandsmuseet, 39
Fyn and the central islands,
  4, 58–69
the arts, 59, 64, 66
casino, 64
emergencies, 69
guided tours, 69
hotels, 59–60, 62–63, 65,
  66.68
markets, 59
nightlife, 59, 63–64, 66
restaurants, 59–60, 61, 62–63,
  65, 66, 67
shopping, 60, 61, 64, 67
sports, 59, 64, 67
transportation, 68–69
visitor information, 69

G

Gamle By, 76
Gammeltorv, 15
Gardens
Copenhagen, 20, 21, 22, 23,
  121–123
Fyn, 61, 64
Gay and lesbian travel, xxi–
  xxii
gay bars, 32
Gefion Springvandet, 17, 18
Genealogy tours, xxxi
Gilleleje, 50
Glaciers, 100
Glasmuseum, 78
Golf
Bornholm, 86–87, 90, 91
Copenhagen, 34
Fyn, 64
Sjælland, 48, 51, 54, 55
Græsholmen, 90
Greenland, 4, 95–104
emergencies, 103
guided tours, 103–104
hotels, 98, 100, 101, 102
pharmacies, 104
restaurants, 100, 101, 102
sightseeing, 97–102
sports, 97
transportation, 102–103
visitor information, 104
Group tours, xxx–xxxi
Group travel, xvi
Gudhjem, 89–90
Guided tours
Bornholm, 93–94
Copenhagen, 42–43
Faroe Islands, 113
Fyn, 69
Greenland, 103–104

Jylland, 82–83
Sjælland, 56–57

H

H. C. Andersens
  Barndomshjem, 62
Hærvejen, 78
Halsskov, 55
Hammeren, 88
Hammershus, 88
Hans Christian Andersen Hus,
  61
Havnar Kirkja, 107
Health and fitness clubs, 34
Health concerns, xxii
Hellgandsklosteret, 79
Helligånds Kirken, 10, 14
Helligdomsklipperne, 89
Helsingør, 46, 48
Hiking
Bornholm, 85, 92
Greenland, 97
Hillerød, 49
Himmelbjerget, 75
Hirschsprungske Samling,
  20, 21
Hjejlen (steamer), 75
Højbro Plads, 11
Højby Kirke, 50
Højerup Kirke, 52
Højesteret, 11
Hollufgård, 62
Holmen, 11, 14
Holmens Kirken, 10, 14
Horseback riding, 34
Hospitalsdalen, 97
Hostels, youth and family,
  xxiv, xxviii
Hotels, xxiii, xxiv, 5–6. ☞
  Also under individual
  islands
Humlebæk, 46
Hvalsey Church, 98

I

Ilulissat/Jakobshavn, 100–
  101
Inns, xxiv
Insurance, xxii–xxiii
health, xxii
rental car, xv
travel, xvi, xxii–xxiii
trip cancellation, xxii
Istedgade, 20, 21

J

Jazz clubs
Copenhagen, 32–33
Fyn, 64
Jylland, 77
Jelling, 75
Jens Bang Stenhus, 78
Jomfru Ane Gade, 79
Jons Kapel, 87
Julianehåb Museum, 97
Jylland, 4, 70–83
the arts, 77, 80
beer-wine cellar, 78, 80

casinos, 75, 77, 80
emergencies, 82
guided tours, 82–83
hotels, 71, 73, 74, 75, 76–77, 79, 80
nightlife, 75, 77, 80
pharmacies, 82
restaurants, 71, 73, 74, 76–77, 79, 80
sightseeing, 71, 73–80
sports, 71
transportation, 76, 81–82
visitor information, 83

K

Kangerlussuaq/Søndre Strømfjord, *100*
Kastellet, *17, 18*
Katvaq, *98*
Kerteminde, *60–61*
Kierkegaard, Søren, *14*
Kirkjubøur, *109–110*
Klaksvík, *110–111*
Knud Rasmussens Fødehjem, *101*
Knuthenborg Safari Park, *54*
Københavns Bymuseum, *20, 21*
Københavns Synagoge, *19, 21*
Københavns Universitet, *19, 21*
Køge, *52*
Køge Kunst Museet, *52*
Køge Museum, *52*
Kolding, *71, 73*
Koldinghus, *71*
Kongaminnið, *107*
Kongelige Bibliotek, *10, 14*
Kongelige Repræsantationlokaler, *11*
Kongelige Stald, *10, 14*
Kongelige Teater, *16, 18, 33*
Kongens Have (Copenhagen), *21*
Kongens Have (Odense), *61*
Kongens Nytorv, *16, 18*
Kronborg Slot, *6, 46, 48*
Kulturhistoriske Museum, *75–76*
Kunsthallen, *62*
Kunstindustrimuseet, *17, 19*
Kværndrup, *66*

L

Ladby, *61*
Ladbyskibet, *61*
Landsbrugs Museum, *89*
Landsmuseet, *98*
Langeland, *67*
Language, *xxiii*
Danish vocabulary, *125–126*
Larsen, Johannes, *60–61*
Legoland, *74, 82*
Lejre Forsøgscenter, *52*
Lindholm Høje, *79*
Liselund Slot, *53*
Little Mermaid, The, *17–18*
Lolland, *54–55*

Louisiana Modern Art Museum, *6, 46*
Luggage, *xxvii*
Lurblæserne, *10, 14*

M

Madsebakke, *88*
Magnus Cathedral, *109*
Mail, *xxv*
Marienlyst Slot, *48*
Marmorkirken, *17, 19*
Medical assistance, *xxii*
Middelaldercentret, *53*
Miðvágur, *111*
Moesgård Forhistorisk Museum, *76*
Mølsted Museum, *38*
Monastery, *79*
Monastery clock, Dominican, *74*
Money, *xxv*
Møn, *52–53*
Møns Klint, *52–53*
Møtergården, *61*
Museet for Fotokunst, *62*
Museet for Moderne Kunst, *39*
Museums, *xxvi, 6*
Bornholm, *86, 89, 91*
Copenhagen, *10, 15–16, 17, 18, 19, 20, 21, 22, 38–39*
Fyn, *59, 61, 62, 65*
Greenland, *97, 98, 101*
Jylland, *73, 75–76, 78, 80*
Sjælland, *46, 48, 51, 52, 54*
Music, *xxxi*
Mykines, *111*
Mykineshólmur, *111*

N

Narsarsuaq, *97*
Nationalmuseet, *6, 10, 14*
Neksø, *91–92*
Neksø Museum, *91*
Nesting Box, *18*
Nielsen, Carl, *61*
Nikolaj Kirken, *10, 14–15*
Norðurlandahúsið, *107*
Nørrebro, *19–23, 30–31*
Norse ruins, *98*
Nuuk/Godthåb, *98, 100*
Ny Carlsberg Glyptotek, *20, 21*
Nyboder, *19*
Nyborg, *59–60*
Nyborg Museum, *59*
Nyborg Slot, *59*
Nyhavn, *16, 19*
Nylars, *92*
Nylars Kirke, *92*
Nytorv, *15*

O

Odense, *61–64*
Odense Castle, *61*
Odsherred, *50*
Omnimax Theater, *22*
Opera, *33*
Østerlars, *90*
Østerlars Kirke, *90*

P

Packing, *xxvii*
Palmehuset, *20*
Passports, *xxvii–xxviii*
Photography, *xiv*

Q

Qaqortoq/Julianehåb, *97–98*
Qassiarsuk, *98*
Qeqertarsuaq/Godhavn, *100*

R

Råbjerg Mile, *80*
Rådhus (Århus), *76*
Rådhus (Copenhagen), *10, 15*
Rådhus Pladsen, *15, 23, 26*
Railroad, *75*
rail passes, *xxxii*
Rasmussen, Knud, *101*
Rebild Park, *79*
Rentals, *xxiv*
Restaurants, *xvii–xviii, 5, 6.*
☞ *Also under individual islands*
Ribe, *73–74*
Ribe Domkirke, *73*
Ribes Vikinger, *73*
Rønne, *86–87*
Rø Plantage, *90*
Rock clubs, *33*
Rosenberg Slot, *6, 20, 21–22*
Roskilde, *50–51*
Roskilde Domkirke, *50*
Royal Court Theater, *15–16*
Roykstovan, *110*
Rundetårn, *20, 22*
Runestener, *75*
Rungstedlund, *45–46*
Running, *34*
Russiske Ortodoks Kirke, *19*

S

Sailing, *5*
St. Albans Church, *18*
St. Knuds Kirke, *62*
St. Olav's Church, *109*
Saksun, *110*
Sandur, *112*
Senior-citizen travel, *xxviii*
Seven Gardens, *64*
Shopping, *xxviii.* ☞ *Also under individual islands*
Silkeborg, *75–76*
Single travelers, *xxx*
Sisimiut/Holsteinsborg, *100*
Sjælland, *44–57*
the arts, *48, 51*
beaches, *53*
emergencies, *56*
guided tours, *56–57*
hotels, *48, 49, 51, 53–54, 55*
nightlife, *48, 51*
pharmacies, *56*
restaurants, *46, 48, 49, 51, 53–54*
sightseeing, *45–46, 48–55*
sports, *45, 48, 51, 54, 55*

transportation, 55–56
visitor information, 57
Sjællands Odde, 50
Skagen, 80
Skagen Museum, 80
Skálafjørður, 110
Skansin, 107
Skt. Nikolai Kirke (Køge), 52
Skt. Nikolai Kirke (Vejle), 74–75
Skt. Olai's Kirke, 48
Slættaratindur, 110
Soccer, 35
Sønderho, 74
Statens Museum for Kunst, 20, 22
Stege, 53
Storebæltsbro Udstillings Center, 55
Strøget, 10, 15, 23, 26, 28–29
Student travel, xxviii
Svaneke, 90–91
Svendborg, 65–66
Svendborgs Omegns Museum, 65
Swimming
Bornholm, 85
Copenhagen, 35
Synagogue, 21

T

Taxes, xxviii–xxix
Taxis, 41
Teatermuseum, 10, 15–16
Telephones, xxix
Tennis, 35
Terrarium, 64
Theater
Copenhagen, 16, 18, 33
Fyn, 64
Theme trips, xxxi
Thermometer, neon, and gilded barometer, 15

Thorvaldsen Museum, 10, 16
Thule, 102
Tilsandede Kirke, 80
Tinganes, 107
Tipping, xxvi
Tivoli (Århus), 76
Tivoli (Copenhagen), 20, 22, 121–123
Tjodhilde Kirke, 98
Tøjhusmuseet, 10, 16
Tórshavn, 107, 109
Tórshavn Park, 107
Tour operators, xviii, xxix–xxxi
Trælleborg, 55
Train travel, xxxi–xxxii
Copenhagen, 40
Fyn, 68–69
Jylland, 81, 82
rail passes, xxxii
Sjælland, 56
Travel agencies, xxxiii
air travel, xiii
Copenhagen, 43
tour operators and, xxx
for traveler's with disabilities, xviii
Travel gear, xxxiii
Traveler's checks, xxvi
Troense, 66–67
Trolleskoven, 88
Tycho Brahe Planetarium, 20, 22–23

U

U.S. government, xxxiii
Uummannaq, 101–102
Uummannaq Church, 101
Uummannaq Museum, 101

V

Vágur, 112
Valdemars Slot, 66–67

Vejle, 74–75
Vesterbro, 20, 23, 28, 30–31
Vestmanna, 109
Viborg, 78
Videos, 124
Viebæltegård, 65–66
Viking artifacts
Fyn, 61
Jylland, 73, 76, 79
Sjælland, 51, 55
Viking Center, 73
Viking Moot, 76
Vikingeskibshallen, 51
Vindmølleparken, 77
Visas, xxvii–xxviii
Visitor information, xxxiii
Bornholm, 94
Copenhagen, 43
Faroe Islands, 113
Fyn, 69
Greenland, 104
Jylland, 83
Sjælland, 57
Viðareiði, 111
Vocabulary, Danish, 125–126
Vor Frelsers Kirken, 10, 16
Vor Frue Kirken, 19, 23

W

Walking tours
Copenhagen, 42–43
Fyn, 69
Jylland, 83
Sjælland, 57
Windsurfing, 92
W.Ø. Larsens Tobakmuseet, 10, 16
World Clock, 15

Z

Zoologiske Have, 23

NOTES

NOTES

NOTES

NOTES

NOTES

NOTES

NOTES

NOTES

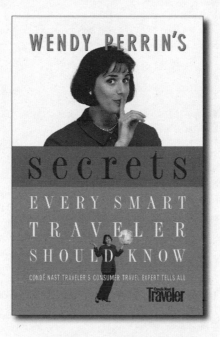

Fodor's Travel Publications

Available at bookstores everywhere, or call 1–800–533–6478, 24 hours a day.

Gold Guides
U.S.

Alaska	Florida	New Orleans	Seattle & Vancouver
Arizona	Hawai'i	New York City	The South
Boston	Las Vegas, Reno,	Pacific North Coast	U.S. & British Virgin
California	Tahoe	Philadelphia & the	Islands
Cape Cod, Martha's	Los Angeles	Pennsylvania Dutch	USA
Vineyard, Nantucket	Maine, Vermont,	Country	Virginia & Maryland
The Carolinas &	New Hampshire	The Rockies	Walt Disney World,
Georgia	Maui & Lāna'i	San Diego	Universal Studios
Chicago	Miami & the Keys	San Francisco	and Orlando
Colorado	New England	Santa Fe, Taos,	Washington, D.C.
		Albuquerque	

Foreign

Australia	Europe	Montréal &	Scotland
Austria	Florence, Tuscany	Québec City	Singapore
The Bahamas	& Umbria	Moscow, St.	South Africa
Belize & Guatemala	France	Petersburg, Kiev	South America
Bermuda	Germany	The Netherlands,	Southeast Asia
Canada	Great Britain	Belgium &	Spain
Cancún, Cozumel,	Greece	Luxembourg	Sweden
Yucatán Peninsula	Hong Kong	New Zealand	Switzerland
Caribbean	India	Norway	Thailand
China	Ireland	Nova Scotia, New	Toronto
Costa Rica	Israel	Brunswick, Prince	Turkey
Cuba	Italy	Edward Island	Vienna & the Danube
The Czech Republic	Japan	Paris	Valley
& Slovakia	London	Portugal	
Eastern &	Madrid & Barcelona	Provence &	
Central Europe	Mexico	the Riviera	
		Scandinavia	

Special-Interest Guides

Adventures to Imagine	Fodor's Gay Guide	Halliday's New	Rock & Roll Traveler
Alaska Ports of Call	to the USA	Orleans Food	USA
Ballpark Vacations	Fodor's How to Pack	Explorer	Sunday in
Caribbean Ports	Great American	Healthy Escapes	San Francisco
of Call	Learning Vacations	Kodak Guide to	Walt Disney World
The Complete Guide	Great American	Shooting Great	for Adults
to America's	Sports & Adventure	Travel Pictures	Weekends in New
National Parks	Vacations	National Parks and	York
Disney Like a Pro	Great American	Seashores of the East	Wendy Perrin's
Europe Ports of Call	Vacations	National Parks of	Secrets Every Smart
Family Adventures	Great American	the West	Traveler Should
	Vacations for	Nights to Imagine	Know
	Travelers with	Rock & Roll Traveler	Worldwide Cruises
	Disabilities	Great Britain and	and Ports of Call
		Ireland	

Fodor's Special Series

**Fodor's Best
Bed & Breakfasts**

America

California

The Mid-Atlantic

New England

The Pacific
Northwest

The South

The Southwest

The Upper Great
Lakes

**Compass American
Guides**

Alaska

Arizona

Boston

Chicago

Colorado

Hawaii

Idaho

Hollywood

Las Vegas

Maine

Manhattan

Minnesota

Montana

New Mexico

New Orleans

Oregon

Pacific Northwest

San Francisco

Santa Fe

South Carolina

South Dakota

Southwest

Texas

Utah

Virginia

Washington

Wine Country

Wisconsin

Wyoming

Citypacks

Amsterdam

Atlanta

Berlin

Chicago

Florence

Hong Kong

London

Los Angeles

Montréal

New York City

Paris

Prague

Rome

San Francisco

Tokyo

Venice

Washington, D.C.

Exploring Guides

Australia

Boston &
New England

Britain

California

Canada

Caribbean

China

Costa Rica

Egypt

Florence & Tuscany

Florida

France

Germany

Greek Islands

Hawaii

Ireland

Israel

Italy

Japan

London

Mexico

Moscow &
St. Petersburg

New York City

Paris

Prague

Provence

Rome

San Francisco

Scotland

Singapore & Malaysia

South Africa

Spain

Thailand

Turkey

Venice

Flashmaps

Boston

New York

San Francisco

Washington, D.C.

Fodor's Gay Guides

Los Angeles &
Southern California

New York City

Pacific Northwest

San Francisco and
the Bay Area

South Florida

USA

Pocket Guides

Acapulco

Aruba

Atlanta

Barbados

Budapest

Jamaica

London

New York City

Paris

Prague

Puerto Rico

Rome

San Francisco

Washington, D.C.

**Languages for
Travelers (Cassette
& Phrasebook)**

French

German

Italian

Spanish

Mobil Travel Guides

America's Best
Hotels & Restaurants

California and
the West

Major Cities

Great Lakes

Mid-Atlantic

Northeast

Northwest and
Great Plains

Southeast

Southwest and
South Central

Rivages Guides

Bed and Breakfasts
of Character and
Charm in France

Hotels and Country
Inns of Character and
Charm in France

Hotels and Country
Inns of Character and
Charm in Italy

Hotels and Country
Inns of Character and
Charm in Paris

Hotels and Country
Inns of Character and
Charm in Portugal

Hotels and Country
Inns of Character and
Charm in Spain

Short Escapes

Britain

France

New England

Near New York City

Fodor's Sports

Golf Digest's
Places to Play

Skiing USA

USA Today
The Complete Four
Sport Stadium Guide

WHEREVER YOU TRAVEL, *H*ELP IS NEVER FAR AWAY.

From planning your trip to providing travel assistance along the way, American Express® Travel Service Offices are always there to help you do more.

Denmark

American Express TFS/Bureau De Change
Amagertorv 18
Copenhagen
45/33/12 23 01

Travel